Selected readings in psychology

Selected readings in

PSYCHOLOGY

Don E. Gibbons, Ph.D.

Assistant Professor of Psychology,
University of Portland,
Portland, Oregon

John F. Connelly, Ph.D.

Assistant Professor of Psychology,
Kansas State College of Pittsburg,
Pittsburg, Kansas

The C. V. Mosby Company

Saint Louis   1970

Preface

To decide what type of selections should be included in the present book of readings, we found it helpful to consider first what we should *not* attempt to include. First of all, we believe that a book of readings designed primarily for classroom use as an adjunct to a standard textbook should not be merely a compendium of the experimental and theoretical articles that have made the greatest contribution to the field of psychology. Every introductory textbook reports these essential findings and speculations within the context of a meaningful discussion that makes them comprehensible to beginning students; to also force these students to read such articles in their original form would appear to impose an unnecessary burden upon them without providing any corresponding increase in educational enrichment. Moreover, most undergraduates do not have the necessary theoretical background and technical vocabulary to enable them to appreciate such articles "in the raw." Even if they are rewritten in nontechnical language, as some editors have done, we believe that their theoretical import can best be comprehended within the framework of meaningful discussion that most textbooks already provide.

On the other hand, we were also convinced that our book of readings should not be merely a collection of popularized articles on psychology. This function is handled quite adequately in the present culture by the mass-circulation magazines, and material that is selected for academic use should possess a comparatively greater amount of theoretical and scientific content.

It would appear to us that there is one function which a book of readings used in conjunction with an introductory textbook may uniquely fulfill. Students begin their study of psychology with a strong phenomenological interest in their own behavior and in the behavior of their fellowman. As they begin to acquire the basic facts and concepts of the field, they would welcome opportunities to apply them in extended discussion of many phenomena that there is simply not room to deal with in an introductory textbook itself. Therefore we have chosen articles from the psychological literature that deal in an interesting yet appropriately didactic manner with topics about which students tend to be curious and which may be used to illustrate and elaborate upon facts and principles that the beginning student needs to master.

In addition, we believe that a book of readings need not be encyclopedic to be useful. To impose upon a student the burden of mastering the content of fifty or sixty articles in addition to his regular textbook would appear to be an impossible goal if thorough comprehension is also to be desired. We believe that sheer mass will never substitute for quality. Consequently, we have kept the total number of selections small to retain a uniformly high standard of quality and relevance to both the interest of the student and the needs of the instructor.

Finally, we believe that a book of readings should not be without the same type of instructor's aids that now accompany most textbooks. We have therefore prepared a set of discussion materials and test questions that will be available to those who adopt the book for classroom use, together with a matrix chart relating each selection to the most appropriate companion chapter in each of the principal introductory psychology textbooks now on the market.

Don E. Gibbons
John F. Connelly

Contents

Part I

The science of psychology

Chapter 1

The more or less scientific method*

Rudolf Flesch

Despite numerous attempts to reduce the scientific method to a few
basic steps and to set forth as completely as possible the rules of procedure that govern their application, the troublesome fact remains that
success in science, as in other areas of human endeavor, is often the
result of creativity or of simply being in the right place at the right
time. How, then, do we go about selecting and training good scientists,
and which orientation or set of procedures is most desirable for an
aspiring scientist to follow?

Perhaps the most famous incident in the history of science occurred in the
third century B.C. in Syracuse, Sicily. The mathematician Archimedes was
taking a bath. His mind was busy with a scientific problem. King Hiero of
Syracuse had ordered a golden crown and suspected the goldsmith of having
cheated him by using some silver instead of the gold he'd been supplied with.
The king had asked Archimedes to prove it.

Suddenly Archimedes noticed that his body caused some water to spill
over. In a flash he realized the solution of the problem: he'd take the crown's
weight in pure gold, dip it into water, and see whether the overflow was the
same as that of the crown. Whereupon he jumped out of the tub, ran home
naked as he was, and shouted to everyone he met: "Eureka! Eureka! . . . I've
found it! I've found it!"

Perhaps the *least* famous incident in the history of science occurred in the
twentieth century A.D. in the United States. The chemist J. E. Teeple was
taking a bath. His mind was busy with a scientific problem. He stepped out of
his bath, reached for a towel, dried himself, shaved, took another bath,
stepped out of it, reached for a towel and discovered that the towel was wet.
Thinking about his scientific problem, he had taken two baths. He had *not*
found the solution to his problem.

The first of these incidents has been retold a million times; the second is

*From *The Art of Clear Thinking* by Rudolf Flesch. Copyright 1951 by Rudolf Flesch.
Reprinted by permission of Harper & Row, Publishers.

trivial. Nevertheless, the second is the one that gives the truer picture of the scientific method.

In the first place, the story about Archimedes puts the spotlight on the happy discovery, giving the impression that this sort of thing is typical of a scientist's life. Actually, "Eureka!" moments are few and far between. Einstein once said, "I think and think, for months, for years; ninety-nine times the conclusion is false. The hundredth time I am right." And that's Einstein, the greatest scientific genius of our time. I leave it to you to estimate the percentage of correct solutions in an ordinary scientist's world. Most of their lives are spent like Mr. Teeple's half-hour in the bathroom, thinking and thinking and getting nowhere.

But there's a more important reason why Archimedes crying "Eureka!" isn't a good picture of a scientist. Today no scientist, dressed or undressed, would dream of telling people "I've found it!" as soon as he has hit upon a bright idea. Even less would he do the modern equivalent—announce his discovery immediately to the press. Just the contrary. He would take care not to breathe a word about it to anyone, but quietly go to his laboratory and run some tests—and more tests—and more tests.

A scientist today doesn't consider a bright idea as a revelation of the truth; he considers it as something to be disproved. Not just proved, mind you; it's his obligation as a scientist to think of every conceivable means and ways to *disprove* it. This habit is so ingrained in him that he doesn't even realize it any more; he automatically thinks of a theory as something to find flaws in. So he does experiments and hunts for every error he can possibly think of; and when he is through with his own experiments, he publishes his findings not in a newspaper but in a scientific journal, inviting other scientists to do some other experiments and prove him wrong.

And when the hunt for errors has subsided and a theory gets established and accepted—do scientists think they've got hold of a new truth? No. To them, all scientific findings are only *tentative* truths, "good until further notice," to be immediately discarded when someone comes along with another theory that explains a few more facts. Absolute truth doesn't even interest them; they get along very happily, thank you, with a set of working hypotheses that are good only at certain times and for certain purposes. The most famous example of this today is the theory of light. There is a wave theory that fits certain investigations, and a particle theory that fits certain others. Years ago physicists stopped trying to find out which is true and which is false. The Danish Nobel prize winner, Niels Bohr, has called this the principle of complementarity, saying that after all "waves" and "particles" are only handy metaphors in dealing with certain facts; so why not use whichever is more practical at the moment? Never mind what light is "really"; let's get on with the job of finding out what it *does*. Or, as one physicist said, "Let's use the particle theory on Mondays, Wednesdays, and Fridays, and the wave theory on Tuesdays, Thursdays, and Saturdays."

For the layman, the most important thing about science is this: that it isn't a search for truth but a search for error. The scientist lives in a world where truth is unattainable, but where it's always possible to find errors in the long-settled or the obvious. You want to know whether some theory is really scientific? Try this simple test: if the thing is shot through with *perhapses* and *maybe's* and hemming and hawing, it's probably science; if it's supposed to be *the* final answer, it is not.

So-called "scientific" books that are supposed to contain final answers are never scientific. Science is forever self-correcting and changing; what is put forth as gospel truth cannot be science.

But what does *science* mean? If someone asked you for a definition, you'd probably be on the spot. If pressed, you might come up with something like the definition in Webster's: "A branch of study . . . concerned with the observation and classification of facts, esp. with the establishment . . . of varifiable general laws. . . ."

That's a pretty good description of what the word means to the average person. Does it mean the same thing to scientists? It does not. Recently President Conant of Harvard, a chemist, published *his* definition of science: "An interconnected series of concepts and conceptual schemes that have developed as a result of experimentation and observation." As you see, the two definitions are almost exact opposites. *You* think science deals with facts; a scientist thinks it deals with concepts. *You* think science tries to establish laws; a scientist thinks it aims at more and more experiments.

And what is the scientific method? Your answer is apt to be: "The classification of facts." President Conant's answer is again different. Look up *Scientific method* in the index of his book, and you'll find this: "Scientific method. *See* Alleged scientific method." In other words, President Conant thinks there *isn't any* scientific method.

That surely is extreme. Even if there is no clearly definable scientific method, there's a way in which scientists work, and it's certainly worth knowing about. Let's look at a careful description by Dr. W. I. B. Beveridge, a British biologist:

The following is a common sequence in an investigation of a medical or biological problem:

(a) The relevant literature is critically reviewed.

(b) A thorough collection of field data or equivalent observational enquiry is conducted, and is supplemented if necessary by laboratory examination of specimens.

(c) The information obtained is marshalled and correlated and the problem is defined and broken down into specific questions.

(d) Intelligent guesses are made to answer the questions, as many hypotheses as possible being considered.

(e) Experiments are devised to test first the likeliest hypotheses bearing on the most crucial questions.

The key word here is *guesses* in (d). In the popular view the emphasis is on (b), the collection of data. But not among scientists. They like to distinguish between "accumulators" and "guessers," and they're pretty much agreed that it's the guessers that are important. In more fancy terms, you could say that the modern emphasis is on deduction rather than induction, or that the Aristotelian method is now more esteemed than the Baconian. What it comes down to is simply this: Our top scientists say we need more ideas rather than more facts; they want more Einsteins who just sit and think rather than Edisons who have a genius for tinkering in the laboratory. After all, Edison, as one of them has said, "was not a scientist and was not even interested in science."

Meanwhile, our research relies far more on accumulating than on guessing. General Electric, with its training courses in "Creative Engineering," is the exception; the American Cancer Society, which is openly resigned to "whittling away at this mass of mystery," is typical of the general rule.

Which is why Dr. Sinnott, director of the Sheffield School of Science at Yale, said recently:

> "It must be ruefully admitted that we have not produced our share of great new germinative ideas in recent years. In atomic research, for example, most of the fundamental theoretical progress was made either by European scientists or men who had received their training abroad. We are strong in application, in development and engineering, but much less so in the fundamental contributions of the theory on which all these are based. . . . We are in danger of being overwhelmed by a mass of undigested results."

And what is the method used by those hard-to-find "guessers"? If we try to analyze it, we come right back to Duncker's description of problem-solving, to his "solutions from below" and "solutions from above." Scientific problems are solved either by finding a seemingly irrelevant key factor or by applying a seemingly unsuitable thought pattern. Which means that scientific discoveries are made in one of two ways: by accident or by hunch.

Take any history of science, and you'll find that it is a history of accidents and hunches. Both types of discoveries are equally fascinating.

If you're interested in accidents, for instance, scientific history looks like this:

In 1786, Luigi Galvani noticed the accidental twitching of a frog's leg and discovered the principle of the electric battery.

In 1822, the Danish physicist Oersted, at the end of a lecture, happened to put a wire conducting an electric current near a magnet, which led to Faraday's invention of the electric dynamo.

In 1858, a seventeen-year-old boy named William Henry Perkin, trying to make artificial quinine, cooked up a black-looking mass, which led to his discovery of aniline dye.

In 1889, Professors von Mering and Minkowski operated on a dog. A laboratory assistant noticed that the dog's urine attracted swarms of flies. He called this to the attention of Minkowski, who found that the urine contained sugar. This was the first step in the control of diabetes.

In 1895, Roentgen noticed that cathode rays penetrated black paper and discovered X-rays.

In 1929, Sir Alexander Fleming noticed that a culture of bacteria had been accidentally contaminated by a mold. He said to himself: "My, that's a funny thing." He had discovered penicillin.

Of course, all these accidents would have been meaningless if they hadn't happened to Galvani, Perkin, Roentgen, and so on. As Pasteur has said, "Chance favors the prepared mind." What is necessary is an accidental event plus an observer with *serendipity*—"the gift of finding valuable or agreeable things not sought for." (Horace Walpole coined that beautiful word.)

On the other hand, if you're interested in hunches, scientific history looks like this, for example:

Harvey describes his discovery of the circulation of the blood:

"I frequently and seriously bethought me, and long revolved in my mind, what might be the quantity of blood which was transmitted, in how short a time its passage might be effected and the like. . . . I began to think whether there might not be a motion, as it were, in a circle."

James Watt invents the steam engine:

"On a fine Sabbath afternoon I took a walk. . . . I had entered the green and had passed the old washing house. I was thinking of the engine at the time. I had gone as far as the herd's house when the idea came into my mind that as steam was an elastic body it would rush into a vacuum, and if a connection were made between the cylinder and an exhausting vessel it would rush into it and might then be condensed without cooling the cylinder. . . . I had not walked further than the golf house when the whole thing was arranged in my mind."

Darwin writes about his theory of evolution:

"I can remember the very spot in the road, whilst in my carriage, when to my joy the solution occurred to me."

Kékule tells how he discovered the benzene ring on top of a London bus:

"I sank into a reverie. The atoms flitted about before my eyes. . . . I saw how two small ones often joined into a little pair; how a larger took hold of two smaller, and a still larger clasped three or even four of the small ones, and how all span around in a whirling round-dance. . . . The cry of the conductor, 'Clapham Road,' woke me up."

Walter B. Cannon discovers the significance of bodily changes in fear and rage:

"These changes—the more rapid pulse, the deeper breathing, the increase of sugar in the blood, the secretion from the adrenal glands—were very diverse and seemed unrelated. Then, one wakeful night, after a considerable collection of these changes had been disclosed, the idea flashed through my mind that they could be nicely integrated if conceived as bodily preparations for supreme effort in flight or in fighting."

Does all this mean that some scientists are good at hunches and some others blessed with serendipity? Not at all. The accidental clue needs a receptive mind; the hunch has to grow from a study of facts. The good guesser works both ways, depending on what he has to go on. Here's one more example that shows a combination of both methods. It is typical of modern scientific research in many ways.

During World War II, a team of psychologists studied the propaganda effect of orientation films. Among other things, they tried to find out whether films changed the opinions and attitudes of soldiers who saw them, and whether and how these changes lasted. They had a hunch that the effect of the films would gradually wear off and that after some time, soldiers would forget the factual details and revert to their original opinion.

This idea may seem rather obvious to you. It seemed obvious to the psychologists too—but, being scientists, they decided to test it anyway. So they gave the soldiers a test after one week and another test after nine weeks.

As expected, the soldiers had forgotten most of the facts in the film during those eight weeks. But, "clearly contrary to the initial expectation," the general propaganda effect of the film—the opinion change—had considerably *increased* between the first and the second test. There was not the slightest doubt about it: the soldiers had forgotten the details of the film, but its message had sunk in deeper.

The research team cheerfully accepted this unexpected fact and immediately proceeded to account for it by a hypothesis. They found that it could be explained through a theory by the British psychologist, Bartlett, published in 1932. Bartlett had written that "after learning, that which is recalled tends to be modified with lapse of time in the direction of omission of all but general content and introduction of new material in line with the individual's attitudes." In other words, as time passes, we're apt to forget details but *reinforce* what we remember of the general idea.

Well, what have we here? Doubtless the research team made a valuable discovery. Yet the whole story is as unlike that of Archimedes in his bath as can be. For one thing, there is no single scientist, but a team of thirteen men and two women. Second, the discovery is exactly the opposite from what the scientists expected to find. Third, it is immediately connected up with an idea thought up by another scientist in another country, twenty years before.

And finally, there is no "Eureka!," no shouting from the housetops, no happy announcement to the world. Instead, after reporting their discovery and stating their hypothesis, the researchers add casually: "These highly speculative suggestions indicate some very interesting areas for future research."

Chapter 2

Is common sense scientifically valid?

Don E. Gibbons and John F. Connelly

A scientific theory is basically a set of assumptions about how to proceed. Everybody, then, has a theory—or indeed a number of theories—about human behavior, and some of these theories are quite pervasive and firmly fixed. In recent years the experimental approach to human behavior has been employed to investigate a number of assumptions about human behavior that have been widely held. In some instances the assumptions of "common sense" have been confirmed and in other instances they have not been confirmed.

Many classroom discussions in beginning psychology courses have to do with the nature and the appropriateness of empirical investigations of behavior in comparison with commonsense assumptions. The following questionnaire may serve as a brief inventory of some of the points that are frequently raised in discussion and may or may not be supported by experimental evidence.

1. T F Only children tend to be spoiled.
2. T F Alcohol in moderate amounts will function as a stimulant.
3. T F It is possible to demonstrate the existence of telepathy by staring at the back of a person's head, which will cause him to turn around.
4. T F Hypnotism, over a period of time, will weaken one's will.
5. T F Man differs from animals in that man is able to make use of abstract concepts, whereas animals are not.
6. T F People born under the influence of certain planets show the influence in their characters.*
7. T F If a mother is a heavy cigarette smoker during pregnancy, she cannot pass the craving on to her children.
8. T F A square jaw is a sign of willpower.*
9. T F Excessive study can occasionally result in impairment of one's mental abilities.
10. T F All men are created equal in capacity for achievement.*
11. T F People of superior intelligence are more apt to become insane than are people of normal intelligence.
12. T F You can estimate an individual's intelligence pretty closely by just looking at his face.*
13. T F An expectant mother by fixing her mind on a subject can influence the character of her unborn child.*

*From Nixon, H. K.: Popular Answers to Some Psychological Questions, *The American Journal of Psychology* **36**:418-423, 1925.

14. T F Man is superior to animals because his conduct is very largely guided by reason.
15. T F A person who does not look you in the eye is likely to be dishonest.*
16. T F A high forehead indicates intellectual superiority.*
17. T F Especially intelligent children are likely to be weak and retarded physically.*
18. T F The study of algebra and geometry is valuable because it teaches you to think logically.
19. T F No defect of body or mind can hold us back if we have enough will-power.*
20. T F The marriage of cousins is practically certain to result in children of inferior intelligence.*
21. T F One of the best ways to improve one's knowledge of English is through the study of Greek and Latin.
22. T F People who have small, closely set eyes are not as intelligent as others.
23. T F It is possible to tell a great deal about a person's character by analyzing his handwriting.
24. T F Man's biological and chemical systems have little to do with his ability to remember.
25. T F Electrical stimulation of the brain is never really pleasant.
26. T F People with bigger brains tend to be smarter.
27. T F LSD cannot affect your heredity.

The answers to all the above questions are "false."

---

*From Nixon, H. K.: Popular Answers to Some Psychological Questions, *The American Journal of Psychology* **36**:418-423, 1925.

Chapter 3

How to talk back to a statistic*

Darrell Huff

Recent ideas in communication theory revolve around the distinction between the "medium" and the "message." The medium of television has become a powerful tool for communication, but the message from this medium can be and often is very perplexing, not only to the general public but even to the statistician! How do we evaluate the essentially statistical messages of television commercials? Or, how do we talk back to the message of the pseudostatistician?

So far, I have been addressing you rather as if you were a pirate with a yen for instruction in the finer points of cutlass work. In this concluding chapter I'll drop that literary device. I'll face up to the serious purpose that I like to think lurks just beneath the surface of this book: explaining how to look a phony statistic in the eye and face it down; and no less important, how to recognize sound and usable data in that wilderness of fraud to which the previous chapters have been largely devoted.

Not all the statistical information that you may come upon can be tested with the sureness of chemical analysis or of what goes on in an assayer's laboratory. But you can prod the stuff with five simple questions, and by finding the answers avoid learning a remarkable lot that isn't so.

WHO SAYS SO?

About the first thing to look for is bias—the laboratory with something to prove for the sake of a theory, a reputation, or a fee; the newspaper whose aim is a good story; labor or management with a wage level at stake.

Look for conscious bias. The method may be direct misstatement or it may be ambiguous statement that serves as well and cannot be convicted. It may be selection of favorable data and suppression of unfavorable. Units of measurement may be shifted, as with the practice of using one year for one comparison and sliding over to a more favorable year for another. An improper measure may be used: a mean where a median would be more informative

*From *How to Lie With Statistics* by Darrell Huff. Pictures by Irving Geis. By permission of W. W. Norton & Co., Inc. Copyright 1954 by Darrell Huff and Irving Geis.

(perhaps all too informative), with the trickery covered by the unqualified word "average."

Look sharply for unconscious bias. It is often more dangerous. In the charts and predictions of many statisticians and economists in 1928 it operated to produce remarkable things. The cracks in the economic structure were joyously overlooked, and all sorts of evidence was adduced and statistically supported to show that we had no more than entered the stream of prosperity.

It may take at least a second look to find out who-says-so. The who may be hidden by what Stephen Potter, the *Lifemanship* man, would probably call the "O.K. name." Anything smacking of the medical profession is an O.K. name. Scientific laboratories have O.K. names. So do colleges, especially universities, more especially ones eminent in technical work. The writer who proved a few chapters back that higher education jeopardizes a girl's chance to marry made good use of the O.K. name of Cornell. Please note that while the data came from Cornell, the conclusions were entirely the writer's own. But the O.K. name helps you carry away a misimpression of "Cornell University says . . ."

When an O.K. name is cited, make sure that the authority stands behind the information, not merely somewhere alongside it.

You may have read a proud announcement by the Chicago *Journal of Commerce*. That publication had made a survey. Of 169 corporations that replied to a poll on price gouging and hoarding, two-thirds declared that they were absorbing price increases produced by the Korean war. "The survey shows," said the *Journal* (look sharp whenever you meet those words!), "that corporations have done exactly the opposite of what the enemies of the American business system have charged." This is an obvious place to ask, "Who says so?" since the *Journal of Commerce* might be regarded as an interested party. It is also a splendid place to ask our second test question:

HOW DOES HE KNOW?

It turns out that the *Journal* had begun by sending its questionnaires to 1,200 large companies. Only fourteen per cent had replied. Eighty-six per cent had not cared to say anything in public on whether they were hoarding or price gouging.

The *Journal* had put a remarkably good face on things, but the fact remains that there was little to brag about. It came down to this: Of 1,200 companies polled, nine per cent said they had not raised prices, five per cent said they had, and eighty-six per cent wouldn't say. Those that had replied constituted a sample in which bias might be suspected.

Watch out for evidence of a biased sample, one that has been selected improperly or—as with this one—has selected itself. Ask the question we dealt with in an early chapter: Is the sample large enough to permit any reliable conclusion?

Similarly with a reported correlation: Is it big enough to mean anything? Are there enough cases to add up to any significance? You cannot, as a casual reader, apply tests of significance or come to exact conclusions as to the adequacy of a sample. On a good many of the things you see reported, however, you will be able to tell at a glance—a good long glance, perhaps—that there just weren't enough cases to convince any reasoning person of anything.

WHAT'S MISSING?

You won't always be told how many cases. The absence of such a figure, particularly when the source is an interested one, is enough to throw suspicion on the whole thing. Similarly a correlation given without a measure of reliability (probable error, standard error) is not to be taken very seriously.

Watch out for an average, variety unspecified, in any matter where mean and median might be expected to differ substantially.

Many figures lose meaning because a comparison is missing. An article in *Look* magazine says, in connection with Mongolism, that "one study shows that in 2,800 cases, over half of the mothers were 35 or over." Getting any meaning from this depends upon your knowing something about the ages at which women in general produce babies. Few of us know things like that.

Here is an extract from the *New Yorker* magazine's "Letter from London" of January 31, 1953.

> The Ministry of Health's recently published figures showing that in the week of the great fog the death rate for Greater London jumped by twenty-eight hundred were a shock to the public, which is used to regarding Britain's unpleasant climatic effects as nuisances rather than as killers. . . . The extraordinary lethal properties of this winter's prize visitation . . .

But how lethal *was* the visitation? Was it exceptional for the death rate to be that much higher than usual in a week? All such things do vary. And what about ensuing weeks? Did the death rate drop below average, indicating that if the fog killed people they were largely those who would have died shortly anyway? The figure sounds impressive, but the absence of other figures takes away most of its meaning.

Sometimes it is percentages that are given and raw figures that are missing, and this can be deceptive too. Long ago, when Johns Hopkins University had just begun to admit women students, someone not particularly enamored of coeducation reported a real shocker: Thirty-three and one-third per cent of the women at Hopkins had married faculty members! The raw figures gave a clearer picture. There were three women enrolled at the time, and one of them had married a faculty man.

A couple of years ago the Boston Chamber of Commerce chose its American Women of Achievement. Of the sixteen among them who were also in *Who's Who*, it was announced that they had "sixty academic degrees and eighteen children." That sounds like an informative picture of the group until you discover that among the women were Dean Virginia Gildersleeve and Mrs. Lillian M. Gilbreth. Those two had a full third of the degrees between them. And Mrs. Gilbreth, of course, supplied two-thirds of the children.

A corporation was able to announce that its stock was held by 3,003 persons, who had an average of 660 shares each. This was true. It was also true that of the two million shares of stock in the corporation three men held three-quarters and three thousand persons held the other one-fourth among them.

If you are handed an index, you may ask what's missing there. It may be the base, a base chosen to give a distorted picture. A national labor organization once showed that indexes of profits and production had risen much more rapidly after the depression than an index of wages had. As an argument for wage increases this demonstration lost its potency when someone dug out the missing figures. It could be seen then that profits had been almost bound to rise more rapidly in percentage than wages simply because profits had reached a lower point, giving a smaller base.

Sometimes what is missing is the factor that caused a change to occur. This omission leaves the implication that some other, more desired, factor is responsible. Figures published one year attempted to show that business was on the upgrade by pointing out that April retail sales were greater than in the year before. What was missing was the fact that Easter had come in March in the earlier year and in April in the later year.

A report of a great increase in deaths from cancer in the last quarter-century is misleading unless you know how much of it is a product of such extraneous factors as these: Cancer is often listed now where "causes unknown" was formerly used; autopsies are more frequent, giving surer diagnoses; reporting and compiling of medical statistics are more complete; and people more frequently reach the most susceptible ages now. And if you are looking at total deaths rather than the death rate, don't neglect the fact that there are more people now than there used to be.

DID SOMEBODY CHANGE THE SUBJECT?

When assaying a statistic, watch out for a switch somewhere between the raw figure and the conclusion. One thing is all too often reported as another.

As just indicated, more reported cases of a disease are not always the same thing as more cases of the disease. A straw-vote victory for a candidate is not always negotiable at the polls. An expressed preference by a "cross section" of a magazine's readers for articles on world affairs is no final proof that they would read the articles if they were published.

Encephalitis cases reported in the central valley of California in 1952 were triple the figure for the worst previous year. Many alarmed residents shipped their children away. But when the reckoning was in, there had been no great increase in deaths from sleeping sickness. What had happened was that state and federal health people had come in in great numbers to tackle a long-time problem; as a result of their efforts a great many low-grade cases were recorded that in other years would have been overlooked, possibly not even recognized.

It is all reminiscent of the way that Lincoln Steffens and Jacob A. Riis, as New York newspapermen, once created a crime wave. Crime cases in the papers reached such proportions, both in numbers and in space and big type given to them, that the public demanded action. Theodore Roosevelt, as president of the reform Police Board, was seriously embarrassed. He put an end to the crime wave simply by asking Steffens and Riis to lay off. It had all come about simply because the reporters, led by those two, had got into competition as to who could dig up the most burglaries and whatnot. The official police record showed no increase at all.

"The British male over 5 years of age soaks himself in a hot tub on an average of 1.7 times a week in the winter and 2.1 times in the summer," says a newspaper story. "British women average 1.5 baths a week in the winter and 2.0 in the summer." The source is a Ministry of Works hot-water survey of "6,000 representative British homes." The sample was representative, it says, and seems quite adequate in size to justify the conclusion in the San Francisco *Chronicle's* amusing headline: BRITISH HE'S BATHE MORE THAN SHE'S.

The figures would be more informative if there were some indication of whether they are means or medians. However, the major weakness is that the subject has been changed. What the Ministry really found out is how often these people said they bathed, not how often they did so. When a subject is as intimate as this one is, with the British bath-taking tradition involved, saying and doing may not be the same thing at all. British he's may or may not bathe oftener than she's; all that can safely be concluded is that they say they do.

Here are some more varieties of change-of-subject to watch out for.

A back-to-the-farm movement was discerned when a census showed half a million more farms in 1935 than five years earlier. But the two counts were not talking about the same thing. The definition of farm used by the Bureau of the Census had been changed; it took in at least 300,000 farms that would not have been so listed under the 1930 definition.

Strange things crop out when figures are based on what people say—even about things that seem to be objective facts. Census reports have shown more people at thirty-five years of age, for instance, than at either thirty-four or thirty-six. The false picture comes from one family member's reporting the ages of the others and, not being sure of the exact ages, tending to round them off to a familiar multiple of five. One way to get around this: ask birth dates instead.

The "population" of a large area in China was 28 million. Five years later it was 105 million. Very little of that increase was real; the great difference could be explained only by taking into account the purposes of the two enumerations and the way people would be inclined to feel about being counted in each instance. The first census was for tax and military purposes, the second for famine relief.

Something of the same sort has happened in the United States. The 1950 census found more people in the sixty-five-to-seventy age group than there were in the fifty-five-to-sixty group ten years before. The difference could not be accounted for by immigration. Most of it could be a product of large-scale falsifying of ages by people eager to collect social security. Also possible is that some of the earlier ages were understated out of vanity.

Another kind of change-of-subject is represented by Senator William Langer's cry that "we could take a prisoner from Alcatraz and board him at the Waldorf-Astoria cheaper. . . ." The North Dakotan was referring to earlier statements that it cost eight dollars a day to maintain a prisoner at Alcatraz, "the cost of a room at a good San Francisco hotel." The subject has been changed from total maintenance cost (Alcatraz) to hotel-room rent alone.

The *post hoc* variety of pretentious nonsense is another way of changing the subject without seeming to. The change of something *with* something else is presented as *because of*. The magazine *Electrical World* once offered a composite chart in an editorial on "What Electricity Means to America."

You could see from it that as "electrical horsepower in factories" climbed, so did "average wages per hour." At the same time "average hours per week" dropped. All these things are long-time trends, of course, and there is no evidence at all that any one of them has produced any other.

And then there are the firsters. Almost anybody can claim to be first in *something* if he is not too particular what it is. At the end of 1952 two New York newspapers were each insisting on first rank in grocery advertising. Both were right too, in a way. The *World-Telegram* went on to explain that it was first in full-run advertising, the kind that appears in all copies, which is the only kind it runs. The *Journal-American* insisted that total linage was what counted and that it was first in that. This is the kind of reaching for a superlative that leads the weather reporter on the radio to label a quite normal day "the hottest June second since 1949."

Change-of-subject makes it difficult to compare cost when you contemplate borrowing money either directly or in the form of installment buying. Six per cent sounds like six per cent—but it may not be at all.

If you borrow $100 from a bank at six per cent interest and pay it back in equal monthly installments for a year, the price you pay for the use of the money is about $3. But another six per cent loan, on the basis sometimes called $6 on the $100, will cost you twice as much. That's the way most automobile loans are figured. It is very tricky.

The point is that you don't have the $100 for a year. By the end of six months you have paid back half of it. If you are charged at $6 on the $100, or six per cent of the amount, you really pay interest at nearly twelve per cent.

Even worse was what happened to some careless purchasers of freezer-food plans in 1952 and 1953. They were quoted a figure of anywhere from six to twelve per cent. It sounded like interest, but it was not. It was an on-the-dollar figure and, worst of all, the time was often six months rather than a year. Now $12 on the $100 for money to be paid back regularly over half a year works out to something like forty-eight per cent real interest. It is no wonder that so many customers defaulted and so many food plans blew up.

Sometimes the semantic approach will be used to change the subject. Here is an item from *Business Week* magazine.

> Accountants have decided that "surplus" is a nasty word. They propose eliminating it from corporate balance sheets. The Committee on Accounting Procedure of the American Institute of Accountants says: . . . Use such descriptive terms as "retained earnings" or "appreciation of fixed assets."

This one is from a newspaper story reporting Standard Oil's record-breaking revenue and net profit of a million dollars a day.

> Possibly the directors may be thinking some time of splitting the stock for there may be an advantage . . . if the profits per share do not look so large. . . .

DOES IT MAKE SENSE?

"Does it make sense?" will often cut a statistic down to size when the whole rigmarole is based on an unproved assumption. You may be familiar with the Rudolf Flesch readability formula. It purports to measure how easy a piece of prose is to read, by such simple and objective items as length of words and sentences. Like all devices for reducing the imponderable to a number and substituting arithmetic for judgment, it is an appealing idea. At least it has appealed to people who employ writers, such as newspaper publishers, even if not to many writers themselves. The assumption in the formula is that such things as word length determine readability. This, to be ornery about it, remains to be proved.

A man named Robert A. Dufour put the Flesch formula to trial on some literature that he found handy. It showed "The Legend of Sleepy Hollow" to be half again as hard to read as Plato's *Republic*. The Sinclair Lewis novel *Cass Timberlane* was rated more difficult than an essay by Jacques Maritain, "The Spiritual Value of Art." A likely story.

Many a statistic is false on its face. It gets by only because the magic of numbers brings about a suspension of common sense. Leonard Engel, in a *Harper's* article, has listed a few of the medical variety.

> An example is the calculation of a well-known urologist that there are eight million cases of cancer of the prostate gland in the United States—which would be enough to provide 1.1 carcinomatous prostate glands for every male in the susceptible age group! Another is a prominent neurologist's estimate that one American in twelve suffers from migraine; since migraine is responsible for a third of chronic headache cases, this would mean that a quarter of us must suffer from disabling headaches. Still another is the figure of 250,000 often given for the number of multiple sclerosis cases; death data indicate that there can be, happily, no more than thirty to forty thousand cases of this paralytic disease in the country.

Hearings on amendments to the Social Security Act have been haunted by various forms of a statement that makes sense only when not looked at closely. It is an argument that goes like this: Since life expectancy is only about sixty-three years, it is a sham and a fraud to set up a social-security plan with a retirement age of sixty-five, because virtually everybody dies before that.

You can rebut that one by looking around at people you know. The basic fallacy, however, is that the figure refers to expectancy at birth, and so about half the babies born can expect to live longer than that. The figure, incidentally, is from the latest official complete life table and is correct for the 1939-1941 period. An up-to-date estimate corrects it to sixty-five-plus. Maybe that will produce a new and equally silly argument to the effect that practically everybody now lives to be sixty-five.

Postwar planning at a big electrical-appliance company was going great guns a few years ago on the basis of a declining birth rate, something that had been taken for granted for a long time. Plans called for emphasis on small-capacity appliances, apartment-size refrigerators. Then one of the planners had an attack of common sense: He came out of his graphs and charts long enough to notice that he and his co-workers and his friends and his neighbors and his former classmates with few exceptions either had three or four children or planned to. This led to some open-minded investigating and charting—and the company shortly turned its emphasis most profitably to big-family models.

The impressively precise figure is something else that contradicts common sense. A study reported in New York City newspapers announced that a working woman living with her family needed a weekly pay check of $40.13 for adequate support. Anyone who has not suspended all logical processes while reading his paper will realize that the cost of keeping body and soul together cannot be calculated to the last cent. But there is a dreadful temptation; "$40.13" sounds so much more knowing than "about $40."

You are entitled to look with the same suspicion on the report, some years ago, by the American Petroleum Industries Committee that the average yearly tax bill for automobiles is $51.13.

Extrapolations are useful, particularly in that form of soothsaying called forecasting trends. But in looking at the figures or the charts made from them, it is necessary to remember one thing constantly: The trend-to-now may be a fact, but the future trend represents no more than an educated guess. Implicit in it is "everything else being equal" and "present trends continuing." And somehow everything else refuses to remain equal, else life would be dull indeed.

For a sample of the nonsense inherent in uncontrolled extrapolation, consider the trend of television. The number of sets in American homes increased around 10,000% from 1947 to 1952. Project this for the next five years and you find that there'll soon be a couple billion of the things, Heaven forbid, or forty sets per family. If you want to be even sillier, begin with a base year that is earlier in the television scheme of things than 1947 and you can just as well "prove" that each family will soon have not forty but forty thousand sets.

A Government research man, Morris Hansen, called Gallup's 1948 election forecasting "the most publicized statistical error in human history." It was a paragon of accuracy, however, compared with some of our most widely used estimates of future population, which have earned a nationwide horse-laugh. As late as 1938 a presidential commission loaded with experts doubted that the U. S. population would ever reach 140 million; it was 12 million more than that just twelve years later. There are textbooks published so recently that they are still in college use that predict a peak population of not more than 150 million and figure it will take until about 1980 to reach it. These fearful underestimates came from assuming that a trend would continue without change. A similar assumption a century ago did as badly in the opposite direction because it assumed continuation of the population-increase rate of 1790 to 1860. In his second message to Congress, Abraham Lincoln predicted the U. S. population would reach 251,689,914 in 1930.

Not long after that, in 1874, Mark Twain summed up the nonsense side of extrapolation in *Life on the Mississippi:*

> In the space of one hundred and seventy-six years the Lower Mississippi has shortened itself two hundred and forty-two miles. That is an average of a trifle over one mile and a third per year. Therefore, any calm person, who is not blind or idiotic, can see that in the Old Oölitic Silurian Period, just a million years ago next November, the Lower Mississippi River was upward of one million three hundred thousand miles long, and stuck out over the Gulf of Mexico like a fishing-rod. And by the same token any person can see that seven hundred and forty-two years from now the Lower Mississippi will be only a mile and three-quarters long, and Cairo and New Orleans will have joined their streets together, and be plodding comfortably along under a single mayor and a mutual board of aldermen. There is something fascinating about science. One gets such wholesale returns of conjecture out of such a trifling investment of fact.

Part II

The biological foundations
of psychology

Chapter 4

The permanent record of the stream
of consciousness*

Wilder Penfield

This and the following article deal with one of the most intriguing
problems in psychology: How do we remember? Both human experimentation (illustrated by the present article) and animal experimentation (illustrated in the next article by McConnell's work with flatworms)
are directed at the question, "What is the mechanism of memory?"
Some researchers say this mechanism might be neural (eg. Penfield),
whereas others say it might be chemical, and both answers are probably correct.

Penfield's argument is briefly as follows: as a neurosurgeon he has
demonstrated that we can electrically stimulate the surface of the brain
of human patients and arouse "memories" of previous experiences.
The brain is composed of nerves, ganglions (collections of nerves), and
synapses (spaces between nerves), so that electrical stimulation must
somehow activate these neural structures, allowing his patients to
remember events that they thought they had "forgotten." Thus even
supposedly "forgotten" events must somehow be recorded in the neural
structures of our brain: the mechanism of memory is at least partially
neural.

While considering how I might fortify my position before this Congress,
composed as it is of leading psychologists from all the world, I took from my
book shelves the two volumes of Psychology by William James. I blew off the
dust that had lain upon them, I fear, since my undergraduate days at Prince-
ton and read his classical chapter on "The Stream of Thought."

Consciousness, he said, is a personal phenomenon. It deals with external
objects, some of which are constant, and it chooses among them. But consciousness is never the same in successive moments of time. It is a stream
forever flowing, forever changing.

It has fallen to my lot, during explorations of the cortex, to demonstrate

*Abridged from *Acta Psychologica* 11:47-69, 1956.

a mechanism in the human brain which preserves the record of the stream of thought. When it becomes necessary to operate under local anesthesia and to stimulate the surface of one of the temporal lobes, it happens occasionally that small parts of that record are activated, bringing back a period of past experience with a startling degree of vividness and detail. The patient then reviews the sights and sounds and thinking of a previous period of time.

• • •

CASE EXAMPLES

Case T. S.: T. S. was a young man of 19 years. He had temporal lobe seizures that were sometimes precipitated by listening to music. He was fond of jazz and also symphonic music.

At the beginning of each attack he experienced what he called a "flash-back."[1]

He explained that this usually had to do with himself and his past but was "much more distinct" than anything he could summon to his memory.

At the time of operation, stimulation of a point on the anterior part of the first temporal convolution on the right caused him to say, "I feel as though I were in the bathroom at school." Five minutes later, after negative stimulations elsewhere, the electrode was reapplied near the same point. The patient then said something about "street corner." The surgeon asked him, "where," and he replied, "South Bend, Indiana, corner of Jacob and Washington." When asked to explain, he said he seemed to be looking at himself—at a younger age.

When the stimulation was repeated the response was quite different. This time he said, "that music, from 'Guys and Dolls.' " When asked which song in the play he referred to, he could not name it. "I was listening to it," he said. "It was an orchestration. . . ."

Such results have been produced many times and we have used every practicable control and verification. The following case may be reported in greater detail.

Case M. M.: The patient M. M. was a woman of 26 years who was afflicted by recurring cerebral seizures. The first manifestation of each attack was a sudden "feeling —as though I had lived through this all before." At times there was also a feeling of fear. On other occasions she experienced what she called a flash-back not unlike those just described in the case of T. S.

The initial feeling of familiarity she described as applying to the whole of any experience she might be having at the moment. On the other hand, the flash-backs were experiences from her earlier life. They came suddenly while she retained awareness of her actual surroundings. She gave the following example: Without warning she seemed to be sitting in the railroad station of a small town, which might be Vanceburg, Kentucky, or perhaps Garrison. "It is winter and the wind is blowing outside and I am waiting for a train." This was apparently an experience from her earlier life but it was one she had "forgotten."

These minor seizures (psychical seizures) were often followed by automatism, periods of irresponsible behaviour of which she would have no memory. During these periods she might fall or walk about in a confused state, speaking unrelated and disjointed words and sentences.

---

[1]Flash-back is an expression used by those familiar with moving picture techniques to describe the presentation of a scene that has occurred in the earlier history of one of the characters of the play.

Thus, in summary, the localized epileptic discharges in the right temporal lobe of this young woman were causing her to experience, from time to time: 1) a sense of false familiarity (déjà vu), 2) a feeling of fear, 3) reproductions of previous experience. The first was an illusion, the second an emotion, the third an hallucination. These are all to be considered psychical phenomena, any one of which the operator might hope to reproduce by stimulation.

• • •

Case R. M.: During stimulation of the superior surface of the left temporal lobe within the fissure of Sylvius, R. M. said: "A guy coming through the fence at the baseball game, I see the whole thing." Afterward he said, "I just happened to watch those two teams play when the fellow came through the fence. . . . That would be like the beginning of an attack, anything might come up." He went on to explain that such scenes from his past came to him suddenly at the beginning of a seizure, when he was thinking of something else, things he had forgotten all about.

One more example may be described. In this case the hallucination had to do with thoughts. It is difficult to discover whether in such cases the thought is divorced from any visual or auditory content or not.

Case A. D.: This patient had temporal lobe seizures introduced by having what he called two thoughts simultaneously.

Stimulation in the first temporal convolution caused him to say, "My thoughts bounced together and I was mixed up for a second."

When the stimulation was repeated, he said, "The same two thoughts came together." After the electrode was withdrawn he explained that one of the thoughts was concerned with what was happening at the present time and the second thought was different but he could not recall it clearly.

When the same area was stimulated after an interval of time, he said, "This is it." When asked whether he had had a memory, he said, "No. It is the thought that crosses." But he could not explain and gave up the effort.

DISCUSSION

The foregoing examples demonstrate the nature of evidence upon which this discussion must be based. I have published other cases elsewhere and shall draw on our total experience in this argument.

Psychical responses

From the patient's point of view there is a great difference between psychical responses and sensory responses to stimulation. When a sensory area is stimulated the patient never seems to feel an object. He does not hear words or music, nor see a person or building. In sensory responses there are no recollections of the past and the subject himself is usually clear that the sensation is not an ordinary experience at all.

What we have referred to as "psychical responses," on the other hand, include many different elements of thought, made up of auditory, visual, somatic, and labyrinthine information, as well as interpretations, perceptions, comparisons, emotions.

Under the heading of psychical, there are two types of response. One is a reproduction of past experience and the other is a sudden alteration in interpretation of present experience. Thus the psychical responses to stimulation, taken together, may be divided into two groups:

1. *Experiential*. This has to do with the past and includes past events and past interpretation.

2. *Interpretive*. This has to do with the present.

Experiential responses

When these flash-backs, these short reproductions of past experience, occurred as epileptic phenomena, Jackson called them "dreamy states." They are the same when produced by stimulation—drawn from the patient's past experience. Let me use the words of the patient M. M. again: "I had a little memory—a scene from a play—they were talking and I could see it," and again, "Oh, . . . familiar memory, in an office somewhere. I could see the desks. I was there and someone was calling to me, a man leaning on a desk with a pencil in his hand."

All the detail of those things to which she had paid attention are still there. Perhaps the pencil in his hand had seemed important, but other images that must have reached her retina during the original experience are now lost, for they were ignored originally. Throughout all of these evoked experiences she continued to be aware of the fact that she was actually in the operating room.

It is clear that a flash-back response is usually completely experiential, including events and also the patient's interpretation. The patient feels the attendant emotion and understands the original meaning.

Interpretive responses

As an example of interpretive responses, take again the case of M. M. When the electrode was applied to another area of the temporal lobe it produced a sudden sense of familiarity which she referred at once to her present experience. She felt the operation had happened before and that she even knew what the surgeon was about to do. This occurred independently of any recollection of the past.

When such interpretations have been described by temporal lobe epileptics, clinicians have long called them "déjà vu" phenomena. They are disturbances of the present process of interpretation. They are illusions, but these illusions take different forms. There may be a false sense of familiarity as already described; or, on the contrary, everything may seem strange or absurd. The relationship of the individual to his environment may seem to be altered. The distance from things seen or heard may seem to be increased or decreased. The patient may say he is far away from himself or from the world.

Allied to these altered interpretations is the production of emotions not justified by the experience. Fear is the commonest emotion produced by stimulation. It was reported as an epileptic aura 22 times out of 271 cases of temporal lobe biopsy and was produced by stimulation 9 times.

All of these are interpretive responses. They correspond with the judgments which a normal individual is making constantly as he compares present experience with past experience. If a decision is to be made as to whether present experience is familiar or appropriate or menacing, the record of past experience must be available and the new record must be somehow classified with similar old records for the purposes of comparison.

Localization

Both types of response, experiential and interpretive, argue for the existence of a permanent ganglionic recording of the stream of consciousness. The record of that stream must be preserved in a specialized mechanism. Otherwise experiential responses to an electrode applied locally would be impossible. It seems likely also that appropriate parts of this same record are somehow utilized when recurring judgments are made in regard to familiarity and meaning of each new experience.

• • •

Doubling of conscious experience

When stimulation produced an experiential response during operative exploration, the patient usually recognized that this was something out of his own past. At the same time he may have been acutely aware of the fact that he was lying upon the operating table. Thus he was able to contemplate and to talk about this doubling of awareness and to recognize it as a strange paradox.

A young man who had recently come from his home in South Africa cried out when the superior surface of his right temporal lobe was being stimulated: "Yes, Doctor, yes, Doctor! Now I hear people laughing—my friends—in South Africa." After stimulation was over he could discuss that double awareness and express his astonishment, for it had seemed to him that he was with his cousins at their home where he and the two young ladies were laughing together. He did not remember what they were laughing at. Doubtless he would have discovered that also, if the strip of experience had happened to begin earlier, or if the surgeon had continued the stimulation a little longer.

This was an experience from his earlier life. It had faded from his recollective memory, but the ganglionic pattern which must have been formed during that experience was still intact and available to the stimulating electrode. It was at least as clear to him as it would have been had he closed his eyes and ears 30 seconds after the event and rehearsed the whole scene "from memory." Sight and sound and personal interpretation, all were re-created for him.

It is significant, however, that during the re-creation of that past experience he was not impelled to speak to his cousins. Instead he spoke to the "Doctor" in the operating room. Herein may lie an important distinction between this form of hallucination and the hallucinations of a patient during a toxic delirium or a psychotic state. In my experience (and relying only on my own memory!) no patient has ever addressed himself to a person who was part of a past experience, unless perhaps it was when he had passed into a state of automatism.[2]

As J. T. lay on the operating table two sets of ganglionic recordings were available to him for his conscious consideration, one that had been laid down during an interval of time that belonged to the past, and another that was being laid down during an equal interval of time in what we may call the

---

[2]During automatism patients sometimes talk about unrelated matters, which might suggest that they were addressing someone, but they never describe hallucinations and there is complete subsequent amnesia.

present. He was evidently able to distinguish between the present experience and the past and so he addressed himself in astonishment to one of the actors in the present experience.

In the recording which he was then making of the present experience, he was including the experience that came to him from the past, together with the sensory information of his present environment in the operating room, and the results of his reasoning in regard to the two recordings.

When such states occurred in an epileptic attack, Hughlings Jackson spoke of a doubling of consciousness. But there is an important difference in the two experiences. Although the sensory elements may be as realistic in one as in the other, the interpretation in the flash-back was all finished while the interpretation of both experiences had to be made and recorded as a part of the present experience!

When we discussed the matter, the patient and I, during the period of convalescence which followed removal of a large portion of his right temporal lobe, he recalled the whole affair and also his own surprise that he should hear his friends so far away and laugh with them while he faced such a serious situation here in Montreal.

One might suggest that, while the right temporal lobe under the influence of stimulation was engaged in the reproduction of the experience from the past, the left temporal lobe was being employed by the patient in the formation of the recording of the whole present experience. Such a suggestion is, of course, no more than a surmise. But that he did make a new record of both experiences somewhere is certain.

There are two elements in the experiential record, first the sensory material of which the subject was originally aware and, second, the interpretation of the sensory material with a conclusion as to its significance. As already pointed out, in order to make the second, or interpretive, element possible, there must be comparison with past experience so that a conclusion may be drawn as to familiarity, strangeness, distance, danger, advantage, and necessity for action. It seems likely that under normal conditions the actual recording of the stream of consciousness may be utilized for the purposes of comparison long after it has been lost to voluntary recall.

Tempo of action

I conclude that the interval of time involvement in the past experience is the same as the time required for its subsequent re-enactment. The action or thought in the re-enactment progresses at the same speed as during the original experience. I make this conclusion about speed from consideration of the following evidence:

The patient N. C., whose case has been described, listened to an orchestra while the electrode was applied. When she hummed the air, accompanying thus the music, the tempo of her humming was the tempo that would be expected of an orchestra.

Let me give another similar example.

D. F. was an intelligent young woman, a secretary and amateur musician. After the anterior end of her right temporal lobe had been amputated, the cut surface of the gray matter was stimulated at a point on the superior surface of the lobe. The stimulus caused her to say that she heard an orchestra playing and she asserted that we had turned on a phonograph. When she hummed the tune, Miss Phoebe Stanley, the operating nurse, recognizing the song, supplied the words of the lyric. The tempo of the patient's humming was certainly the tempo that would be expected of an orchestra playing that air.

And so, since the music is reproduced at a normal tempo regardless of the number of electrical impulses per second which may be varied from 30 to 100, I would conclude that the rate of movement in the re-created experience is the same as that of the original occurrence.

Further, and more important, verification of this conclusion is to be found in the fact that no patient has suggested that the people who walked or spoke or called during the hallucination did so at an unusual or unexpected rate of speed.

The patient's interpretation of an experiential response

Some patients call the response a dream. Others state that it is a flash-back from their own life history. All agree that it is more vivid than anything that they could recall voluntarily.

G. F. was caused to hear her small son, Frank, speaking in the yard outside her own kitchen, and she heard the "neighborhood sounds" as well. Ten days after operation she was asked if this was a memory. "Oh, no," she replied. "It seemed more real than that." Then she added: "Of course, I have heard Frankie like that many, many times, thousands of times."

This response to stimulation was a single experience. Her memory of such occasions was a generalization. Without the aid of the electrode, she could not recall any one of the specific instances nor hear the honking of automobiles that might mean danger to Frankie, or cries of other children or the barking of dogs that would have made up the "neighborhood sounds" on each occasion.

The patients have never looked upon an experiential response as a remembering. Instead of that it is a hearing—and seeing—again, a living-through moments of past time. Do you remember Dickens' Christmas Carol, and how Old Scrooge seemed to re-live certain boyhood experiences under the strange spell of the "Spirit of Christmas Past"? It seems to be a little like that.

D. F. listened to an orchestra in the operating room but did not recall where she had heard it "that way." It was a song she had never learned to sing or play. Perhaps she had been oblivious of her surroundings while she listened to the orchestra in that previous period of time. T. S. heard music and seemed to be in the theatre where he had heard it. A. Br. heard the singing of a Christmas song in her church at home in Holland. She seemed to be there in the church and was moved again by the beauty of the occasion just as she had been on that Christmas Eve some years before.

Content of the record

The nature of the contents of the record of the stream of consciousness may be guessed from the words of the patients that I have quoted tonight and of patients included in previous publications. It may be surmised also, by any clinician, from critical study of the content of the temporal lobe seizures which Hughlings Jackson called dreamy states. It may be guessed from the fact that when you meet a friend after many years you detect the little changes in him in a way that proves you had not lost the detail of original experiences. It may well be that seeing him renders details of the original record available for comparison, details which were lost to voluntary recollection.

The recording has strong visual and auditory components but always it is an unfolding of sight and sound and also, though rarely, of sense of position. The experience goes forward. There are no still pictures.

Curiously enough, no patient has yet reported pain or taste or smell during an experiential response. These sensations, without recollection of previous experience, were elicited by the electrode only from sensory areas. They were considered by the patient to be no more than present sensations, not elements in a past experience. It should be said, however, that the failure to get a response of any particular type has little statistical value, for the total number of patients from whom psychical responses have been elicited is, after all, small.[3]

One might seek to discover whether reasoning, which is divorced from awareness of sensory phenomena, finds any place in the cortical record. It is difficult for me to explore this possibility which involves certain questions of philosophical analysis. But it may be pointed out that patients do sometimes speak of unexpected thoughts coming into mind as a warning of the onset of a focal seizure. They usually report that this confuses them so that the account they give of the matter is not clear.

An example was presented above (Case A. D.) of the production of two thoughts by temporal stimulation. The patient said that one thought had to do with what was going on at the present time and the second thought was different, but the effect upon him was confusion and inability to explain. It might seem that two lines of reasoning or thinking could not co-exist without interference and that, if thoughts were really re-activated, they confused the patient's present effort to rationalize.

However that may be, it seems clear that the final interpretation and the understanding of any experience are recorded with the experience. This interpretation and understanding may be considered the end result or the conclusion of rationalization. Certainly, at the times of re-activation, the patient has no difficulty in perceiving his former understanding of a situation along with the objective aspects of the situation itself.

Memory contrasted with the record

It is clear that each successive recording is somehow classified and compared with previous recordings so that, little by little, each separate song is "learned" and becomes a unit in the memory, and all the familiar things in a man's life undergo the same change. A poem or an elocution may be "committed to memory." But memory, as we ordinarily think of it, is something

---

[3]My associate Dr. Sean Mullan informs me that there have been 87 cases of temporal lobe epilepsy in which electrical exploration was carried out during the past three years. In only 22 of them did stimulation produce echoes of past experiences. We have explored the cortex in 271 temporal lobe cases in all, which suggests that not over 60 patients had experiential responses. In no cases where the epileptogenic focus was located in central or frontal regions have there been such responses.

more, and a great deal less, than any recording, unless that recording was made unusually vivid by fear or joy or special meaning. Then perhaps the detail of an original experience and the patient's memory of it might be identical.

The psychical responses of the "flash-back" variety were, for the most part, quite unimportant moments in the patient's life: standing on a street corner, hearing a mother call her child, taking a part in a conversation, listening to a little boy as he played in the yard. If these unimportant minutes of time were preserved in the ganglionic recordings of these patients, why should it be thought that any experience in the stream of consciousness drops out?

The evidence suggests that nothing is lost, that the record of each man's experience is complete. The time taken up by deep sleep or coma must drop out and it must be left an open question as to whether or not the time taken up by reasoning is included in the record.

CONCLUSION

In conclusion it is evident that the brain of every man contains an unchanging ganglionic record of successive experience. The psychical responses which have been produced by electrical stimulation, during craniotomy and cortical exploration, demonstrate that this record embraces and retains the elements that once were incorporated in his stream of thought.

Simply expressed, the conditions which bring about these psychical responses, both experiential and interpretive, are these: The stimulating electrode, delivering for example 60 impulses per second, is applied to a point on the temporal cortex of a man who is fully awake. The ganglion cells of the cortex are hyper-irritable and ready to react because, for years, small electrical discharges have been playing over the cortical blanket day and night from a neighboring epileptogenic focus.

Thousands of these conditioned ganglion cells may well be reached directly by the stimulating current and they have neuronal connections that pass through the gray matter that covers the temporal lobe and also inward to the central integrating circuits of the brain stem. But instead of mass activity, a selective and highly patterned ganglionic action results.

Let me describe what seems to happen by means of a parable: Among the millions and millions of nerve cells that clothe certain parts of the temporal lobe on each side, there runs a thread. It is the thread of time, the thread that has run through each succeeding, wakeful hour of the individual's past life. Think of this thread, if you like, as a pathway through an unending sequence of nerve cells, nerve fibers, and synapses. It is a pathway which can be followed again because of the continuing facilitation that has been created in the cell contacts.

When, by chance, the neurosurgeon's electrode activates some portion of that thread, there is a response as though that thread were a wire recorder, or a strip of cinematographic film, on which are registered all those things of which the individual was once aware, the things he selected for his attention in that interval of time. Absent from it are the sensory impulses he ignored, the talk he did not heed.

Time's strip of film runs forward, never backward, even when resurrected from the past. It seems to proceed again at time's own unchanged pace. It would seem, once one section of the strip has come alive, that a functional all-or-nothing principle steps in so as to protect the other portions of the film from activation by the electric current. As long as the electrode is held in place, the experience of a former day goes forward. There is no holding it still, no turning it back. When the electrode is withdrawn it stops as suddenly as it began.[4]

We have found a way of activating the anatomical record of the stream of consciousness. It is evident, therefore, that the ganglionic mechanism which preserves man's experiential record is either present, in duplicate, in the temporal cortex of each hemisphere, where stimulation produces these responses; or it is located in duplicate in the hippocampal zones of each side where direct stimulation does not produce the responses; or, finally, it is located more centrally in the brain where the closest functional connection is maintained with the stimulable zones of the temporal lobes.

However that may be, and whatever the mechanism involved, it is certain that in the temporal cortex lie the keys of activation of the record.

During any given period of waking time each individual forms a record of the stream of consciousness. The record is the final expression, and the outcome, of the action of central integration of nerve impulses. The formation of this record is subject to the selecting and limiting influences of attention. As the record is formed, it includes the elements of consciousness. Possibly, like a film, its contents are projected on the screen of man's awareness before it is replaced by subsequent experience. Thus it might seem that the record of the stream of consciousness is more than a record. It represents one of the final stages in the neuronal integration which makes consciousness what it is.

Probably no man can, by voluntary effort, completely re-activate any portion of the record of the stream of thought. Except for a few seconds or minutes after the event, he seems to have no voluntary mechanism that rivals the electrode. Memory, as ordinarily conceived, is quite a different phenomenon. It seems likely, however, that the original record continues to be available in some sort of way for the purposes of the comparison and interpretation of each new experience, as long as a man may live and keep his wits.

The stream of consciousness flows inexorably onward, as described in the words of William James. But, unlike a river, it leaves behind it a permanent record that seems to be complete for the waking moments of a man's life, a record that runs, no doubt, like a thread along a pathway of ganglionic and synaptic facilitations in the brain. This pathway is located partly or wholly in the temporal lobes.

There is hope in all this that physiology and psychology, and philosophy, too, may be drawn more closely together and that, with the opening of a new chapter of understanding of the localization of function within the human brain, some light may yet be thrown upon the mind of man.

---

[4]A particular strip can sometimes be repeated by interrupting the stimulation and then reapplying it at the same or a nearby point, for the threshold of evocation of that particular response is lowered for a time by the first stimulus. Graham Brown and Sherrington described local facilitation and intensification of motor responses by repeated stimulation at a single point in the anthropoid cortex, and we have found the same to be true for man in motor and sensory areas of the cortex.

Chapter 5

Memory transfer through cannibalism in planarians*

James V. McConnell

The search for the engram—the unit of memory—is not a new endeavor, but looking for this memory unit in the chemistry of the body is a recent development. James V. McConnell's work with the flatworm constitutes one of the beginnings of this new trend in memory theory. Starting with a demonstration that even flatworms are able to learn, proceeding with research suggesting that what one flatworm learns can somehow be chemically transferred to another flatworm, and hypothesizing that the chemical transfer agent (and presumably the memory unit) might be ribonucleic acid, McConnell and a host of other researchers have touched off a new area of controversy in psychology and society in general. An unequivocal answer to the question, "What and where is the engram?" is still absent; but already popular magazines are speculating about the "memory pill."

The following article makes no pretense of "settling" the issue, but it does provide an interesting account of much of the early work with flatworms. It presents an outline of how this research has been related to the chemicals ribonucleic acid (RNA) and deoxyribonucleic acid (DNA) and admits that we are still far short of an adequate total theory of memory. As one reads this article, however, it is difficult not to think of the era of the "memory pill."

The research that I am going to outline today had its start several years ago, and I trust you will allow me to give you a few of the pertinent background details, if only to convince you that our work is more serious than it sometimes sounds, and of sufficient scope at least to approach respectability. It was in 1953, when I was a graduate student at the University of Texas, that a fellow student, Robert Thompson, suggested to me that we attempt to condition a planarian, or common flatworm. Having avoided the rigors of introductory Zoology up to that point, my only prior experience with worms had

*From *Journal of Neuropsychiatry* **3**:42-48, 1962.

been at the business end of a fishing pole. I soon discovered, however, that fishing worms are round, while planarians are flat. Planarians are also usually less than an inch in length, and rather interesting in their own right.

Flatworms occupy a unique niche on the phylogenetic scale, being the lowest organisms to possess bilateral symmetry, a rude form of encephalization, and a human, synaptic-type nervous system. According to some psychological theories—the ones that postulate that learning is a matter of reshuffling connections among neurons—the planarian should be the lowest organism to be able to demonstrate "true" learning. As far as we knew in 1953, no one had ever demonstrated unequivocally that these organisms could indeed be trained. Since then, of course, we have discovered the usual obscure reference that antedates our work by 30 years—it appears in Dutch and was published in a little-read European journal—but I am not at all sure that even this knowledge would have deterred us. At any rate, Thompson and I set out in 1953 to attempt classical conditioning in planarians.

Imagine a trough gouged out of plastic, 12 inches in length, semi-circular in cross-section, and filled with pond water. At either end are brass electrodes attached to a power source. Above the trough are two electric light bulbs. Back and forth in the trough crawls a single flatworm, and in front of the apparatus sits the experimenter, his eye on the worm, his hands on two switches. When the worm is gliding smoothly in a straight line on the bottom of the trough, the experimenter turns on the lights for 3 seconds. After the light has been on for two of the three seconds, the experimenter adds one second of electric shock, which passes through the water and causes the worm to contract. The experimenter records the behavior of the worm during the two-second period after the light has come on but before the shock has started. If the animal gives a noticeable turning movement or a contraction prior to the onset of the shock, this is scored as a "correct" or "conditioned" response.

From this brief description of the experimental paradigm, many of you will recognize that Thompson and I were attempting to establish a form of Pavlovian conditioning in our experimental animals (Group E), and according to our data, we were successful. Planarians occasionally give a mild and presumably innate response to the onset of the light even when it has not been previously paired with shock, so we ran a control group that received just trials of photic (light) stimulation (Group LC); we also ran a control group that received just shock, occasionally interspersing a test trial of light alone (Group SC). All animals were given 150 trials. Over that period of time, as Tables 3 and 4 show, the experimental animals, which received light paired with shock, showed a significant increase in responsivity, while the control groups showed either no change at all or a significant decline.

Hence Thompson and I concluded that we had accomplished what we set out to accomplish—namely, we had proven that worms could be conditioned.

Those of you who have ever chopped up a planarian in a Zoology course will know that these animals have enormous powers of regeneration. A large specimen may be cut into perhaps 50 pieces, each of which will eventually regenerate into a complete organism. It was while we were running that first experiment that Thompson and I wondered aloud, feeling rather foolish as we did so, what would happen if we conditioned a flatworm, then cut it in

Table 3. Mean turns, contractions, and combined responses on the first 50 and last 50 trials for Groups E (experimental) and LC (light control)

Group	Response	First 50 trials	Last 50 trials	Diff.	p
E	Turns	12.6	16.6	4.0	.01
	Contractions	1.2	5.0	3.8	.01
	Combined	13.8	21.6	7.8	.01
LC	Turns	11.7	7.6	−4.1	.01
	Contractions	0.6	2.1	1.5	
	Combined	12.3	9.7	−2.6	

Table 4. Mean turns, contractions, and combined responses on the first 15 and last 15 test trials for Group SC (shock control)

Response	First 15 test trials	Last 15 test trials	Diff.*
Turns	5.4	4.2	−1.2
Contractions	0.2	0.4	0.2
Combined	5.6	4.6	−1.0

*None of the differences is significant at the .05 level of confidence.

two and let both halves regenerate. Which half would retain the memory? As it happened, we never got around to performing that experiment at Texas, for Thompson received his doctorate soon after we finished our first study and went on to Lousiana State University and bigger and better things—namely, rats. When I went to the University of Michigan in 1956, however, I was faced with the difficult problem that in the academic world, one must publish or perish. The only thing I knew much about was flatworms, so I talked two bright young students, Allan Jacobson and Daniel Kimble, into performing the obvious experiment on learning and regeneration.

Kimble, Jacobson and I did the following. We took our experimental animals and trained them to a criterion of 23 responses out of any block of 25 trials. When they had reached this criterion, we assumed that they were properly conditioned and immediately cut them in half across the middle. Head and tail sections were then put in individual bowls and allowed about 4 weeks to regenerate. At the end of this period, these experimental animals (Group E) were re-trained to the same criterion and savings scores calculated. We also ran a group of worms which were cut, allowed to regenerate, and then were conditioned for the first time—this to tell us if cutting and subsequent regeneration in any way sensitized the animals to conditioning (Group RC). Another control group was conditioned, then allowed to rest uncut for a month before being retested (Group TC)—this to tell us how much forgetting we could expect in our experimental animals had we not cut them in half.

In all honesty I must admit that we did not obtain the results we had expected. We had assumed that the regenerated heads would show fairly

Table 5. Number of trials to criterion for Group E (experimental)

S	Original training	Retest head	Retest tail
E1	99	50	51
E2	191	37	24
E3	97	48	72
E4	83	35	44
E5	200	30	25
M	134	40	43.2

Table 6. Number of trials to criterion for Group RC (regeneration control)

S	Head	Tail
RC1	134	150
RC2	188	179
RC3	276	85
RC4	395	300
RC5	250	325
M	248.6	207.8

Table 7. Number of trials for Group TC (time control)

S	Original training	Retest
TC1	123	24
TC2	153	25
TC3	195	62
TC4	131	43
TC5	325	45
M	185.4	39.8

complete retention of the response for, after all, the head section retained the primitive brain and "everybody knows" that the brain is where memories are located. And, as Tables 5, 6, and 7 indicate, the heads did show just as much retention as did the uncut control animals. We had also hoped, in our heart of hearts, that perhaps the tails would show a slight but perhaps significant retention of some kind, merely because we thought this would be an interesting finding. We were astounded, then, to discover that the tails not only showed as much retention as did the heads, but in many cases did much better than the heads and showed absolutely no forgetting whatsoever. Obviously memory, in the flatworm, was being stored throughout the animal's body, and as additional proof of this we found that if we cut the worm into three or even more pieces, each section typically showed clear-cut retention of the conditioned response.

It was at this time that we first postulated our theory that conditioning caused some chemical change throughout the worm's body, and it was also about then that Reeva Jacobson came along to help us test what seemed at

Table 8. Number of trials to criterion for totally regenerated animals

S	Original training	Retest after total regeneration
1	200	166
2	325	143
3	300	220
4	327	51
5	75	62
6	381	94
mean	268	122.7
SD	102	60

the time to be rather an odd hypothesis. She took planarians, cut off their tails, and conditioned the heads before any regeneration could take place. Then she let her animals grow new tails. She next removed these new tails and let them grow new heads, ending up with apparently completely reformed organisms. These total regenerates, as we called them, were then tested for any "savings" of the original conditioning. By now we knew what to expect from planarians, and so we weren't too surprised when Reeva's regenerated flatworms showed a significant retention of what the original organism had learned. True, as Table 8 suggests, these total regenerates did not demonstrate the complete retention that our original animals had shown, but they did remember enough so that our hypothesis seemed vindicated.

By now, worms were in the *Zeitgeist*. Edward Ernhart, working with Carl Sherrick at Washington University, demonstrated not only that flatworms could learn a two-unit T-maze, but also that this maze habit was retained by their animals following cutting and regeneration. Again, the tails remembered at least as much as did the heads. Ernhart is perhaps most famous, however, for a more recent study of his. If one takes a flatworm and splits the head straight down the middle, time and time again, the two halves will not heal together but will each regenerate into a complete head. One ends up, then, with a two-headed worm. Ernhart compared the length of time it took two-headed animals to be conditioned with the length of time it took one-headed (or normal) animals to reach the same criterion and found that he had validated an old aphorism—two heads are indeed better than one.

Roy John and William Corning, working at the University of Rochester, became quite interested in the chemical theory of learning about this time, and undertook one of the most spectacular pieces of research yet to come from any worm laboratory. John reasoned that learning in flatworms had to be mediated, at least in part, by some molecular change within the organism's cells. Since Hydén had found changes in RNA in nerve cells as a result of experience, John believed that RNA might be implicated in learning and retention in planarians. So he and Corning conditioned a number of flatworms, cut them in half, and let them regenerate in a weak solution of ribonuclease, which breaks up RNA. When they compared their experimental animals with a number of controls, they found evidence that the experimental heads were relatively unaffected by the ribonuclease, while the tails showed complete forgetting. The tails could be retrained, but it took approximately as long the second time as it had the first.

Ralph Gerard, the noted neurophysiologist, interprets the data as follows: There are probably two distinct but related physiological mechanisms for learning in planarians. The first such mechanism is the familiar one of neural interconnections which are reshuffled in the brain due to the animal's experiences—the so-called circuit-diagram model, if I may be permitted the analogy. Structural changes in the neural pathways in the brain would presumably not be altered by ribonuclease, which accounts for the fact that the Rochester head-regenerates showed no real forgetting. The second type of memory mechanism, however, involves a change in the coding of the RNA molecules in the cells throughout the worm's body. Presumably whenever the animal learns, the RNA is altered appropriately so that when regeneration takes place, the altered RNA builds the memory into the regenerated animal right from the start. If the RNA were destroyed by the ribonuclease, it is likely that the DNA in the cells would replace the lost RNA, but this replacement RNA would not carry the changed code since the DNA was presumably unaffected by the learning.

If all of this sounds rather complex, you must forgive me. I am not at all sure that at this early date we have more than the vaguest notion just how learning could affect RNA nor how, much less why, this altered RNA might build the memory into the regenerating tissue. The important thing to remember is that John's hunch that RNA might be involved in memory seems to have been substantiated.

Before further discussing RNA and memory, I should like to detail, briefly, some other research that Roy John and Bill Corning, at Rochester, and my own group of worm runners at the University of Michigan and at the Britannica Center in Palo Alto have been pursuing jointly. In 1957, when we got our first results on retention of learning following regeneration, and came up with our chemical hypothesis, it seemed to us that we might be able to transfer a memory from a trained animal to an untrained animal if we could somehow get the right chemicals out of the first worm and into the second. We spent several years trying to test this admittedly wild notion without much success. First we tried grafting the head of a trained animal onto the tail of an untrained planarian, but this never worked very well. If one reads introductory zoology tests, one often gets the notion this little operation is most easy to perform. Sadly enough, the best average on record is three successes out of 150 attempts and we simply did not have 150 trained heads to waste. We tried grinding the trained worms up and injecting the pieces into untrained animals, but we never could master the injection techniques. It was only some time after we began this work that it occurred to us that we could let the animals do the transferring for us. For, under the proper conditions, one worm will eat another. And since planarians have but the most rudimentary of digestive tracts, there seemed an excellent chance that the tissue from the food worm would pass into the body of the cannibal relatively unchanged.

So, with Barbara Humphries as our chief experimenter, we conditioned a number of worms, chopped them into small pieces and hand-fed the pieces to untrained cannibals. We also took the precaution of feeding a number of un-trained worms to untrained cannibals for a control or comparison group. Our first pilot study gave us such unbelievable results that we immediately insti-tuted several changes in our procedure and repeated the study not once, but four times. And each time the results were quite significant—and still rather unbelievable. I should mention before going any further that the chief pro-cedural change we made was the institution of a "blind" running technique which helped guard against experimenter bias. Under this blind procedure, the person actually training the worms never knows anything about the ani-mals he runs—we follow an elaborate coding system in which each animal's code letter is changed daily. The experimenter then doesn't know which ani-mal is in which group, nor even which animal is which from day to day. Thus, as far as we could tell, we could not have unconsciously tampered with the data.

The results of this work, as Table 9 shows, were somewhat startling. In all five studies, it was clear that the cannibals which had fed on trained worms gave approximately half again as many conditioned responses during the first days of training as did the cannibals which had fed on untrained worms. In our studies, the differences between the two groups tended to disappear after the first few days as the control animals approached criterion. The experimen-tal animals were presumably so close to criterion right from the start that the slope of their learning curve was much less than that of the controls.

Table 9. Number of responses in first 25 training trials for cannibals fed conditioned planarians (experimentals) and for cannibals fed unconditioned planarians (controls). Number of responses in first 25 trials

Experimentals	Controls
4	1
6	1
7	3
8	4
8	4
8	4
9	5
10	5
10	5
10	6
11	6
12	6
13	6
14	7
14	7
15	10
15	10
15	11
15	11
17	16
18	22
19	
mean 11.73	7.14

I would also like to mention a couple of fortunate mistakes we made which do not prove anything but which are interesting evidence in their own right. One time our elaborate coding system broke down and a control animal was fed a piece of conditioned worm. For several days prior to this feeding, the control animal had been responding at an average of 2 or 3 times out of any 25 trials. Immediately following this inadvertent meal of conditioned tissue, the animal performed at criterion level, giving 23 responses out of the next 25 trials. Then there was one group of cannibals which we accidentally fed animals that had been given a number of conditioning trials, but which were not even close to criterion when we cut them up. The cannibals which ate these trained but not-yet-conditioned worms showed absolutely no transfer effect at all.

Now, if we had been the only ones to have obtained such results, our findings might be dismissed as the achievement of crackpots. Luckily for us, Corning, Karpick, and John instituted their own program of cannibalism shortly after we did and so far have run two large and very well controlled studies, both using the blind technique, and have obtained results which are essentially identical to ours.

And, as if this were not enough, our work has just been replicated by a high school student. Let me quote briefly from the Washington *Post* of 25 March, 1962. "A 17-year-old girl's rather startling answer to a rather startling question—'Is Knowledge Edible?'—brought her one of the two top prizes in a Northern Virginia Science Fair yesterday. Tentatively, Ruth Ann Ziegler's answer is 'yes.'

"What Miss Ziegler found was that a worm who eats an educated worm learns things twice as fast as his brother who eats an uneducated worm. Hence her title, 'Is Knowledge Edible?'

"By electrical shocks she taught flatworms to respond to light. An ordinary flatworm needs about 260 shocks before he responds without one. He is then 'conditioned.'

"Experiments taught Miss Ziegler that a worm fed the head of an unconditioned worm needs an average of 264 shocks. A worm fed an unconditioned tail needs 269.

"But a worm fed a conditioned tail takes only 168 shocks and a worm fed a conditioned head a mere 140 shocks.

"This experiment was part of Miss Ziegler's effort to see if conditioned learning is affected by chemicals and, if it is, if it can be passed on through regeneration and ingestion. It's apparently 'yes' all the way."

Frankly, we are not quite sure where all of this work leaves us—except that we are most definitely out on a limb of some kind. At the moment, a number of laboratories around the country are starting investigations into the biochemistry of learning, using planarians as their tools. Specifically, several of us are attempting to extract RNA, DNA and other biochemicals from conditioned worms to feed to untrained cannibals. If we can show, for example, that RNA and only RNA causes the memory transfer, we can surely hope to determine the subtle molecular differences between "trained" and "untrained" RNA. If this could be done, we would be one step closer to cracking the problem of the molecular properties of memory—perhaps a giant step closer at that, particularly if it turns out that teaching the animals different sorts of habits causes different sorts of changes in the RNA molecules. But perhaps that is too much to hope for at the present.

Now, in conclusion, let me attempt to tie all of this research together. We have shown that planarians are capable of learning, that this learning survives cutting and regeneration, that the memory storage mechanism has a bio-chemical component (probably RNA) which is widely distributed throughout the animal's body, and that learning seems to be transferrable from one animal to another via cannibalistic ingestion. If memory in higher organisms is also mediated via biochemical changes, and if these changes are specific to the habits learned, we might eventually discover a substance (probably RNA with a deliberately modified structure) which would facilitate learning if it were incorporated into animal or human bodies. If so, the research we have been doing with our lowly flatworms may have practical consequences we never dreamed of when we began our work some nine years ago.

Chapter 6

Imprinting*

Eckhard H. Hess

Students of behavior generally agree that the early experiences of animals (including man) have a profound effect on their adult behavior. Some psychologists go so far as to state that the effect of early experience upon adult behavior is inversely correlated with age. This may be an oversimplification, but in general it appears to hold true. Thus, the problem of the investigator is not so much to find out *whether* early experience determines adult behavior as to discover *how* it determines adult behavior.

Three statements are usually made about the effects of early experience. The first is that early habits are very persistent and may prevent the formation of new ones. This, of course, refers not only to the experimental study of animals but also to the rearing of children. The second statement is that early perceptions deeply affect all future learning. This concept leads to the difficult question whether basic perceptions—the way we have of seeing the world about us—are inherited or acquired. The third statement is simply that early social contacts determine the character of adult social behavior. This is the phenomenon of imprinting.

At the turn of the century, Craig, experimenting with wild pigeons, found that in order to cross two different species it was first necessary to rear the young of one species under the adults of the other. Upon reaching maturity the birds so reared preferred mates of the same species as their foster parents. Other interspecies sexual fixations have been observed in birds and fishes.

Heinroth and his wife successfully reared by hand the young of almost every species of European birds. They found that many of the social responses of these birds were transferred to their human caretaker. Lorenz extended these experiments, dealing especially with greyleg geese.

Lorenz was the first to call this phenomenon "imprinting," although earlier workers had observed this effect. He was also the first to point out that it appeared to occur at a critical period early in the life of an animal. He postulated that the first object to elicit a social response later released not only that response but also related responses such as sexual behavior. Imprinting, then, was related not only to the problem of behavior but also to the general biological problem of evolution and speciation.

Although imprinting has been studied mainly in birds, it also has been ob-

*From *Science* 130:133-141, July 17, 1959. Copyright 1959 by American Association for the Advancement of Science.

served to occur in other animals. Instances of imprinting have been reported in insects, in fish, and in some mammals. Those mammals in which the phenomenon has been found—sheep, deer, and buffalo—are all animals in which the young are mobile almost immediately after birth. Controlled experimental work with mammals, however, has just begun.

The first systematic investigations of imprinting were published in 1951. Simultaneously in this country and in Europe, the work of Ramsay and Fabricius gave the first indication of some of the important variables of the process. Ramsay worked with several species of ducks and a variety of breeds of chickens. He noticed the importance of the auditory component in the imprinting experiment and the effect of changes in coloring on parental recognition as well as on recognition of the parents by the young. His findings also showed that color is an essential element in recognition, while size or form seemed to be of less importance. Most of Ramsay's experiments dealt with exchange of parents and young and did not involve the use of models or decoys as imprinting objects, although he also imprinted some waterfowl on such objects as a football or a green box.

Fabricius carried on experiments with several species of ducklings and was able to determine approximately the critical age at which imprinting was most successful in several species of ducks. In some laboratory experiments he found it impossible to do imprinting in ducklings with a silent decoy— something which my coworkers and I were easily able to do a few years later in our Maryland laboratory. After the appearance of this pioneer work by Ramsay and by Fabricius, no relevant papers appeared until 1954. At that time Ramsay and Hess published a paper on laboratory approach to the study of imprinting. The basic technique was modified slightly the following year and then was continued in the form described below. Papers in 1956 by Margaret Nice and by Hinde, Thorpe, and Vince include most of the pertinent materials published up to 1956 since Lorenz's classic statement of the problem.

Since 1956, however, there has been an increasing number of papers on imprinting in a variety of journals. However, most investigators report experiments which are primarily designed to look for ways in which imprinting can be likened to associative learning and are not primarily carried out to investigate the phenomenon itself. Later we shall return to a consideration of these experiments; for the present we shall concern ourselves mainly with the program carried out since 1951 at McDonogh and at Lake Farm Laboratory, Maryland, and at our laboratories at the University of Chicago.

EXPERIMENTAL STUDIES

Our laboratory in Maryland had access to a small duck pond in which we kept relatively wild mallards. The birds laid their eggs in nesting boxes, so the eggs could be collected regularly. After storage for a few days, the eggs were incubated in a dark, forced-air incubator. About two days before hatching, the eggs were transferred to a hatching incubator. Precautions were taken to place the newly hatched bird into a small cardboard box (5 by 4 by 4 inches) in such a way that it could see very little in the dim light used to carry out the procedure.

Each bird was given a number, which was recorded on the box itself as well as in our permanent records. The box containing the bird was then placed in a still-air incubator, used as a brooder, and kept there until the bird was to be imprinted. After the young bird had undergone the imprinting procedure, it was automatically returned to the box, and the box was then transferred to a fourth incubator, also used as a brooder, and kept there until the bird was to be tested. Only after testing was completed was the duckling placed in daylight and given food and water.

The apparatus we constructed to be used in the imprinting procedure consisted of a circular runway about 5 feet in diameter. This runway was 12 inches wide and 12½ feet in circumference at the center. Boundaries were formed by walls of Plexiglas 12 inches high. A mallard duck decoy, suspended from an elevated arm radiating from the center of the apparatus, was fitted internally with a loud-speaker and a heating element. It was held about 2 inches above the center of the runway. The arms suspending the decoy could be rotated by either of two variable-speed motors. The speed of rotating and intermittent movement could be regulated from the control panel located behind a one-way screen about 5 feet from the apparatus. The number of rotations of both the decoy and the animal were recorded automatically. Tape recorders with continuous tapes provided the sound that was played through the speaker inside the decoy. A trap door in the runway, operated from the control panel, returned the duckling to its box.

Imprinting procedure. The young mallard, at a certain number of hours after hatching, was taken in its box from the incubator and placed in the runway of the apparatus. The decoy at this time was situated about 1 foot away. By means of a cord, pulley, and clip arrangement, the observer released the bird and removed the box. As the bird was released, the sound was turned on in the decoy model, and after a short interval the decoy began to move about the circular runway. The sound we used in the imprinting of the mallard ducklings was an arbitrarily chosen human rendition of "*gock*, gock, gock, gock, gock." The decoy emitted this call continually during the imprinting process. The duckling was allowed to remain in the apparatus for a specified amount of time while making a certain number of turns in the runway. At the end of the imprinting period, which was usually less than 1 hour, the duckling was automatically returned to its box and placed in an incubator until it was tested for imprinting strength at a later hour.

Testing for imprinting. Each duckling to be tested was mechanically released from its box halfway between two duck models placed 4 feet apart. One of these was the male mallard model upon which it had been imprinted; the other was a female model which differed from the male only in its coloration. One minute was allowed for the duckling to make a decisive response to the silent models. At the end of this time, regardless of the nature of the duckling's response, sound was turned on simultaneously for each of the models. The male model made the "gock" call upon which the duckling had been imprinted, while the female model gave the call of a real mallard female calling her young.

Four test conditions followed each other in immediate succession in the testing procedure. They were: (i) both models stationary and silent; (ii) both models stationary and calling; (iii) the male stationary and the female calling; (iv) the male stationary and silent and the female moving and calling. We estimated these four tests to be in order of increasing difficulty. The time of response and the character of the call note (pleasure tones or distress notes) were recorded. Scores in percentage of positive responses were then recorded for each animal. If the duckling gave a positive response to the imprinting object (the male decoy) in all four tests, imprinting was regarded as complete, or 100 percent.

DETERMINATION OF THE "CRITICAL PERIOD"

To determine the age at which an imprinting experience was most effective we imprinted our ducklings at various ages after hatching. In this series of experiments the imprinting experience was standard. It consisted in having the duckling follow the model 150 to 200 feet around the runway during a period of 10 minutes. It appears that some imprinting occurs immediately after hatching, but a maximum score is consistently made only by those ducklings imprinted in the 13- to 16-hour-old group.

Social facilitation in imprinting. In order to find whether imprinting would occur in those ducklings which were past the critical age for imprinting —that is, over 24 hours of age—we attempted to imprint these older ducklings in the presence of another duckling which had received an intensive imprinting experience. Ducklings ranging in age from 24 to 52 hours were given 100 feet of following experience during a period of 30 minutes. The average score for the ducklings was 50 percent; this shows that some imprinting can occur as a result of social facilitation. Two conclusions can be drawn. (i) Social facilitation will extend the critical age for imprinting. (ii) The strength of imprinting in these older ducklings is significantly less than that when the animal is imprinted alone at the critical age under the same time and distance conditions; under the latter circumstances the average score made is between 80 and 90 percent. A further indication of this dissipation of imprintability with increasing age is obtained when we average the scores for those animals which were between 24 and 32 hours old. The average score for these animals was 60 percent, while the score made by older animals ranging in age from 36 to 52 hours was 43 percent. One last item points to the difference; even when the time and distance were increased during imprinting of the older ducklings there were no perfect scores. With such a large amount of distance to travel during the imprinting period, approximately 40 percent of the animals would be expected to make perfect scores if they were imprinted during the critical period.

FIELD TESTS OF IMPRINTING

In this same exploratory vein we have also carried out some studies under more normal environmental conditions. To do this we took animals imprinted in our apparatus and placed them in the duck-pond area, where they could either stay near a model placed at the water's edge or follow the model as it was moved along the surface of the duck pond, or go to real mallards which had just hatched their ducklings. Imprinted ducklings did not follow the live mallard females who had young of an age similar to that of the experimental animals. In fact, they avoided her and moved even closer to the decoy. Naive mallards, about a day old, from our incubator, immediately joined such live females and paid no attention to the decoys. These records, which we captured on motion-picture film, offer proof that what we do in the laboratory is quite relevant to the normal behavior of the animals and is not a laboratory artifact.

COLOR AND FORM PREFERENCES IN IMPRINTING OBJECTS

An examination of the importance of the form and color of an imprinting object is relevant to any inquiry concerning factors contributing to the strength of imprinting.

Eight spheres approximately 7 inches in diameter in the colors red, orange, yellow, green, and blue, and in achromatic shades of near-black, near-white, and neutral grey were presented to 95 young Vantress broiler chicks as imprinting objects. The imprinting procedure was essentially the same as that described above in the duckling experiments. All the animals were exposed to one of the spheres during the critical period. Each imprinting experience lasted for a total of 17 minutes, during which time the imprinting object moved a distance of 40 feet.

Twenty-four hours after imprinting, each animal was tested in a situation where the object to which it had been imprinted was presented, together with the remaining four colored spheres if the animal had been imprinted to a colored sphere, or with the remaining two achromatic spheres, if the animal had been imprinted to one of the achromatic spheres.

It was found that the stimuli differed significantly in the degree to which they elicited the following-reaction. The stimuli, ranked in their effectiveness for eliciting following during imprinting, from the highest to the lowest, are: blue, red, green, orange, grey, black, yellow, white. These colors, in the same order, were increasingly less effective in terms of the scores made during the testing period. We concluded from this that the coloring of a stimulus is more important than its reflectance.

In order to determine also form preferences in imprinting objects, we took the same spheres we used in determining color preferences and added superstructures of the same coloring, so that the spheres had heads, wings, and tails.

The addition of superstructures had a definite effect on the ease with which the following-reaction could be elicited: the plain ball was found to be the most efficient; the ball with wing and tail-like superstructures, less so; and the ball to which wings, tail, and head had been added, least efficient. We even presented a stuffed brown Leghorn rooster to the chicks, and it was found to be the least efficient model of all in eliciting the following response.

AUDITORY IMPRINTING IN THE EGG

Some investigators of imprinting have felt that vocalization of the incubating parent might cause imprinting to that vocalization even before the young fowl hatched. This seemed a likely hypothesis, so we carried out the following experiment. About 30 mallard eggs were incubated in an incubator with a built-in loud-speaker. For 48 hours before hatching these mallards were exposed to a constantly played taped recording of a female mallard calling her young. Eggs were removed just before hatching and placed in a different incubator. Later, when tested, these young made no significantly greater choice of this source of sound than of the "gock" call used in our normal imprinting procedure. [A preliminary experiment was reported earlier.] Auditory imprinting, while the mallard is still in the egg, is therefore considered to be unlikely.

LAW OF EFFORT

We decided to vary independently the factors of time of exposure and the actual distance traveled by the duckling during the imprinting period. Since previous results had indicated that a 10-minute exposure period was sufficient to produce testable results, we decided to run a series of animals, varying the distance traveled but keeping the time constant at 10 minutes. We therefore used one circumference of the runway ($12\frac{1}{2}$ feet) as a unit and ran groups of animals for zero, one, two, four, and eight turns. This resulted in imprinting experiences in which the ducklings moved about 1 foot, $12\frac{1}{2}$ feet, 25 feet, 50 feet, and 100 feet, respectively. All ducklings were imprinted when they were between 12 and 17 hours of age, in order to keep the variable of critical period constant. The results showed that increasing the distance over which the duckling had to follow the imprinting object increased the strength of imprinting. A leveling-off of this effect appears to occur after a distance of about 50 feet.

In order to determine the effect of length of exposure time on imprinting strengths, we chose a distance that could be traversed by ducklings in periods of time as short as 2, 10, and 30 minutes. The scores made by animals imprinted for 2, 10, and 30 minutes, respectively, while traveling a distance of $12\frac{1}{2}$ feet were essentially identical. Moreover, there is no significant difference between the findings for ducklings allowed to follow for a distance of 100 feet during a 10-minute period and those allowed 30 minutes to cover the same distance.

The strength of imprinting appeared to be dependent not on the duration of the imprinting period but on the effort exerted by the duckling in following the imprinting object. To confirm this notion we tried two supplementary experiments. In the first, we placed 4-inch hurdles in the runway so that the ducklings not only had to follow the model but also had to clear the obstacles. As we suspected, the birds which had to climb the hurdles, and thus expend more effort, made higher imprinting scores than those which traveled the same distance without obstacles. In the second experiment we allowed the duckling to follow the decoy up an inclined plane, with similar results. After further experiments we came to the conclusion that we could write a formula for imprinting: the strength of imprinting equals the logarithm of the effort expended by the animal to get to the imprinting object during the imprinting period, or $I_s = \log E$.

Previous accounts in the literature on imprinting have made the following of a moving object a necessary condition of imprinting. Our results, as formulated in the law of effort, indicate that the amount of walking done by the animal during the imprinting period is of primary significance. The following experiment was therefore carried out. Two identical decoys were spaced 3 feet apart. A light over each decoy could be turned on and off so that only the model giving the "gock" call was illuminated in the darkened experimental apparatus, and the illumination was made to coincide with the call. When the duckling reached the lighted and calling model, the light and sound were turned off in the model and turned on in the other, which was 3 feet away. In this manner we could shuttle the animal back and forth and have it cover a distance similar to that used in the normal imprinting situation, where it walks behind a moving object.

Animals were run at four shuttles and 16 shuttles. The results show scores similar to those obtained previously for the 12½-foot and 50-foot distances. They indicate, again, that imprinting strength is a function of the distance walked by the duckling, regardless of whether or not the more complex perception of *following* a moving object is involved.

FEAR BEHAVIOR AND LOCOMOTORY ABILITY

In the light of the "critical period" results, the question arises as to what developmental changes might be taking place that would account for the limits of the critical period.

During the very early hours of their lives, animals show no fear. We conducted an experiment with 137 White Rock chicks of different ages and found that there is no fear up to 13 to 16 hours after hatching. Afterwards, the proportion of animals from age group to age group begins gradually to increase up to the age of 33 to 36 hours, when all animals show fear. Fear responses will prevent an animal from engaging in the kind of social behavior necessary for imprinting to take place, since a fearful animal will avoid rather than follow a potential imprinting object.

On the other hand, fear behavior cannot account for the limitation of imprinting before the peak of maximum effectiveness. Since the strength of imprinting is dependent on locomotor activity, we postulated that the ability to move about might thus be an important factor. The ability to move about is a growth function and would limit the onset of the critical period. Hence, we tested 60 Vantress broiler chicks of White Rock stock of different ages to determine the development of increasing locomotor ability.

The two curves we obtained, from these two experimental studies—one for increasing locomotor ability and one for increasing incidence of fear behavior with increasing age—were found to be in substantial agreement with the limits of the critical period. In fact, in plotting these two curves together, we obtained a hypothetical "critical period" for imprinting which strongly resembled the empirical one obtained for that breed.

It seems likely that all animals showing the phenomenon of imprinting will have a critical period which ends with the onset of fear. Thus, we can predict in a series of animals, knowing only the time of onset of fear, the end of imprintability for that species. Even in the human being one could thus theoretically place the end of maximum imprinting at about 5½ months, since observers have placed the onset of fear at about that time.

INNATE BEHAVIOR PATTERNS AND IMPRINTING

Most commonly the following-reaction to a certain model has been taken as a means of observing the progress of imprinting during the first exposure to the imprinting object and also as an indicator of the effectiveness of this exposure. However, the following-reaction is always accompanied by other innate behaviors which may also be observed and recorded. For the present purpose, the emission of "distress notes" or "contentment tones," maintenance of silence, and fixation of an object were checked for individual animals for a 2-minute period at the beginning of an imprinting session.

To differentiate between the "distress notes" and the "contentment tones" of chickens is comparatively easy, even for the layman who has never become familiar with them. "Distress notes" are a series of high-intensity, medium-pitch tones of approximately $\frac{1}{4}$-second duration in bursts of five to ten. Little pitch modulation occurs in this kind of call. "Contentment tones," on the other hand, are a series of high-pitch, low-intensity notes emitted in bursts of three to eight and with considerable pitch modulation during emission. The duration of the individual tones is much shorter, $\frac{1}{12}$ of a second or less. During distress notes the animal usually holds it head high; during contentment tones it holds it head beak down. The designations *distress notes* and *contentment tones* are merely labels and should not necessarily be taken literally.

The subjects were 124 Vantress broiler chicks which had never experienced light until the time of the experiment. The experimental situation was much like the first 2 minutes of an imprinting experiment.

We found that the behavior of the animals changed markedly with age. The younger the animals were, the more pronounced was their striving to move under the cover of the nearby model. Although it was considerably more difficult for the younger animals to cover even the short distance between their original location and the model because of their poor locomotor ability, the time it took these younger animals to reach the model was much shorter than the time it took the older animals. However, the mode of locomotion for these younger animals was not walking but, rather, a kind of tumbling; they used both feet and wings as supports, and thus left them exhausted after reaching the model a few inches away.

These results concerning behavior patterns during imprinting offer still further corroborating evidence for the location of the critical period as empirically determined. The emission of distress notes by animals older than 17 hours, even in the presence of an object that offers warmth and shelter, may be taken as an indication that a new phase of the animals' perception of their environment has set in. This behavior obstructs imprinting under the conditions of our laboratory arrangement. The high incidence of animals emitting contentment tones in the presence of the model is gradually replaced by an increasing number of animals emitting distress notes. No similar displacement occurs in animals remaining silent. The emission of contentment tones decreased as the animals became older, and the emission of distress notes increased at the same time.

The most important interpretation of these findings is that elicitation of following-behavior by various means after the critical period may not touch upon imprinting phenomena at all. Conventional training methods may be employed to overcome the fear response which the animals show after 17 hours, and it is not impossible to induce them, for example, to follow human beings. However, during the critical period, habituation or learning proper need not be considered as far as lowering of fear behavior is concerned, since at that time there is little or no fear present in the animals.

DRUG STUDIES

The rapid drop in imprinting, then, appears to be coupled with the developing emotional response of fear—a response that makes imprinting impossible. To examine this aspect of imprinting, reduction of the emotional response by means of a tranquilizing drug seemed a logical step. Meprobamate was chosen because of evidence that it would reduce emotionality without markedly influencing motility or coordination. Preliminary experiments with dosages of meprobamate showed clearly that the emotionality of the ducklings was markedly reduced. In fact, the ducklings showed no fear of strange objects or persons, even though they were at an age where marked fear is normally a certainty.

To obtain the maximal information from this experiment, we then decided to test animals under the following four conditions: (i) drug at 12 hours of age, imprinting at 24 hours of age when the effect of the drug had worn off; (ii) drug at 12 hours of age, imprinting at 14 to 16 hours of age, test when the drug effect had worn off; (iii) imprinting at 16 hours, test under drug later; and (iv) drug at 24 hours, imprinting at 26 hours, test when the drug effect had worn off.

In general, the procedure for imprinting and testing was the same as that which has been described. Control animals were given distilled water, and chlorpromazine and Nembutal were used to obtain additional information. The results are shown in Table I.

It is obvious that, while meprobamate reduces fear or emotional behavior, it also makes imprinting almost impossible. It does not, however, interfere with the effects of imprinting. This is clear from the results of test (iii). Chlorpromazine allows a high degree of imprinting under all conditions, whereas Nembutal reduces imprintability at all points except under the conditions of test (iii).

From the data, it appears that we might interpret the action of the drugs

Table 1. Percentage of positive response made by ducklings under different conditions of testing and drug administration

Conditions	Control H_2O	Mepro-bamate (25 mg/kg)	Nembutal (5 mg/kg)	Chlor-promazine (15 mg/kg)
Drug at 12 hr, imprinting at 24 hr	14	54	31	57
Drug at 12 hr, imprinting at 14-16 hr.	62	8	28	63
Imprinting without drug at 16 hr, test under drug	61	65	61	58
Drug at 24 hr, imprinting at 26 hr	19	17	16	59

as follows. If we assume that meprobamate and chlorpromazine reduce metabolism, then we could expect the high imprinting scores found at 24 hours of age [test (i)], because metabolism had been slowed and we had thus stretched out the imprinting or sensitive period. This did not occur when we used Nembutal or distilled water. The second point deals with the reduction of emotionality. In test (iv) we had little evidence of emotionality in the meprobamate and the chlorpromazine groups. Emotionality did occur in the control and in the Nembutal group. Thus far, the only way we can interpret this former result is to consider the law of effort. Here we had found that the strength of imprinting was a function of effort or of distance traveled. It may be that, since meprobamate is a muscle relaxant, these effects of meprobamate cut into the muscular tension or other afferent consequences and thus nullify the effectiveness of the imprinting experience. Since, under the same circumstances, we attain perfectly good imprinting in all cases with chlorpromazine, this notion becomes even more tenable.

CEREBRAL LESIONS

In addition to drug effects we also studied the results of cerebral lesions on the imprinting behavior of chicks. This was done partly because we had noticed a loss of the fear response in some chicks that had undergone operations—chicks which were old enough to have this response fully developed.

Chicks with a type 1 lesion showed good imprinting at the age of 3 days. This is considerably better than the finding for the control chicks, which only occasionally show this behavior so late in their first few days. Even with this lesion, chicks at 5 and at 7 days showed no imprinting.

Chicks with type 2 lesion showed no imprinting, although some that had been prepared earlier gave no evidence of fear responses to strange objects.

Completely decerebrate animals were run only at 2 days of age, and they followed well, but the tests were inconclusive insofar as imprinting strength was concerned.

Athough the number of animals used in this study is still small, this seems to be a fruitful avenue of approach. Control animals that have had sham operations act essentially like normal chicks. Other experiments involving electrical stimulation are being undertaken, since such stimulation may reinforce imprinting behavior.

GENETIC STUDIES

We have also considered the genetic side of imprinting. We kept ducklings which were highly imprintable and bred them separately from ducklings which showed very little imprinting response. We thus had two groups of offspring, those produced by "imprinters" and those produced by "non-imprinters." There was a clear and significant difference in the imprinting behavior of the two groups, even in the first generation. The offspring of imprintable parents were easily imprinted; those of less imprintable parents were difficult to imprint. The "imprinter" ducklings had imprinting test scores more than three times better than those of the "non-imprinter" ducklings. Similar results were also obtained in a study of bantam chicks. We are also following up those animals which have had experimental imprinting experiences to determine what influence, if any, these experiences have on their behavior as adults. So far the results are inconclusive, but they do suggest that experimental imprinting of mallards affects their behavior as adults, particularly with respect to courtship patterns.

Birds of various species show differing degrees of imprintability. Domestic fowl do show imprinting responses, but the results are not as clear as for wild

Table 2. Number and imprintability of different experimental animals. Most of the animals were imprinted in runway and mallard decoy situations. Some of the Vantress broilers were imprinted on colored spheres, and the sheep were imprinted on human beings

Animal	*No.**	*Imprintability†*
Ducks		
Wild mallard	3500	E +
Domesticated mallard	150	E
Peking	200	G
Rouen	100	F
Wood	50	P
Black	50	G
Total	4050	
Geese		
Canada	30	E +
Pilgrim	50	G
Total	80	
Chickens		
Jungle fowl	100	G
Cochin bantam	300	G
New Hampshire Red	100	G
Rhode Island Red	100	G
Barred Rock	200	G
Vantress broiler	500	G +
White Rock	100	F
Leghorn	200	P
Total	1600	
Other Fowl		
Pheasant	100	P
Eastern bobwhite quail	50	G
California valley quail	20	E
Turkey	30	F
Total	200	
Mammals		
Sheep	2	G
Guinea pig	12	G
Total	14	
Total	5944	

*Estimated for fowl, actual for mammals.
†E, excellent; G, good; F, fair; P, poor.

birds. We have had good success in imprinting some breeds of chicks, and the best imprinters among them are the Vantress broilers. Leghorns, on the other hand, appear to be too highly domesticated to give clear results. Other animals we have used in our experimentation are two kinds of geese, black ducks, wood ducks, turkeys, pheasants, quail, Peking ducks, and Rouens. The various breeds we have so far used in our work and the degree of imprintability found in each are shown in Table 2.

IMPRINTING IN MAMMALS

The guinea pig is similar to the chick and the duckling in that it is mobile and reasonably self-sufficient soon after birth. For this reason we used it in exploratory work. We first developed a method of obtaining the young from the mother with minimal parental contact. This was done by Caesarean section. However, further work showed that it was sufficient to obtain the young within an hour after they were born, and for the moment we are doing this. Guinea pigs imprint on human beings and follow them about as do the fowl with which we have been working. The maximum effectiveness of the imprinting experience seems to be over by the second day. So far, in using our imprinting apparatus with our usual duck decoy we have obtained best results sometime before the end of the first day of age. Work is being continued so that we can have a more standardized procedure before beginning a major program in this area.

IMPRINTING AND LEARNING

The supposed irreversibility of imprinting has been particularly singled out by some investigators to show that imprinting is nothing but "simple learning" —whatever that is. We do have some isolated instances which point to a long-range effect, but systematic work is just now beginning in our laboratories. Canada goslings, imprinted on human beings for a period of a week or two, will from that time on respond to their former caretaker with the typical "greeting ceremony," as well as accept food out of his hand. This occurs in spite of the fact that they normally associate entirely with the Canada geese on our duck pond. A more striking case is that of a jungle fowl cock which was imprinted by me and kept away from his own species for the first month. This animal, even after 5 years—much of that time in association with his own species—courts human beings with typical behavior, but not females of his own species. This certainly is a far-reaching effect and is similar to the finding of Räber, who reported on a male turkey whose behavior toward human beings was similar. An increased amount of homosexual courtship in mallards has been observed with some of our laboratory imprinted animals, which, while not a statistically valuable finding, perhaps points also to long-range, irreversible effects.

Imprinting is currently receiving much attention, and papers on the subject are being published at an impressive rate. Unfortunately, most experimenters appear to be certain that imprinting is identical with simple association learning and design their experiments as studies in association learning. In many instances the animals are too old when used in the experiments to fall within the critical age for imprinting, with the result that only association learning can occur. Papers falling into this category are those of Jaynes, Moltz, and James.

Our own experiments on the relation between association learning with food as a reward and imprinting during the critical period show four distinct differences.

In the first place, learning a visual discrimination problem is quicker and more stable when practice trials are spaced by interspersing time periods between trials than when practice trials are massed by omitting such intervening time periods. With imprinting, however, massed practice is more effective than spaced practice, as shown by our law of effort. Secondly, *recency* in experience is maximally effective in learning a discrimination; in imprinting, *primacy* of experience is the maximally effective factor. The second difference is illustrated by the following experiment. Two groups of 11 ducklings each were imprinted on two different imprinting objects. Group 1 was first imprinted on a male mallard model and then on a female model. Group 2, on the other hand, was first imprinted on a female model and subsequently on a male model. Fourteen of the 22 ducklings, when tested with both models present, preferred the model to which they first had been imprinted, showing primacy. Only five preferred the model to which they had been imprinted last, showing recency, and three showed no preference at all.

In addition, it has been found that the administration of punishment or painful stimulation increases the effectiveness of the imprinting experience, whereas such aversive stimulation results in avoidance of the associated stimulus in the case of visual discrimination learning.

Finally, chicks and ducklings under the influence of meprobamate are able to learn a color discrimination problem just as well as, or better than, they normally do, whereas the administration of this drug reduces imprintability to almost zero.

Imprinting, then, is an obviously interesting phenomenon, and the proper way to approach it is to make no assumptions. To find out its characteristics, to explore its occurrence in different organisms, and to follow its effects would seem a worth-while program of study.

What can we say in conclusion about the general nature of imprinting? Our best guess to date is that it is a rigid form of learning, differing in several ways from the usual association learning which comes into play immediately after the peak of imprintability. In other words, imprinting in our experiments results in the animal learning the rough, generalized characteristics of the imprinting object. Its detailed appreciation of the *specific* object comes as a result of normal conditioning—a process which in the case of these animals takes a much longer time and is possible days after the critical period for imprinting has passed. It is an exciting new field and is certainly worthy of study.

Part III

Learning

Chapter 7

Conditioned emotional reactions*

John B. Watson and Rosalie Raynor

This classic study presents a model of the connecting of emotional responses to previously neutral stimuli by means of classical conditioning procedures. The infant used in the following investigation possessed a comparatively placid disposition; but one would suspect that a child who was either more alert or more tense than the subject discussed would not only acquire a conditioned response more rapidly but would also react more intensely and for a longer time. According to one theorist, H. J. Eysenck, such constitutional differences in conditionability might be great enough to help determine whether one individual becomes neurotic under the stress of daily living, whereas another does not.

Experimental work has been done so far on only one child, Albert B. This infant was reared almost from birth in a hospital environment; his mother was a wet nurse in the Harriet Lane Home for Invalid Children. Albert's life was normal: he was healthy from birth and one of the best developed youngsters ever brought to the hospital, weighing twenty-one pounds at nine months of age. He was on the whole stolid and unemotional. His stability was one of the principal reasons for using him as a subject in this test. We felt that we could do him relatively little harm by carrying out such experiments as those outlined below.

At approximately nine months of age we ran him through the emotional tests that have become a part of our regular routine in determining whether fear reactions can be called out by other stimuli than sharp noises and the sudden removal of support. In brief, the infant was confronted suddenly and for the first time successively with a white rat, a rabbit, a dog, a monkey, with masks with and without hair, cotton wool, burning newspapers, etc. A permanent record of Albert's reactions to these objects and situations has been preserved in a motion picture study. Manipulation was the most usual reaction called out. *At no time did this infant ever show fear in any situation.*

*From *Journal of Experimental Psychology* 3:1-14, 1920.

These experimental records were confirmed by the casual observations of the mother and hospital attendants. No one had ever seen him in a state of fear and rage. The infant practically never cried.

Up to approximately nine months of age we had not tested him with loud sounds. The test to determine whether a fear reaction could be called out by a loud sound was made when he was eight months, twenty-six days of age. The sound was that made by striking a hammer upon a suspended steel bar four feet in length and three-fourths of an inch in diameter. The laboratory notes are as follows:

> "One of the two experimenters caused the child to turn its head and fixate her moving hand; the other, stationed back of the child, struck the steel bar a sharp blow. The child started violently, his breathing was checked and the arms were raised in a characteristic manner. On the second stimulation the same thing occurred, and in addition the lips began to pucker and tremble. On the third stimulation the child broke into a sudden crying fit. This is the first time an emotional situation in the laboratory has produced any fear or even crying in Albert."

The sound stimulus, thus, at nine months of age, gives us the means of testing several important factors. I. Can we condition fear of an animal, *e.g.*, a white rat, by visually presenting it and simultaneously striking a steel bar? II. If such a conditioned emotional response can be established, will there be a transfer to other animals or other objects? III. What is the effect of time upon such conditioned emotional responses? IV. If after a reasonable period such emotional responses have not died out, what laboratory methods can be devised for their removal?

I. The establishment of conditioned emotional responses. At first there was considerable hesitation upon our part in making the attempt to set up fear reactions experimentally. A certain responsibility attaches to such a procedure. We decided finally to make the attempt, comforting ourselves by the reflection that such attachments would arise anyway as soon as the child left the sheltered environment of the nursery for the rough and tumble of the home. We did not begin this work until Albert was eleven months, three days of age. Before attempting to set up a conditioned response we, as before, put him through all of the regular emotional tests. *Not the slightest sign of a fear response was obtained in any situation.*

The steps taken to condition emotional responses are shown in our laboratory notes.

11 months 3 days

1. White rat suddenly taken from the basket and presented to Albert. He began to reach for rat with left hand. Just as his hand touched the animal the bar was struck immediately behind his head. The infant jumped violently and fell forward, burying his face in the mattress. He did not cry, however.

2. Just as the right hand touched the rat the bar was again struck. Again the infant jumped violently, fell forward and began to whimper.

In order not to disturb the child too seriously no further tests were given for one week.

11 months 10 days

1. Rat presented suddenly without sound. There was steady fixation but no tendency at first to reach for it. The rat was then placed nearer, whereupon tentative reaching movements began with the right hand. When the rat nosed the infant's left hand, the hand was immediately withdrawn. He started to reach for the head of the animal with the forefinger of the left hand, but withdrew it suddenly before contact. It is thus seen that the two joint stimulations given the previous week were not without effect. He was tested with his blocks immediately afterwards to see if they shared in the process of conditioning. He began immediately to pick them up, dropping them, pounding them, etc. In the remainder of the tests the blocks were given frequently to quiet him and to test his general emotional state. They were always removed from sight when the process of conditioning was under way.

2. Joint stimulation with rat and sound. Started, then fell over immediately to right side. No crying.

3. Joint stimulation. Fell to right side and rested upon hands, with head turned away from rat. No crying.

4. Joint stimulation. Same reaction.

5. Rat suddenly presented alone. Puckered face, whimpered and withdrew body sharply to the left.

6. Joint stimulation. Fell over immediately to right side and began to whimper.

7. Joint stimulation. Started violently and cried, but did not fall over.

8. Rat alone. The instant the rat was shown the baby began to cry. Almost instantly he turned sharply to the left, fell over on left side, raised himself on all fours and began to crawl away so rapidly that he was caught with difficulty before reaching the edge of the table.

This was as convincing a case of a completely conditioned fear response as could have been theoretically pictured. In all, seven joint stimulations were given to bring about the complete reaction. It is not unlikely had the sound been of greater intensity or of a more complex clang character that the number of joint stimulations might have been materially reduced. Experiments designed to define the nature of the sounds that will serve best as emotional stimuli are under way.

II. **When a conditioned emotional response has been established for one object, is there a transfer?** Five days later Albert was again brought back into the laboratory and tested as follows:

11 months 15 days

1. Tested first with blocks. He reached readily for them, playing with them as usual. This shows that there has been no general transfer to the room, table, blocks, etc.

2. Rat alone. Whimpered immediately, withdrew right hand and turned head and trunk away.

3. Blocks again offered. Played readily with them, smiling and gurgling.

4. Rat alone. Leaned over to the left side as far away from the rat as possible, then fell over, getting up on all fours and scurrying away as rapidly as possible.

5. Blocks again offered. Reached immediately for them, smiling and laughing as before.

The above preliminary test shows that the conditioned response to the rat had carried over completely for the five days in which no tests were given. The question as to whether or not there is a transfer was next taken up.

6. Rabbit alone. The rabbit was suddenly placed on the mattress in front of him. The reaction was pronounced. Negative responses began at once. He leaned as far away from the animal as possible, whimpered, then burst into tears. When the rabbit was placed in contact with him he buried his face in the mattress, then got up on all fours and crawled away, crying as he went. This was a most convincing test.

7. The blocks were next given him, after an interval. He played with them as before. It was observed by four people that he played far more energetically with them than ever before. The blocks were raised high over his head and slammed down with a great deal of force.

8. Dog alone. The dog did not produce as violent a reaction as the rabbit. The moment fixation occurred the child shrank back and as the animal came nearer he attempted to get on all fours but did not cry at first. As soon as the dog passed out of his range of vision he became quiet. The dog was then made to approach the infant's head (he was lying down at the moment). Albert straightened up immediately, fell over to the opposite side and turned his head away. He then began to cry.

9. The blocks were again presented. He began immediately to play with them.

10. Fur coat (seal). Withdrew immediately to the left side and began to fret. Coat put close to him on the left side, he turned immediately, began to cry and tried to crawl away on all fours.

11. Cotton wool. The wool was presented in a paper package. At the end the cotton was not covered by the paper. It was placed first on his feet. He kicked it away but did not touch it with his hands. When the hand was laid on the wool he immediately withdrew it but did not show the shock that the animals or fur coat produced in him. He then began to play with the paper, avoiding contact with the wool itself. He finally, under the impulse of the manipulative instinct, lost some of his negativism to the wool.

12. Just in play W. put his head down to see if Albert would play with his hair. Albert was completely negative. Two other observers did the same thing. He began immediately to play with their hair. W. then brought the Santa Claus mask and presented it to Albert. He was again pronouncedly negative.

11 months 20 days

1. Blocks alone. Played with them as usual.

2. Rat alone. Withdrawal of the whole body, bending over to the left side, no crying. Fixation and following with eyes. The response was much less marked than on first presentation the previous week. It was thought best to freshen up the reaction by another joint stimulation.

3. Just as the rat was placed on his hand the rod was struck. Reaction violent.

4. Rat alone. Fell over at once to left side. Reaction practically as strong as on former occasion but no crying.

5. Rat alone. Fell over at once to left side. Got up on all fours and started to crawl away. On this occasion there was no crying, but strange to say, as he started away he began to gurgle and coo, even while leaning far over to the left side to avoid the rat.

6. Rabbit alone. Leaned over to left side as far as possible. Did not fall over. Began to whimper but reaction not so violent as on former occasions.

7. Blocks again offered. He reached for them immediately and began to play.

All of the tests so far discussed were carried out upon a table supplied with a mattress, located in a small, well-lighted dark-room. We wished to test next whether conditioned fear responses so set up would appear if the situation were markedly altered. We thought it best before making this test to freshen the reaction both to the rabbit and to the dog by showing them at the moment the steel bar was struck. It will be recalled that this was the first time any effort had been made to directly condition response to the dog and rabbit. The experimental notes are as follows:

8. The rabbit at first was given alone. The reaction was exactly as given in test (6) above. When the rabbit was left on Albert's knees for a long time he began tentatively to reach out and manipulate its fur with forefingers. While doing this the steel rod was struck. A violent fear reaction resulted.

9. Rabbit alone. Reaction wholly similar to that on trial (6) above.

10. Rabbit alone. Started immediately to whimper, holding hands far up, but did not cry. Conflicting tendency to manipulate very evident.

11. Dog alone. Began to whimper, shaking head from side to side, holding hands as far away from the animal as possible.

12. Dog and sound. The rod was struck just as the animal touched him. A violent negative reaction appeared. He began to whimper, turned to one side, fell over and started to get up on all fours.

13. Blocks. Played with them immediately and readily.

On this same day and immediately after the above experiment Albert was taken into the large well-lighted lecture room belonging to the laboratory. He was placed on a table in the center of the room immediately under the skylight. Four people were present. The situation was thus very different from that which we obtained in the small dark-room.

1. Rat alone. No sudden fear reaction appeared at first. The hands, however, were held up and away from the animal. No positive manipulatory reactions appeared.

2. Rabbit alone. Fear reaction slight. Turned to left and kept face away from the animal but the reaction was never pronounced.

3. Dog alone. Turned away but did not fall over. Cried. Hands moved as far away from the animal as possible. Whimpered as long as the dog was present.

4. Rat alone. Slight negative reaction.

5. Rat and sound. It was thought best to freshen the reaction to the rat. The sound was given just as the rat was presented. Albert jumped violently but did not cry.

6. Rat alone. At first he did not show any negative reaction. When rat was placed nearer he began to show negative reaction by drawing back his body, raising his hands, whimpering, etc.

7. Blocks. Played with them immediately.

8. Rat alone. Pronounced withdrawal of body and whimpering.

9. Blocks. Played with them as before.

10. Rabbit alone. Pronounced reaction. Whimpered with arms held high, fell over backward and had to be caught.

11. Dog alone. At first the dog did not produce the pronounced reaction. The hands were held high over the head, breathing was checked, but there was no crying. Just at this moment the dog, which had not barked before, barked three times loudly when only about six inches from the baby's face. Albert immediately fell over and broke into a wail that continued until the dog was removed. The sudden barking of the hitherto quiet dog produced a marked fear response in the adult observers!

From the above results it would seem that emotional transfers do take place. Furthermore it would seem that the number of transfers resulting from an experimentally produced conditioned emotional reaction may be very large. In our observations we had no means of testing the complete number of transfers which may have resulted.

III. The effect of time upon conditioned emotional responses. We have already shown that the conditioned emotional response will continue for a period of one week. It was desired to make the time test longer. In view of the imminence of Albert's departure from the hospital we could not make the interval longer than one month. Accordingly, no further emotional experimentation was entered into for thirty-one days after the above test. During the month, however, Albert was brought weekly to the laboratory for tests upon right and left-handedness, imitation, general development, etc. No emotional tests whatever were given and during the whole month his regular nursery routine was maintained in the Harriet Lane Home. The notes on the test given at the end of this period are as follows:

1 year 21 days

1. Santa Claus mask. Withdrawal, gurgling, then slapped at it without touching. When his hand was forced to touch it, he whimpered and cried. His hand was forced to touch it two more times. He whimpered and cried on both tests. He finally cried at the mere visual stimulus of the mask.

2. Fur coat. Wrinkled his nose and withdrew both hands, drew back his whole body and began to whimper as the coat was put nearer. Again there was the strife between withdrawal and the tendency to manipulate. Reached tentatively with left hand but drew back before contact had been made. In moving his body to one side his hand accidentally touched the coat. He began to cry at once, nodding his head in a very peculiar manner (this reaction was an entirely new one). Both hands were withdrawn as far as possible from the coat. The coat was then laid on his lap and he continued nodding his head and whimpering, withdrawing his body as far as possible, pushing the while at the coat with his feet but never touching it with his hands.

3. Fur coat. The coat was taken out of his sight and presented again at

the end of a minute. He began immediately to fret, withdrawing his body and nodding his head as before.

4. Blocks. He began to play with them as usual.

5. The rat. He allowed the rat to crawl towards him without withdrawing. He sat very still and fixated it intently. Rat then touched his hand. Albert withdrew it immediately, then leaned back as far as possible but did not cry. When the rat was placed on his arm he withdrew his body and began to fret, nodding his head. The rat was then allowed to crawl against his chest. He first began to fret and then covered his eyes with both hands.

6. Blocks. Reaction normal.

7. The rabbit. The animal was placed directly in front of him. It was very quiet. Albert showed no avoiding reactions at first. After a few seconds he puckered up his face, began to nod his head and to look intently at the experimenter. He next began to push the rabbit away with his feet, withdrawing his body at the same time. Then as the rabbit came nearer he began pulling his feet away, nodding his head, and wailing "da da." After about a minute he reached out tentatively and slowly and touched the rabbit's ear with his right hand, finally manipulating it. The rabbit was again placed in his lap. Again he began to fret and withdrew his hands. He reached out tentatively with his left hand and touched the animal, shuddered and withdrew his whole body. The experimenter then took hold of his left hand and laid it on the rabbit's back. Albert immediately withdrew his hand and began to suck his thumb. Again the rabbit was laid in his lap. He began to cry, covering his face with both hands.

8. Dog. The dog was very active. Albert fixated it intensely for a few seconds, sitting very still. He began to cry but did not fall over backwards as on his last contact with the dog. When the dog was pushed closer to him he at first sat motionless, then began to cry, putting both hands over his face.

These experiments would seem to show conclusively that directly conditioned emotional responses as well as those conditioned by transfer persist, although with a certain loss in the intensity of the reaction, for a longer period than one month. Our view is that they persist and modify personality throughout life. It should be recalled again that Albert was of an extremely phlegmatic type. Had he been emotionally unstable probably both the directly conditioned response and those transferred would have persisted throughout the month unchanged in form.

IV. "Detachment" or removal of conditioned emotional responses. Unfortunately Albert was taken from the hospital on the day the above tests were made. Hence the opportunity of building up an experimental technique by means of which we could remove the conditioned emotional responses was denied us.

Chapter 8

Desensitization of a post-traumatic phobia*

Malcom Kushner

If emotional responses can be established by conditioning, then it should be possible to employ conditioning techniques to unlearn emotional reactions that are undesirable. The following article describes one such technique.

The patient was a seventeen-year-old youth whose automobile was struck at an intersection by a hit-and-run driver approximately one month prior to being seen. He was not physically injured beyond sustaining a bumped knee. Immediately following the accident the patient became very upset, tense, and anxious. His appetite was poor, he had considerable difficulty falling asleep, and had become obviously more grouchy and irritable. He was afraid to drive his car and while never a very good student, he began to do even more poorly. He complained of not being able to concentrate in school, being very much ill at ease, and his grades deteriorated so badly that just prior to coming for treatment he tried to enlist in the Air Force rather than be expelled from school. He failed to pass the Air Force mental examination, however.

When first seen the patient was very tense and quiet. Although his appearance and dress conformed to the usual stereotype of the "hot rodder" his behavior was quite reserved and polite. Being unable to drive a car presents a considerable difficulty for a young man today but for this patient it was even more of a problem inasmuch as he was a member of an organized drag-racing club, was an avid "hot rodder" and car tinkerer. Most of his energies, interests, and the object of his working after school had been to support his car. To feel anxious around cars, uneasy when being driven by others, and to be unable to drive his own car was for this young man one of the most difficult situations imaginable and reflected the intensity of his fears. The patient had a prior history of being somewhat "wild" but he felt that he had settled down since meeting his girl friend whom he intended to marry. On first impression it was thought that there might be some ulterior motives contributing in part to the patient's reactions, that is, his talk of now leaving school in light of his poor prior performance and nonacademic interests and also considering the fact that his case was being handled by a lawyer. It was decided to utilize a systematic desensitization approach as a means of reducing this patient's high anxiety level at home and to try to do this in varied settings as well. It was determined to see the patient three times a week.

The systematic desensitization approach as described by Wolpe consists of presenting to the patient a series of imaginary, graded situations representing his area of difficulty, beginning with one which is minimally anxiety-provoking, and gradually, step by step, approaching the situation which ordinarily evokes maximal anxiety in him. It is important that the increments be made in steps which at no time are overwhelmingly disturbing to the patient, or reinforcement of his fears is a possibility. An important element of procedure requires the patient to be completely relaxed as he imagines each situation. This is in recognition of Jacobson's findings that muscular relaxation inhibits anxiety, thereby making its expression physiologically impossible. If the patient is completely relaxed and the situation elicits no anxiety, this, in effect, conditions him to tolerate the situation and enables him to proceed to the next step, and so forth, until he finally is able to visualize himself in the phobic situation without undue anxiety. Experience has shown that the nonanxious attitude in the imaginary situation transfers to the real life conditions, eliminating the need to present the actual objects or situations. Exercises in deep muscle relaxation are initially provided the patient to prepare him for this procedure. Wolpe and others utilize hypnosis or hypnoidal states as a means of inducing relaxation. As Wolpe noted, this writer has found that effective results may be obtained with subjects who are able to relax sufficiently without the need for hypnosis.

In the second session, three days later, the patient indicated feeling somewhat better. An effort was made to go into his background, particularly his schooling and aspirations, in somewhat more detail. He was not too bright and had just managed to get by in school prior to the accident. He now felt that he would not be able to pass the semester as a result of his problems and would probably have to drop out of school. He claimed that he could not concentrate in class, read magazines and, in general, was not attentive. A discussion with the patient's mother revealed essentially the same bits of historical information as reported by the patient. She also indicated that he appeared to be less anxious and fidgety and he appeared to her to be somewhat more relaxed since initiating treatment. As a result of getting this additional information it was felt even more that secondary gains played an important role in the clinical picture. Nevertheless it was felt that the anxiety and the phobic condition could be diminished through relaxation and desensitization. Once again the relaxation procedures were described and practiced and the patient proved very adept at this. Because he was able to relax so readily the desensitization technique began at that session. Each imaginary situation was repeated once before proceeding to the next step. The initial instruction to the patient was to imagine himself looking at his car as it was prior to the accident. Since he did not report any feelings of tension or anxiety at this level, the next step was for him to imagine himself leaning against his car. From there the final situation for that session was for the patient to imagine himself sitting in his car without the ignition turned on. In each of these three imaginary situations the patient reported no feelings of tension or anxiety. Too rapid presentation of situations in the hierarchy was avoided to prevent the patient from being overwhelmed; hence this session was terminated after three steps in the series.

The third session was two days later and at the beginning the patient reported that he was able to fall asleep much more readily when he attempted to relax while in bed and that he felt much better, particularly in school. He stated that he had learned to relax before going into his classes and as a result had been able to take better notes. He reported getting a "C" on a quiz, which encouraged him considerably. Clinically he appeared to be more responsive and less agitated. The desensitization series continued, beginning this session with the last situation of the preceding meeting, that is, the patient sitting in his car with the ignition turned off. He then was asked to imagine himself sitting in his car and turning on the ignition, with the car stationary but the motor idling. He did not signal that he was upset by this thought and the next step was to have the patient imagine himself backing out of his driveway and turning the car so that he was in position to drive off. Here, also, there was no signal of disturbance. The patient was then instructed to imagine himself driving the car around the block on which he lived and approaching an intersection on the way. At this point the patient showed some signs of growing tense although he did not signal this to the therapist. (Close observation of a patient will reveal changes in breathing rate, facial contortions, and so forth that are indicative of increased tension.) He was then told to "erase" the thought and relax. This same situation was repeated about one minute later and once more there was some evidence of disturbance although not as much as before. The desensitization was then stopped for the day.

On the first three visits the patient was accompanied by his mother who drove the car. On the fourth visit, which was ten days after first being seen, the patient drove through heavy downtown traffic accompanied by his girl friend. His face was much more relaxed, he smiled more frequently, was not irritable, and claimed that he was able to relax himself to sleep in five minutes or so. He also felt that he was able to concentrate in school. He no longer was thinking about quitting and, though worried about whether he would pass on his next report card, he felt that he could nevertheless get by the semester. The desensitization hierarchy of responses continued, beginning this session with asking the patient to imagine himself driving along a straight road with no intersections. In the next step he was to imagine that he was approaching an intersection with no traffic appearing, and finally he was asked to imagine himself driving in the same situation but with another car nearing the intersection to his right at which there was a "Stop" sign. This was a reconstruction of the situation leading to his accident. At this point he reported only very little anxiety. The entire series was run through again and when the intersection situation was again presented the anxiety was practically all gone. At this point the session was terminated. The next day the patient's mother spoke with the therapist and reported that his improvement was considerable, corroborating the patient's report.

In the fifth session, twelve days after first being seen, the patient indicated continued improvement. He reported feeling practically as well as before the accident. He stated that he had failed four subjects in school but he felt that he was now able to concentrate once more and confidently expected to pass the final six weeks. He appeared to be much more relaxed, was more spontaneous, and in general was responsive, alert, and happy. The desensitization program was resumed at this point, picking up with the patient imagining himself driving along a straight road with no traffic; following this, he was taken through various intersection situations, none of which elicited anxiety. His progress was excellent in the office and he reported practically no difficulty while driving on the highway. It was decided to see him for one more session.

The sixth and final session was held two and one-half weeks following the first contact with the patient. At this time the patient considered himself ninety percent better. He had no trouble sleeping at night, his appetite was normal, he was no longer irritable, and his concentration in school had improved considerably. Relaxation techniques were reinforced at this last session and he was instructed in the various ways that he could bring these to bear and thus make his everyday activities more effective. The patient was discharged and a three-month follow-up revealed still further improvement with no exacerbation of his earlier symptoms.

It was felt that the rapid emission of his symptoms was mainly due to the quickness with which the patient adapted to the relaxation principles as well as to the acute nature of the problem. If, as was suggested above, secondary gain factors were involved in this case, they played no significant role in offsetting the effectiveness of the procedure used.

Chapter 9

"Superstition" in the pigeon*

B. F. Skinner

In everyday life a number of otherwise puzzling behaviors can be understood in terms of the accidental shaping of responses that are unwittingly reinforced. For example, a child may be reinforced by a few moments of parental attention if he hits his sister, and he may then reinforce his parents with a few moments of silence if he is not spanked. Soon the pattern is well established, and the mother "just can't understand what's making him act like such a rotten kid. He must take after his father's side of the family." The article by Skinner illustrates this type of fortuitous shaping of responses under laboratory conditions.

To say that a reinforcement is contingent upon a response may mean nothing more than that it follows the response. It may follow because of some mechanical connection or because of the mediation of another organism; but conditioning takes place presumably because of the temporal relation only, expressed in terms of the order and proximity of response and reinforcement. Whenever we present a state of affairs which is known to be reinforcing at a given drive, we must suppose that conditioning takes place, even though we have paid no attention to the behavior of the organism in making the presentation. A simple experiment demonstrates this to be the case.

A pigeon is brought to a stable state of hunger by reducing it to 75 percent of its weight when well fed. It is put into an experimental cage for a few minutes each day. A food hopper attached to the cage may be swung into place so that the pigeon can eat from it. A solenoid and a timing relay hold the hopper in place for five sec. at each reinforcement.

If a clock is now arranged to present the food hopper at regular intervals *with no reference whatsoever to the bird's behavior,* operant conditioning usually takes place. In six out of eight cases the resulting responses were so clearly defined that two observers could agree perfectly in counting instances. One bird was conditioned to turn counter-clockwise about the cage, making

*From *Journal of Experimental Psychology* 38:168-172, 1948. Copyright 1948 by American Psychological Association. Used with permission of the author and American Psychological Association.

two or three turns between reinforcements. Another repeatedly thrust its head into one of the upper corners of the cage. A third developed a "tossing" response, as if placing its head beneath an invisible bar and lifting it repeatedly. Two birds developed a pendulum motion of the head and body, in which the head was extended forward and swung from right to left with a sharp movement followed by a somewhat slower return. The body generally followed the movement and a few steps might be taken when it was extensive. Another bird was conditioned to make incomplete pecking or brushing movements directed toward but not touching the floor. None of these responses appeared in any noticeable strength during adaptation to the cage or until the food hopper was periodically presented. In the remaining two cases, conditioned responses were not clearly marked.

The conditioning process is usually obvious. The bird happens to be executing some response as the hopper appears; as a result it tends to repeat this response. If the interval before the next presentation is not so great that extinction takes place, a second "contingency" is probable. This strengthens the response still further and subsequent reinforcement becomes more probable. It is true that some responses go unreinforced and some reinforcements appear when the response has not just been made, but the net result is the development of a considerable state of strength.

With the exception of the counter-clockwise turn, each response was almost always repeated in the same part of the cage, and it generally involved an orientation toward some feature of the cage. The effect of the reinforcement was to condition the bird to respond to some aspect of the environment rather than merely to execute a series of movements. All responses came to be repeated rapidly between reinforcements—typically five or six times in 15 sec.

The effect appears to depend upon the rate of reinforcement. In general, we should expect that the shorter the intervening interval, the speedier and more marked the conditioning. One reason is that the pigeon's behavior becomes more diverse as time passes after reinforcement. A hundred photographs, each taken two sec. after withdrawal of the hopper, would show fairly uniform behavior. The bird would be in the same part of the cage, near the hopper, and probably oriented toward the wall where the hopper has disappeared or turning to one side or the other. A hundred photographs taken after 10 sec., on the other hand, would find the bird in various parts of the cage responding to many different aspects of the environment. The sooner a second reinforcement appears, therefore, the more likely it is that the second reinforced response will be similar to the first, and also that they will both have one of a few standard forms. In the limiting case of a very brief interval the behavior to be expected would be holding the head toward the opening through which the magazine has disappeared.

Another reason for the greater effectiveness of short intervals is that the longer the interval, the greater the number of intervening responses emitted without reinforcement. The resulting extinction cancels the effect of an occasional reinforcement.

According to this interpretation the effective interval will depend upon the rate of conditioning and the rate of extinction, and will therefore vary with the drive and also presumably between species. Fifteen sec. is a very effective interval at the drive level indicated above. One minute is much less so. When a response has once been set up, however, the interval can be lengthened. In one case it was extended to two min., and a high rate of responding was maintained with no sign of weakening. In another case, many hours of responding were observed with an interval of one min. between reinforcements.

In the latter case, the response showed a noticeable drift in topography. It began as a sharp movement of the head from the middle position to the left. This movement became more energetic, and eventually the whole body of the bird turned in the same direction, and a step or two would be taken. After many hours, the stepping response became the predominant feature. The bird made a well defined hopping step from the right to the left foot, meanwhile turning its head and body to the left as before.

When the stepping response became strong, it was possible to obtain a mechanical record by putting the bird on a large tambour directly connected with a small tambour which made a delicate electric contact each time stepping took place. By watching the bird and listening to the sound of the recorder it was possible to confirm the fact that a fairly authentic record was being made. It was possible for the bird to hear the recorder at each step, but this was, of course, in no way correlated with feeding. The record obtained when the magazine was presented once every min. resembles in every respect the characteristic curve for the pigeon under periodic reinforcement of a standard selected response. A well marked temporal discrimination develops. The bird does not respond immediately after eating, but when 10 or 15 or even 20 sec. have elapsed it begins to respond rapidly and continues until the reinforcement is received.

In this case it was possible to record the "extinction" of the response when the clock was turned off and the magazine was no longer presented at any time. The bird continued to respond with its characteristic side to side hop. More than 10,000 responses were recorded before "extinction" had reached the point at which few if any responses were made during a 10 or 15 min. interval. When the clock was again started, the periodic presentation of the magazine (still without any connection whatsoever with the bird's behavior) brought out a typical curve for reconditioning after periodic reinforcement . . . The record had been essentially horizontal for 20 min. prior to the beginning of this curve. The first reinforcement had some slight effect and the second a greater effect. There is a smooth positive acceleration in rate as the bird returns to the rate of responding which prevailed when it was reinforced every min.

When the response was again extinguished and the periodic presentation of food then resumed, a different response was picked up. This consisted of a progressive walking response in which the bird moved about the cage. The response of hopping from side to side never reappeared and could not, of course, be obtained deliberately without making the reinforcement contingent on the behavior.

The experiment might be said to demonstrate a sort of superstition. The bird behaves as if there were a causal relation between its behavior and the presentation of food, although such a relation is lacking. There are many analogies in human behavior. Rituals for changing one's luck at cards are good examples. A few accidental connections between a ritual and favorable consequences suffice to set up and maintain the behavior in spite of many unreinforced instances. The bowler who has released a ball down the alley but continues to behave as if he were controlling it by twisting and turning his arm and shoulder is another case in point. These behaviors have, of course, no real effect upon one's luck or upon a ball halfway down an alley, just as in the present case the food would appear as often if the pigeon did nothing—or, more strictly speaking, did something else.

It is perhaps not quite correct to say that conditioned behavior has been set up without any previously determined contingency whatsoever. We have appealed to a uniform sequence of responses in the behavior of the pigeon to obtain an over-all net contingency. When we arrange a clock to present food every 15 sec., we are in effect basing our reinforcement upon a limited set of responses which frequently occur 15 sec. after reinforcement. When a response has been strengthened (and this may result from one reinforcement), the setting of the clock implies an even more restricted contingency. Something of the same sort is true of the bowler. It is not quite correct to say that there is no connection between his twisting and turning and the course taken by the ball at the far end of the alley. The connection was established before the ball left the bowler's hand, but since both the path of the ball and the behavior of the bowler are determined, some relation survives. The subsequent behavior of the bowler may have no effect upon the ball, but the ball has an effect upon the bowler. The contingency, though not perfect, is enough to maintain the behavior in strength. The particular form of the behavior adopted by the bowler is due to induction from responses in which there is actual contact with the ball. It is clearly a movement appropriate to changing the ball's direction. But this does not invalidate the comparison, since we are not concerned with what response is selected but with why it persists in strength. In rituals for changing luck the inductive strengthening of a particular form of behavior is generally absent. The behavior of the pigeon in this experiment is of the latter sort, as the variety of responses obtained from different pigeons indicates. Whether there is any unconditioned behavior in the pigeon appropriate to a given effect upon the environment is under investigation.

The results throw some light on incidental behavior observed in experiments in which a discriminative stimulus is frequently presented. Such a stimulus has reinforcing value and can set up superstitious behavior. A pigeon will often develop some response such as turning, twisting, pecking near the locus of the discriminative stimulus, flapping its wings, etc. In much of the work to date in this field the interval between presentations of the discriminative stimulus has been one min. and many of these superstitious responses are short-lived. Their appearance as the result of accidental correlations with the presentation of the stimulus is unmistakable.

Chapter 10

Cognitive maps in rats and men*

Edward C. Tolman

I shall devote the body of this paper to a description of experiments with rats. But I shall also attempt in a few words at the close to indicate the significance of these findings on rats for the clinical behavior of men. Most of the rat investigations, which I shall report, were carried out in the Berkeley laboratory. But I shall also include, occasionally, accounts of the behavior of non-Berkeley rats who obviously have misspent their lives in out-of-State laboratories. Furthermore, in reporting our Berkeley experiments I shall have to omit a very great many. The ones I *shall* talk about were carried out by graduate students (or underpaid research assistants) who, supposedly, got some of their ideas from me. And a few, though a very few, were even carried out by me myself.

Let me begin by presenting diagrams for a couple of typical mazes, an alley maze and an elevated maze. In the typical experiment a hungry rat is put at the entrance of the maze (alley or elevated), and wanders about through the various true path segments and blind alleys until he finally comes to the food box and eats. This is repeated (again in the typical experiment) one trial every 24 hours and the animal tends to make fewer and fewer errors (that is, blind-alley entrances) and to take less and less time between start and goal-box until finally he is entering no blinds at all and running in a very few seconds from start to goal. The results are usually presented in the form of average curves of blind-entrances, or of seconds from start to finish, for groups of rats.

All students agree as to the acts. They disagree, however, on theory and explanation.

(1) First, there is a school of animal psychologists which believes that the maze behavior of rats is a matter of mere simple stimulus-response connections. Learning, according to them, consists in the strengthening of some of these connections and in the weakening of others. According to this "stimulus-response" school the rat in progressing down the maze is helplessly responding to a succession of external stimuli—sights, sounds, smells, pressures, etc. impinging upon his external sense organs—plus internal stimuli coming from the viscera and from the skeletal muscles. These external and

---

*Abridged from *Psychological Review* 55:189-196, 1948. Copyright 1948 by American Psychological Association, by permission.

internal stimuli call out the walkings, runnings, turnings, retracings, smellings, rearings, and the like which appear. The rat's central nervous system, according to this view, may be likened to a complicated telephone switchboard. There are the incoming calls from sense-organs and there are the outgoing messages to muscles. Before the learning of a specific maze, the connecting switches (synapses according to the physiologist) are closed in one set of ways and produce the primarily exploratory responses which appear in the early trials. *Learning*, according to this view, consists in the respective strengthening and weakening of various of these connections; those connections which result in the animal's going down the true path become relatively more open to the passage of nervous impulses, whereas those which lead him into the blinds become relatively less open.

It must be noted in addition, however, that this stimulus-response school divides further into two subgroups.

(a) There is a subgroup which holds that the mere mechanics involved in the running of a maze is such that the crucial stimuli from the maze get presented simultaneously with the correct responses more frequently than they do with any of the incorrect responses. Hence, just on a basis of this greater frequency, the neural connections between the crucial stimuli and the correct responses will tend, it is said, to get strengthened at the expense of the incorrect connections.

(b) There is a second subgroup in this stimulus-response school which holds that the reason the appropriate connections get strengthened relatively to the inappropriate ones is, rather, the fact that the responses resulting from the correct connections are followed more closely in time by need-reductions. Thus a hungry rat in a maze tends to get to food and have his hunger reduced *sooner* as a result of the true path responses than as a result of the blind alley responses. And such immediately following need-reductions or, to use another term, such "positive reinforcements" tend somehow, it is said, to strengthen the connections which have most closely preceded them. Thus it is as if—although this is certainly not the way this subgroup would themselves state it—the satisfaction-receiving part of the rat telephoned back to Central and said to the girl: "Hold that connection; it was good; and see to it that you blankety-blank well use it again the next time these same stimuli come in." These theorists also assume (at least some of them do some of the time) that, if bad results—"annoyances," "negative reinforcements"—follow, then this same satisfaction-and-annoyance-receiving part of the rat will telephone back and say, "Break that connection and don't you dare use it next time either."

So much for a brief summary of the two subvarieties of the "stimulus-response," or telephone switchboard school.

(2) Let us turn now to the second main school. This group (and I belong to them) may be called the field theorists. We believe that in the course of learning something like a field map of the environment gets established in the rat's brain. We agree with the other school that the rat in running a maze is exposed to stimuli and is finally led as a result of these stimuli to the responses which actually occur. We feel, however, that the intervening brain processes are more complicated, more patterned and often, pragmatically

speaking, more autonomous than do the stimulus-response psychologists. Although we admit that the rat is bombarded by stimuli, we hold that his nervous system is surprisingly selective as to which of these stimuli it will let in at any given time.

Secondly, we assert that the central office itself is far more like a map control room than it is like an old-fashioned telephone exchange. The stimuli, which are allowed in, are not connected by just simple one-to-one switches to the outgoing responses. Rather, the incoming impulses are usually worked over and elaborated in the central control room into a tentative, cognitive-like map of the environment. And it is this tentative map, indicating routes and paths and environmental relationships, which finally determines what responses, if any, the animal will finally release.

Finally, I, personally, would hold further that it is also important to discover in how far these maps are relatively narrow and strip-like or relatively broad and comprehensive. Both strip maps and comprehensive maps may be either correct or incorrect in the sense that they may (or may not), when acted upon, lead successfully to the animal's goal. The differences between such strip maps and such comprehensive maps will appear only when the rat is later presented with some change within the given environment. Then, the narrower and more strip-like the original map, the less will it carry over successfully to the new problem; whereas, the wider and the more comprehensive it was, the more adequately it will serve in the new set-up. In a strip map the given position of the animal is connected by only a relatively simple and single path to the position of the goal. In a comprehensive map a wider arc of the environment is represented, so that, if the starting position of the animal be changed or variations in the specific routes be introduced, this wider map will allow the animal still to behave relatively correctly and to choose the appropriate new route.

But let us turn, now, to the actual experiments. The ones, out of many, which I have selected to report are simply ones which seem especially important in reinforcing the theoretical position I have been presenting. This position, I repeat, contains two assumptions: First, that learning consists not in stimulus-response connections but in the building up in the nervous system of sets which function like cognitive maps, and second, that such cognitive maps may be usefully characterized as varying from a narrow strip variety to a broader comprehensive variety.

The experiments fall under five heads: (1) "latent learning," (2) "vicarious trial and error" or "VTE," (3) "searching for the stimulus," (4) "hypotheses" and (5) "spatial orientation."

"Latent Learning" Experiments. The first of the latent learning experiments was performed at Berkeley by Blodgett. It was published in 1929. Blodgett not only performed the experiments, he also originated the concept. He ran three groups of rats through a six-unit alley maze. He had a control group and two experimental groups. These animals were run in orthodox fashion. That is, they were run one trial a day and found food in the goal-box at the end of each trial. Groups II and III were the experimental groups. The animals of Group II were not fed in the maze for the first six days but only in their home cages some two hours later. On the seventh day the rats found food at the end of the maze for the first time and continued to find it

on subsequent days. The animals of Group III were treated similarly except that they first found food at the end of the maze on the third day and continued to find it there on subsequent days. It will be observed that the experimental groups as long as they were not finding food did not appear to learn much. (Their error curves did not drop.) But on the days immediately succeeding their first finding of the food their error curves did drop astoundingly. It appeared, in short, that during the non-rewarded trials these animals had been learning much more than they had exhibited. This learning, which did not manifest itself until after the food had been introduced, Blodgett called "latent learning." Interpreting these results anthropomorphically, we would say that as long as the animals were not getting any food at the end of the maze they continued to take their time in going through it—they continued to enter many blinds. Once, however, they knew they were to get food, they demonstrated that during these preceding non-rewarded trials they had learned where many of the blinds were. They had been building up a "map," and could utilize the latter as soon as they were motivated to do so.

Honzik and myself repeated the experiments (or rather he did and I got some of the credit) with 14-unit T-mazes, and with larger groups of animals, and got similar results. We used two control groups—one that never found food in the maze (HNR) and one that found it throughout (HR). The experimental group (HNR–R) found food at the end of the maze from the 11th day on and showed the same sort of a sudden drop.

But probably the best experiment demonstrating latent learning was, unfortunately, done not in Berkeley but at the University of Iowa, by Spence and Lippitt. Only an abstract of this experiment has as yet been published. However, Spence has sent a preliminary manuscript from which the following account is summarized. A simple Y-maze with two goal-boxes was used. Water was at the end of the right arm of the Y and food at the end of the left arm. During the training period the rats were run neither hungry nor thirsty. They were satiated for both food and water before each day's trials. However, they were willing to run because after each run they were taken out of whichever end box they had got to and put into a living cage, with other animals in it. They were given four trials a day in this fashion for seven days, two trials to the right and two to the left.

In the crucial test the animals were divided into two subgroups one made solely hungry and one solely thirsty. It was then found that on the first trial the hungry group went at once to the left, where the food had been, statistically more frequently than to the right; and the thirsty group went to the right, where the water had been, statistically more frequently than to the left. These results indicated that under the previous non-differential and very mild rewarding conditions of merely being returned to the home cages the animals had nevertheless been learning where the water was and where the food was. In short, they had acquired a cognitive map to the effect that food was to the left and water to the right, although during the acquisition of this map they had not exhibited any stimulus-response propensities to go more to the side which became later the side of the appropriate goal.

There have been numerous other latent learning experiments done in the Berkeley laboratory and elsewhere. In general, they have for the most part all confirmed the above sort of findings. . . .

Part IV

Perception

Chapter 11

What a "bummer" is really like*

Thomas De Quincey

Around the turn of the century, William James decided to experiment with the effects of opium on himself in an effort to increase his creativity and powers of insight. In the middle of one drug-induced dream, he suddenly felt a flash of inspiration. Certain that the secret of the universe had suddenly been revealed to him, he managed to write down the content of his inspirational flash before losing consciousness. On awakening, he found to his dismay that what he had actually written was, "Hogamus, higamous: Men are polygamous; higamous, hogamous—women monogamous!" So much for the secret of the universe! Today we know that the physiological effect of most hallucinogenic drugs is simply to facilitate the transmission of nerve impulses across the synapse, either in specific parts of the nervous system or in the nervous system as a whole; what the drugged individual perceives as new and deeper levels of reality or awareness is really the continuing reverberations of his own nerve impulses. And if some of his feelings or thoughts should happen to be unpleasant ones . . .

The first notice I had of any important change going on in this part of my physical economy was from the re-awaking of a state of eye oftentimes incident to childhood. I know not whether my reader is aware that many children have a power of painting, as it were, upon the darkness all sorts of phantoms: in some that power is simply a mechanic affection of the eye; others have a voluntary or semi-voluntary power to dismiss or summon such phantoms; or, as a child once said to me, when I questioned him on this matter, "I can tell them to go, and they go; but sometimes they come when I don't tell them to come." He had by one-half as unlimited a command over apparitions as a Roman centurion over his soldiers. In the middle of 1817 this faculty became increasingly distressing to me: at night, when I lay awake in bed, vast processions moved along continually in mournful pomp; friezes of never-ending stories, that to my feelings were as sad and solemn as stories drawn from times before Œdipus or

*Abridged from Thomas De Quincey's *Confessions of an English Opium-Eater,* New York, 1860, Ticknor & Fields.

Priam, before Tyre, before Memphis. And, concurrently with this, a corresponding change took place in my dreams; a theatre seemed suddenly opened and lighted up within my brain, which presented nightly spectacles of more than earthly splendour. And the four following facts may be mentioned, as noticeable at this time:

1. That, as the creative state of the eye increased, a sympathy seemed to arise between the waking and the dreaming states of the brain in one point—that whatsoever I happened to call up and to trace by a voluntary act upon the darkness was very apt to transfer itself to my dreams; and at length I feared to exercise this faculty; for, as Midas turned all things to gold that yet baffled his hopes and defrauded his human desires, so whatsoever things capable of being visually represented I did but think of in the darkness immediately shaped themselves into phantoms for the eye; and, by a process apparently no less inevitable, when thus once traced in faint and visionary colours, like writings in sympathetic ink, they were drawn out, by the fierce chemistry of my dreams, into insufferable splendour that fretted my heart.

2. This and all other changes in my dreams were accompanied by deep-seated anxiety and funereal melancholy, such as are wholly incommunicable by words. I seemed every night to descend—not metaphorically, but literally to descend—into chasms and sunless abysses, depths below depths, from which it seemed hopeless that I could ever re-ascend. Nor did I, by waking, feel that I *had* re-ascended. Why should I dwell upon this? For indeed the state of gloom which attended these gorgeous spectacles, amounting at last to utter darkness, as of some suicidal despondency, cannot be approached by words.

3. The sense of space, and in the end the sense of time, were both powerfully affected. Buildings, landscapes, &c., were exhibited in proportions so vast as the bodily eye is not fitted to receive. Space swelled, and was amplified to an extent of unutterable and self-repeating infinity. This disturbed me very much less than the vast expansion of time. Sometimes I seemed to have lived for seventy or a hundred years in one night; nay, sometimes had feelings representative of a duration far beyond the limits of any human experience.

4. The minutest incidents of childhood, or forgotten scenes of later years, were often revived. I could not be said to recollect them; for, if I had been told of them when waking, I should not have been able to acknowledge them as parts of my past experience. But, placed as they were before me in dreams like intuitions, and clothed in all their evanescent circumstances and accompanying feelings, I *recognized* them instantaneously. I was once told by a near relative of mine that, having in her childhood fallen into a river, and being on the very verge of death but for the assistance which reached her at the last critical moment, she saw in a moment her whole life, clothed in its forgotten incidents, arrayed before her as in a mirror, not successively, but simultaneously; and she had a faculty developed as suddenly for comprehending the whole and every part. This, from some opium experiences, I can believe; I have, indeed, seen the same thing asserted twice in modern books, and accompanied by a remark which probably is true—viz. that the dread book of account which the Scriptures speak of is, in fact, the mind itself of each individual. Of this, at least, I feel assured, that there is no such thing as ultimate *forgetting;* traces once impressed upon the memory are indestructible; a thou-

sand accidents may and will interpose a veil between our present consciousness and the secret inscriptions on the mind. Accidents of the same sort will also rend away this veil. But alike, whether veiled or unveiled, the inscription remains for ever; just as the stars seem to withdraw before the common light of day, whereas, in fact, we all know that it is the light which is drawn over them as a veil, and that they are waiting to be revealed whenever the obscuring daylight itself shall have withdrawn.

Having noticed these four facts as memorably distinguishing my dreams from those of health, I shall now cite a few illustrative cases; and shall then cite such others as I remember, in any order that may give them most effect as pictures to the reader. . . .

. . . Over every form, and threat, and punishment, and dim sightless incarceration, brooded a killing sense of eternity and infinity. Into these dreams only it was, with one or two slight exceptions, that any circumstances of physical horror entered. All before had been moral and spiritual terrors. But here the main agents were ugly birds, or snakes, or crocodiles, especially the last. The cursed crocodile became to me the object of more horror than all the rest. I was compelled to live with him; and (as was always the case in my dreams) for centuries. Sometimes I escaped, and found myself in Chinese houses. All the feet of the tables, sofas, &c., soon became instinct with life: the abominable head of the crocodile, and his leering eyes, looked out at me, multiplied into ten thousand repetitions; and I stood loathing and fascinated. So often did this hideous reptile haunt my dreams that many times the very same dream was broken up in the very same way: I heard gentle voices speaking to me (I hear everything when I am sleeping), and instantly I awoke; it was broad noon, and my children were standing, hand in hand, at my bedside, come to show me their coloured shoes, or new frocks, or to let me see them dressed for going out. No experience was so awful to me, and at the same time so pathetic, as this abrupt translation from the darkness of the infinite to the gaudy summer air of highest noon, and from the unutterable abortions of miscreated gigantic vermin to the sight of infancy and innocent *human* natures. . . .

Then suddenly would come a dream of far different character—a tumultuous dream—commencing with a music such as now I often heard in sleep—music of preparation and of awakening suspense. The undulations of fast-gathering tumults were like the opening of the Coronation Anthem; and, like *that,* gave the feeling of a multitudinous movement, of infinite cavalcades filing off, and the tread of innumerable armies. The morning was come of a mighty day—a day of crisis and of ultimate hope for human nature, then suffering mysterious eclipse, and labouring in some dread extremity. Somewhere, but I knew not where—somehow, but I knew not how—by some beings, but I knew not by whom—a battle, a strife, an agony, was travelling through all its stages—was evolving itself, like the catastrophe of some mighty drama, with which my sympathy was the more insupportable from deepening confusion as to its local scene, its cause, its nature, and its undecipherable issue. I (as is usual in dreams where, of necessity, we make ourselves central to every movement) had the power, and yet had not the power, to decide it. I had the power, if I could raise myself to will it; and yet again had not the power, for the weight of twenty Atlantics was upon me, or the oppression of inexpiable guilt. "Deeper than ever plummet sounded," I lay inactive. Then, like a chorus, the passion deepened. Some greater interest was at stake, some mightier cause, than ever yet the sword had pleaded, or trumpet had proclaimed. Then came sudden alarms; hurryings to and fro; trepidations of innumerable fugitives, I knew not whether from the good cause or the bad; darkness and lights; tempest and human faces; and at last, with the sense that all was lost, female forms, and the features that were worth all the world to me; and but a moment allowed—and clasped hands, with heartbreaking partings, and then—everlasting farewells! and, with a sigh such as the caves of hell sighed when the incestuous mother uttered the abhorred name of Death, the sound was reverberated—everlasting farewells! and again, and yet again reverberated—everlasting farewells!

And I awoke in struggles, and cried aloud, "I will sleep no more!"

Now, at last, I had become awestruck at the approach of sleep, under the condition of visions so afflicting, and so intensely life-like as those which persecuted my phantom-haunted brain. More and more also I felt violent palpitations in some internal region, such as are commonly, but erroneously, called palpitations of the heart—being, as I suppose, referable exclusively to derangements in the stomach. These were evidently increasing rapidly in frequency and in strength. Naturally, therefore, on considering how important my life had become to others besides myself, I became alarmed; and I paused seasonably; but with a difficulty that is past all description. Either way it seemed as though death had, in military language, "thrown himself astride of my path." Nothing short of mortal anguish in a physical sense, it seemed, to wean myself from opium; yet, on the other hand, death through overwhelming nervous terrors—death by brain-fever or by lunacy—seemed too certainly to besiege the alternative course. Fortunately I had still so much of firmness left as to face that choice, which, with most of instant suffering, showed in the far distance a possibility of final escape.

This possibility was realized: I *did* accomplish my escape. And the issue of that particular stage in my opium experiences (for such it was—simply a provisional stage, that paved the way subsequently for many milder stages, to which gradually my constitutional system accommodated itself) was, pretty nearly in the following words, communicated to my readers in the earliest edition of these *Confessions:*

I triumphed. But infer not, reader, from this word *"triumphed,"* a condition of joy or exaltation. Think of me as of one, even when four months had passed, still agitated, writhing, throbbing, palpitating, shattered; and much, perhaps in the situation of him who has been racked, as I collect the torments of that state from the affecting account of them left by a most innocent sufferer in the time of James I. Meantime, I derived no benefit from any medicine whatever, except ammoniated tincture of valerian. The moral of the narrative is addressed to the Opium-Eater; and therefore, of necessity, limited in its application. If he is taught to fear and tremble, enough has been effected. But he may say that the issue of my case is at least a proof that opium, after an eighteen years' use, and an eight years' abuse, of its powers, may still be renounced; and that he may chance to bring to the task greater energy than I did, or that, with a stronger constitution, he may obtain the same results with less. This may be true; I would not presume to measure the efforts of other men by my own. Heartily I wish him more resolution; heartily I wish him an equal success. Nevertheless, I had motives external to myself which he may unfortunately want; and these supplied me with conscientious supports, such as merely selfish interests might fail in supplying to a mind debilitated by opium.

Lord Bacon conjectures that it may be as painful to be born as to die. That seems probable; and, during the whole period of diminishing the opium, I had the torments of a man passing out of one mode of existence into another, and liable to the mixed or the alternate pains of birth and death. The issue was not death, but a sort of physical regeneration; and I may add that ever since, at intervals, I have had a restoration of more than youthful spirits.

One memorial of my former condition nevertheless remains: my dreams are not calm; the dread swell and agitation of the storm have not wholly subsided; the legions that encamped in them are drawing off, but not departed; my sleep is still tumultuous; and, like the gates of Paradise to our first parents when looking back from afar, it is still (in the tremendous line of Milton)—

With dreadful faces thronged and fiery arms.

Chapter 12

Set-breaking as a learned response*

Don E. Gibbons

> If a set is a readiness to perceive a particular situation in a certain way, and if a learning set is a readiness to proceed in a particular manner when faced with a given type of problem, then the stronger these tendencies become, the greater should be their interference with the development of novel or creative approaches to problems for which no previously established procedures are useful. But perhaps we can also learn, by appropriate training, to break those patterns of perception and response that are no longer effective.

Because we are continually generalizing from past situations, certain problems may normally arouse associations which will facilitate solution and others will tend to arouse associations which will block solution. If inappropriate past experience is deliberately provided, a wrong response set may be aroused by a problem which would otherwise be fairly simple (Duncker, 1945; Guetzkow, 1951; Luchins, 1942). On the other hand, it seems likely that appropriate training may act to *negate* the effect of competing associations in a "difficult" problem which would normally initiate an inappropriate response set.

Such an "ability to surmount set" probably depends to some extent on the availability of alternative procedures within the response repertoire of the individual, which might lead more directly to solution (Judson, Cofer, & Gelfand, 1956; Scheerer & Huling, 1960). If this is the case, this availability is probably influenced to some extent by the presence or absence of a set to *look for alternatives;* and if the presence of such a set overcomes a tendency to respond in a limited number of ways when confronted with a problem, it may be termed a "set-breaking set."

The present study constitutes an attempt to create a set-breaking set which would generalize within the experimental situation. Each S was given a problem which was structured to provide a greater or a lesser number of manipulanda designed to interfere with successful solution. Ss in the experimental group were given prior training in development of multiple solutions to prob-

---

*From *Psychological Reports* 17:203-208, 1965. Reprinted with permission of author and publisher.

lems which may be difficult only if a narrow set for solution exists. Set-breaking was defined as increased frequency of solutions to the forms of the experimental problem by this group.

The predictions were as follows: (a) Ss who had undergone the training were expected to produce a greater number of solutions within a shorter average time for the experimental problems, *i.e.*, positive transfer from the training situation was anticipated. (b) A smaller number of solutions and a longer average time to solution were expected for the more highly structured problem. (c) The increased number of solutions and decreased average time to solution for the trained Ss was expected to be more marked for the less structured than for the more structured problem.

METHOD
Subjects

Ss were 72 introductory psychology students, 36 males and 36 females. Half of the students of each sex were randomly assigned to the control and experimental groups.

Apparatus

A 30-in. metal pipe was stationed in an upright position and capped at the bottom, with a small wine bottle cork placed inside. The inside diameter of the pipe was approximately 1.5 in., which was sufficient to allow the cork to drop freely to the bottom. The pipe was placed upon a table along with a yardstick, hammer, pliers, and a chisel. There were also one open box each of drinking straws, paper clips, and toothpicks.

A second table was placed approximately 6 ft. away, and slightly to one side but not out of S's sight. In the *less structured condition,* only a full bucket of water was on this table. In the *more structured condition,* instead of the bucket there were four uncapped 7-Up bottles, three of which were full of water and one partly full, a deck of playing cards, a used ash tray, and one copy each of the magazines "True" and "Esquire." A fifth 7-Up bottle full of water was placed on the floor in front of this second table, as though it had been carelessly left there by somebody who had forgotten to drink it. Three chairs were drawn up to this table, one of the magazines was opened and turned upside down, and drinking straws were placed in two of the bottles on the table in a manner designed to give the impression that this particular part of the room had recently been used as a social area.

Procedure

Control Ss were administered the experimental problem before the training session was held, and the remainder were given the problem afterwards. The training session itself involved presenting Ss with a series of problems whose answers appeared to the writer to be "unconventional," and requesting them to supply the correct solution. They were told that the problems were being considered for use in a test designed to measure creativity. After a problem had been presented and they had been given 3 min. in which to solve it, they were given the correct answer. It was pointed out that the apparent difficulty of the problem stemmed from the fact that certain unnecessary assumptions were often made. Ss were encouraged to look for and eliminate these unnecessary assumptions while solving the remaining problems. Except for routine classroom administrative chores and frequent student questions requesting clarification of the solution to a particular problem, this activity occupied the entire 50-min. period. If a student had seen any of the training problems before or if he arrived at the correct answer before the end of the allotted time, he was requested not to reveal the answer to the others.

Training problems

The following problems were administered in the training session: (a) The word "Polk" is pronounced by Westerners in a similar manner to the word "folk." Also, the word "yoke" is pronounced in a similar way to the word "joke." How do *you* pronounce the word used to designate the white of an egg? (b) Take the Roman numeral nine and add one symbol to make it six. (c) Imagine that you had a plank exactly 12 ft. long and 3 ft. wide. How could you use this plank to cover completely a hole which is *exactly* 6 ft. long and 6 ft. wide, assuming that tools are available if you need them? (d) Given three rows of three dots each, each row directly above the other, how can you connect these nine dots by four successive straight lines drawn without retracing or removing the pencil from the paper? (e) Imagine you have six matches. Draw a sketch illustrating how you could make four equilateral triangles with them.[1]

No attempt was made to relate the lecture to the experimental problem situation. At the start of the previous class period, E had announced that he would like all of the students to participate in a psychological experiment as part of their introductory course work. To equalize demands on the instructor's time, it was requested that half of them sign up for the experiment during the first half of the week (*e.g.*, before the training problems were administered, although this was not mentioned) and the rest sign up during the second half of the week. A list of those requested to sign up during each of these times was then read and subsequently checked to ensure compliance. These two randomly-assigned groups made up the trained and untrained groups for the experimental problem.

Ss were also randomly assigned one of the two conditions of the experimental problem. E first inverted the pipe, showed S the cork, and then replaced them. S was asked, "How would you get the cork out without disturbing the pipe—without turning it upside down, unscrewing the cap, or breaking the base? You may use anything in this end of the room. When you think of the solution, tell me how you would do it. You will have 3 min." After first inquiring if S remembered having seen a similar problem before (none did), E started a stopwatch and retired to a desk at the opposite end of the room.

---

[1]Answers: (a) The white of an egg is *not* the yoke but the albumin. (b) Place an "s" in front of the numeral. (c) Cut the plank into two 12-ft. by 3-ft. segments. (d) You need not remain within the dots: draw a diagonal line through dots 1, 5, and 9, then through dots 2 and 3, extending this line far enough that you can draw a line back through dots 6 and 7, and from dot 7 draw a line back to dot 1. (e) Construct a pyramid so that one of the triangles lies flat and the other three are the sides.

RESULTS

Results are reported as (a) the average time taken by each group to solve the problem and (b) the number of Ss reaching the correct solution. For the purpose of statistical analysis, Ss who did not solve the experimental problem within 3 min. were assigned the maximum solution time of 180 sec.

The prediction that Ss undergoing the training lecture on set-breaking would solve the problem more rapidly and more frequently than Ss without training was supported by the analysis of variance for seconds to solution ($p = .05$) and by the analysis of frequency of solution ($p = .01$). [That is, the differences between the experimental and control groups in seconds to solution and in frequency of solution were so large that if this experiment had been repeated over and over these differences would be expected to occur by chance alone no more than five per cent of the time in the first comparison and one per cent of the time in the second comparison.]

The second prediction, that Ss confronted with the more highly structured problem would take longer to solve it and do so less frequently, was not supported, although the obtained differences were in the predicted direction.

It was expected that trained Ss would show an increased number of solutions and decreased time to solution for the less structured than for the more structured problem. But the interaction of training and problem structure was not sufficiently large to support this prediction, although the results were again in the predicted direction.

Finally, it was observed that female Ss took longer to solve the problem and produced fewer correct solutions. The analysis of variance for time to solution was statistically significant ($p = .01$), as was the chi-square test for frequency of solution ($p = .0005$).

DISCUSSION

There seems to be one aspect of problem solving which previous methods approach but do not explicitly focus on. As a result of negative transfer of procedures, or sets, S often approaches a problem with unnecessary assumptions which have inhibitory effects. An inappropriate set may occasionally be avoided by any one of several methods. Re-formulation of a problem may eliminate it, for example, because S is then faced with a slightly different problem (Wertheimer, 1945); if the disfunctional assumptions involve only part of a problem, they may occasionally be avoided by attending to other aspects of the problem or by shifting one's perspective from the parts of the problem to the problem as a whole (Maier, 1933). The blocking effect of the unnecessary assumptions may be reduced by practice which strengthens the correct response or related associations (Judson, Cofer, & Gelfand, 1956). A similar result can be obtained by training which focuses explicitly on novel uses or associations, especially if such training is prolonged and intensive (Meadow & Parnes, 1959). There seem to be certain problems, however, which some Ss are not able to solve until they *explicitly remove* the unnecessary assumptions which act to block solution. If S is asked, for example, to "take the Roman numeral nine and add one symbol to make it six," he is unable to solve this problem as long as he assumes that the answer or the figure added must also be a Roman numeral. No amount of re-formulation and/or flexibility in approach is going to help as long as he continues to operate within the framework of this erroneous assumption. When the assumption is removed, the answer is straightforward. Behavior necessary for solution might be labeled "set-breaking," in contrast to the "detour" or "practice" approaches above.

Of course, what may actually have been learned during the training session was perhaps a generalized suspicion of problem-solving situations related to the subject matter of psychology or psychological experiments, especially the present one. Being alert for a "trick," the trained Ss may have simply been more open to novel methods of solution. However, set-breaking may itself be viewed as nothing more than being alert for the possibility of "trick" solutions or hidden shortcut methods when confronted with a problem-solving situation.

From Ss' performance, it appears that the two levels of experimental problem structure were not different enough in the numbers of competing associations to produce a significant difference between them in number of solutions or in time to solution. Since the trained group did do significantly better than the untrained group, this small difference in problem difficulty probably accounts in large part for the lack of interaction between training and problem structure.

Because the inhibitory effects of a set can be overcome in many ways, as previously noted, the fact that the observed results are not independent of the sex of S should not be surprising. The comparatively greater success of the male Ss may have been due to greater familiarity with the mechanical or quasi-mechanical situations or a greater ego-involvement.

REFERENCES

Duncker, K.: On problem solving, *Psychological Monographs* **58:** No. 5 (Whole No. 270), 1945.

Guetzkow, H.: An analysis of the operation of set in problem-solving behavior, *Journal of General Psychology* **45:**219-244, 1951.

Judson, A., Cofer, C., and Gelfand, S.: Reasoning as an associative process: II. "Direction" in problem solving as a function of prior reinforcement of relevant responses, *Psychological Reports* **2:**501-507, 1956.

Luchins, A.: Mechanization in problem solving: the effect of "Einstellung," *Psychological Monographs* **54:** No. 6 (Whole No. 248), 1942.

Maier, N.: An aspect of human reasoning, *British Journal of Psychology* **24:**144-155, 1933.

Meadow, A., and Parnes, S.: Evaluation of training in creative problem solving, *Journal of Applied Psychology* **43:**189-194, 1959.

Scheerer, M., and Huling, M.: Cognitive embeddedness in problem solving: a theoretical and experimental analysis. In B. Kaplan and S. Wapner (Eds.): *Perspectives in psychological theory*, New York, 1960, International Universities Press, pp. 256-302.

Wertheimer, M.: *Productive thinking*, New York, 1945, Harper.

Part V

Motivation

Chapter 13

Habit*

William James

The following selection is condensed from the book "Psychology: Briefer Course," which was first published during the latter part of the nineteenth century. Despite their comparative age, the works of William James are more frequently cited in the popular press than those of any other psychologist. By conceiving of the organism as an active system of energy rather than as a passive mechanism that must be acted on by some external energy source or drive, James has anticipated the thinking of many contemporary writers in the areas of motivation and learning. Note the similarity between James' discussion of the faculty of will and the assumptions regarding willpower commonly held by the public at large. Why have these views been generally rejected by later psychologists?

"Habit a second nature? Habit is ten times nature!" the Duke of Wellington once said; and the degree to which this is true no one probably can appreciate as well as the veteran soldier. Daily drill and years of discipline end by fashioning a man completely over again in most of his conduct.

Habit is the enormous fly-wheel of society, its most precious conservative agent. It alone prevents the hardest and most repulsive walks of life from being deserted by those brought up to tread therein. It keeps the fisherman and the deck-hand at sea through the winter; it holds the miner in his darkness, and nails the countryman to his lonely farm through all the months of snow. Already by the age of twenty-five you can see the professional mannerisms settling down on the young salesman, on the young doctor, on the young minister, on the young attorney. You see the little lines of cleavage running through the character, the tricks of thought, the prejudices, the ways of the "shop," from which the man can soon no more escape than his coat-sleeve can suddenly fall into a new set of folds.

If the period between twenty and thirty is the critical one in the formation of intellectual and professional habits, the period below twenty is more important still for the fixing of personal habits such as speech and manners. Hardly

*Abridged from *Psychology: Briefer Course,* New York, 1900, Henry Holt & Co., Inc., pp. 142-150.

ever is a language learned after twenty spoken without a foreign accent; hardly ever can a youth who has suddenly become wealthy unlearn the nasality and other habits of speech bred in him by the associations of his growing years.

The great thing, then, is *to make our nervous system our ally instead of our enemy.* We must make automatic and habitual, as early as possible, as many useful actions as we can, and guard against growing into ways that are likely to be disadvantageous to us, as we should guard against the plague. The more of the details of our daily life we can hand over to the effortless custody of automatism, the more our highest powers of mind will be set free for their own proper work. There is no more miserable human being than one in whom nothing is habitual but indecision, and for whom the lighting of every cigar, the drinking of every cup of coffee, the time of rising and going to bed every day, and the beginning of every bit of work are subjects of express deliberation.

In the acquisition of a new habit, or the leaving off of an old one, we must take care to *launch ourselves with as strong and decided an initiative as possible.* Accumulate all the possible circumstances which reinforce the right motives; put yourself in situations that encourage the new way; make engagements incompatible with the old; take a public pledge if the case allows. In short, envelop your resolution with every aid you know. This will give your new beginning such a momentum that the temptation to break down will not occur as soon as it otherwise might; and every day during which a breakdown is postponed adds to the chances of its never occurring at all.

A second maxim is, *never suffer an exception to occur until the new habit is securely rooted in your life.* Each lapse is like letting fall a ball of string which one has carefully wound up: a single slip undoes more than a great many turns will wind again.

The need of securing success at the outset is imperative. Failure at first is apt to dampen the energy of all future attempts, whereas past experiences of success give one added vigor. Goethe said to a man who consulted him about an enterprise but mistrusted his own powers, "Ach! You need only blow on your hands!" And the remark illustrates the effect on Goethe's spirits of his own habitually successful career.

The question of "tapering off" in abandoning such habits as drinking and smoking is a question about which experts differ within certain limits, and in regard to what may be best for an individual case. In the main, however, all expert opinion would agree that an abrupt acquisition of the new habit is the best way, *if there be a real possibility of carrying it out.* We must be careful not to give the will so stiff a task as to insure its defeat at the very outset; but, *provided one can stand it,* a sharp period of suffering and then a free time is the best thing to aim at, whether in giving up a habit like that of drinking, or in simply changing one's hours of rising or of work. It is surprising how soon a desire will die if it is *never* fed.

One must first learn the art of making a decision before he can learn to make himself over again. He who every day makes a fresh resolve is like one who, arriving at the edge of the ditch he is to leap, forever stops and returns for a fresh run. Without unbroken advance, there is no such thing as an accumulation of the forces available for self improvement.

A final maxim may be added to the preceding: *seize the very first possible opportunity to act on every resolution you make, and on every prompting you may experience in the direction of the habits you aspire to gain.* It is not in the moment of their forming, but in the moment of their producing motor effects, that resolutions and aspirations communicate a new "set" to the brain. With mere good intentions, the road to Hell is proverbially paved. There is no more contemptible type of human character than that of the nerveless sentimentalist and dreamer who spends his life in a weltering sea of sensibility and emotion, but who never does a manly concrete deed.

In order to facilitate the development of new habits in the future, and to make subsequent changes more easily, we may offer the following suggestion: *keep the faculty of effort alive in you by a little gratuitous exercise every day.* That is, be systematically ascetic or heroic in little unnecessary points; do every day or two something for no other reason than that you would rather *not* do it, so that when the hour of need draws nigh it may find you not unnerved and untrained to stand the test. Asceticism of this sort is like the insurance which a man pays on his house and goods. The payment does him no good at the time and it possibly may never bring him a return. But if a fire *does* come, his having paid it will save him from ruin. So with the man who has daily accustomed himself to habits of concentrated attention and self-denial in unnecessary things.

Nothing we ever do, then, is in strict scientific literalness wiped out. The drunken Rip Van Winkle, in Jefferson's play, excuses himself by saying, "I won't count this time." Well, he may not count it, and a kind Heaven may not count it; but it is being counted nevertheless. Down among his nerve cells and fibres the molecules are counting it, registering and storing it up to be used against him when the next occasion arises. Of course, as we become permanent drunkards by so many separate drinks, so we become saints in the moral, and authorities and experts in the practical and scientific spheres, by so many separate acts and hours of work. Let no one have any anxiety about the end result of his education, whatever line of work he may intend to enter. If he keeps faithfully busy each hour of the working day, he may safely leave the final result to itself. He can with perfect certainty count on waking up some fine morning to find himself one of the competent ones of his generation in whatever pursuit he may have singled out.

Chapter 14

Fear*

Harold Ellis Jones and Mary Cover Jones

What makes one stimulus either reinforcing or aversive and another
not? One traditional answer is based on whether a stimulus reduces or
arouses tension—either by itself or because it has been appropriately
paired with one that does. But to fully understand just how and when
certain stimuli will be effective in modifying behavior, it is necessary
to understand the factors that make it possible to have a particular
state of tension or arousal in the first place. As demonstrated in this
classic study, these factors include not merely physiological conditions,
but also cognitive, developmental, and experiential ones.

Among poets and novelists the emotional life has always been a subject of
leading concern. Philosophers and "arm-chair" psychologists have at times inclined to a different emphasis; immersed in the affairs of reason, it is natural
that they should ignore emotion, and assume intellect to be a prime determiner
in human activity. Hence we have the theories of such thinkers as Spencer and
John Stuart Mill, who conceived of behavior as a rational pursuit of comfort
and a calculating avoidance of pain. During the past decade the psychoanalyst
and the behaviorist, following the poet's insight but armed with a heavier burden of facts, have from differing angles stressed the role of emotions in human
adjustment, and have led us to think of personality not merely in terms of the
development of intellectual processes, but also in terms of those organic drives
and cravings which underlie our conscious life. We have begun to realize that
much of our conduct which we formerly believed to be rationally planned, is
really the direct outcome of impulse and emotion. Rational explanations may
occur as afterthoughts. (Perhaps afterthoughts are the commonest kind of
thoughts.) The child in the nursery who asks to have his door open at night
gives as a plausible reason the fact that his room will be better aired, and he
may really believe this to be the deliberately thought-out origin of his desire.

*From *Childhood Education* 5: no. 3, January, 1928. Reprinted by permission of
Association for Childhood Education International, 3615 Wisconsin Avenue, N.W.,
Washington, D. C., and of the authors. Copyright © (1928) by the Association.

A younger child, however, will frankly and noisily insist that he wants the door open because he is *afraid* to be shut up alone. As we grow older and more thoughtful, we become increasingly skilled in cloaking our emotional desires with ingenious embroideries of reason. It is necessary to have a poet's naïveté, or a scientist's carefully regulated freedom from illusion, if we are to understand the real significance of impulsive and emotional factors in our everyday conduct.

The development of mental tests has provided another source of influence which has resulted, particularly among educators, in assigning too much regard to the verbal and intellectual phases of behavior. Though we are as yet unable to measure emotions as competently as the testers measure intelligence, we are nevertheless beginning to sense the significance of the emotional patterning which lies at the basis of temperament. Even in the field of the intellect, while it is true that our basic capacity to learn is a matter of intelligence, our *desire* to learn is to a large extent affected by emotional drives, and the processes which blur and interfere with learning are chiefly processes which involve disturbance in our emotional life.

It becomes quite obvious, then, that we need to pay closer attention to the nature of these emotional factors, and to study the methods by which emotions can be investigated and controlled.

THE "PRIMARY" EMOTIONS

What are the fundamental human relations? Dr. Watson, basing his views upon the observation of young infants in experimental situations, proposes three elementary emotional patterns: *rage,* the response of an infant to being hampered in its movements; *fear,* the response to pain, a loud sound, or to loss of support; and *love,* the response to cuddling or stroking sensitive skin areas. The complex play of emotions in the life of an adult is regarded as the outcome of *conditioning* among these simple and instinctive modes of reaction; if the child two years of age is afraid of other things than of the stimuli mentioned above, this is because a process of association has intervened, so that his fear has become transferred from loud sounds to various visual objects, odors, contact stimuli, and the like, which have been habitually associated with loud sounds.

This behaviorist formula has been accepted widely in the current popular literature, although it is by no means a matter for full agreement among psychologists. Its prestige arises from the fact that it is based upon observation rather than speculation, a condition which inspires confidence among laymen as well as among scientists. In other textbooks of psychology, however, we find a somewhat different listing of the primary emotions. Floyd Allport, in a study of facial expressions as an index of the emotions, reports five somewhat distinct emotional patterns: the pain-grief group of expressions, the surprise-fear group, anger, disgust, and pleasure. Various nuances and complications of emotion are regarded as resulting from mixtures of these primary patterns, and from the association with varying trains of ideas. Thus, a baby's facial expressions of surprise or fear (brows raised, eyes wide open, nose dilated, mouth opened, lips depressed at corners, etc.) may in the adult show characteristic special changes in amazement, dismay, disillusionment, terror, horror, and anxiety.

It should be noted that Watson's three basic emotions, with their stimuli, were derived from studies of very young infants. With older children it is possible that the list would need to be supplemented both as to the stimuli which by *original nature* may provoke emotion, and as to the pattern which the emotion takes. We are here assuming that changes in emotional pattern may not be wholly due to learning, but may to some extent occur as the result of an innate process of ripening, either of a general responsiveness, or of special response dispositions.

WHAT DO CHILDREN FEAR?

This point of view may be illustrated in connection with some of our experiments on children's fears. As children grow older, they begin to show differences in the number and kinds of things of which they are afraid. The only general statement which seems to cover all the cases of fear which we have observed in children is that children tend to be afraid of things that require them to make sudden and unexpected adjustment. Stimuli which are startlingly strange, which are presented without due preparation, or which are painful or excessively intense, belong in this category. For example, in our study of the reactions of preschool children to flashlights, darkness, false-faces, snakes, rabbits, frogs, and the like, it was found that the animal which most often caused fear was the frog, the fear not usually appearing at first sight of the frog, but at sight of the frog suddenly jumping. Likewise, a child was often afraid of a jack-in-the-box; a species of beetle which suddenly snaps up in the air when placed on its back was fairly efficient in arousing alarm; while caterpillars and earthworms produced no more than a mild curiosity in the younger children.

While traces of these childhood fears may last throughout life, affecting adult behavior profoundly, the overt expression of fear is apt to be less marked as childhood is outgrown: partly because the adult meets fewer unfamiliar situations (encounters fewer stimuli for which his action system contains no ready adjustment) and partly because he has learned to mask and repress the more conspicuous symptoms of emotion. From watching individuals of different ages in similar test situations, it is evident that the effectiveness of a stimulus and the type of emotional response are greatly affected by maturity. From the diffuse responsiveness of the infant, to the blunted and inhibited reaction of the blasé adult, the variety of unpredictable behavior in fear producing situations provides a rich field for research.

How does the sight of a snake affect a baby, a toddler, a youth, a grandfather? A few cases, chosen from our laboratory notes, show an interesting developmental sequence.

EXPERIMENTS WITH YOUNG CHILDREN
Experimental situation

A pen eight by ten feet by six inches high was built on the nursery floor. Within this a number of blocks and toys were scattered, and two black suitcases were placed flat on the floor near the wall. The suitcases could be opened easily by a child; one contained a familiar mechanical toy, the other contained a snake of a harmless variety (*Spilotes corais*) about six feet in length and slightly under four inches in girth at the middle of the body. When free in the pen, the snake glided actively about, showing a powerful and agile type of movement, and frequently protruding a black forked tongue about an inch in length. If the child did not open the suitcase containing the snake, an observer was able to do so from a concealed position behind a screen, by pulling a string attached to the lid of the case.

Subject 1: Irving, age one year three months. Irving sat in the pen, playing idly with the ball and blocks. After being released, the snake glided slowly toward Irving, whipping up his head and deflecting his course when within 12 inches of the infant. Irving watched unconcerned, fixating the snake's head on the middle of his body, and letting his gaze wander frequently to other objects in the pen. The snake furnished only a mild incentive to his attention.

Subject 3: Enid, age one year seven months. Enid sat passively in the pen, playing with blocks in an unsystematic fashion. The snake was released and moved fairly rapidly about the pen. Enid showed no interest, giving the snake only casual glances and continuing to play with her blocks when it was within two feet of her. When (later) the snake was held by the observer directly in front of her face, she showed no changes in facial expression, but presently reached out her hand and grasped the snake tightly about the neck.

Subject 8: Sol, age two years three months. When the snake began moving about the pen, Sol watched closely, holding his ground when the snake came near, but making no effort to touch it. He resisted when an attempt was made to have him pick up the snake (this was the same guarded reaction that he had shown previously with the rabbit and white rat). He stood unmoved when the snake was thrust toward him, and showed no overt response, save an attempt to follow visually, when the head of the animal was swung in front and in back of him, neck writhing and tongue darting. After the snake was returned to the suitcase he went to it again and lifted the lid, looked within and then closed it in a business-like manner.

Subject 11: Laurel, age three years eight months. Laurel opened the suitcase, picking out two blocks which were lying against the snake's body. The snake was immobile and she evidently had no differential reaction to it. The snake was taken out. Laurel: "I don't want it." Avertive reactions, moved off, then stood up and started to leave the pen, although without apparent stir or excitement: "Let's put him back in the box." Laurel: "I don't want it." Experimenter: "Come and help me put him back." After slight urging she came over and assisted, using both hands in picking up the snake and dropping him quickly when she reached the suitcase.

Subject 12: Edward, age four years two months. Edward sat down in the pen and began playing constructively with the blocks. At sight of the snake he asked: "Can it drink water?" Experimenter: "Do you know what it is?" Edward: "It's a fish." He puckered his brows and made slight avertive reactions when the snake was swung within a foot of him, but this was overcome through adaptation in three trials. When encouraged to touch the snake he did so, tentatively, but soon grasped it without hesitation at the neck and body.

Subject 15: Ely, age six years seven months. On opening the suitcase he smiled and looked within for nearly a minute, making no effort to reach, and dropping the cover quickly when the snake moved. The snake thrust the lid up with his head, and glided out into the room. Ely took up a post of observation outside the pen. Experimenter: "Do you like him?" Ely nodded in the affirmative, and smiled. Experimenter: "Touch him like this." Ely very hesitatingly touched his back, and withdrew his hand quickly, later consenting to stroke him. He asked: "Does he have teeth?" a reasonable enough inquiry. When the snake moved in his direction he drew away and looked distressed, but was persuaded to help pick up and to put him back in the suitcase.

Of 15 children, seven showed complete absence of fear indications; their age range was from 14 to 27 months, with a median of 20 months. Eight individuals showed "guarded" reactions, two of these revealing distinct fear, and two showing marked avertive responses when the snake gave the appearance of aggression; the other four being classified as "unafraid but wary." The age range of the "guarded" group was from 26 to 79 months, with a median of 44 months. The only case of a child under three years showing fear was Doris, age 26 months, and her reaction changed markedly the following day, as indicated by the report of the group response.

The suitcase was taken into the nursery when nine children were present. Most of them recognized it, and one of the older children said, "There's an animal in there." Several of the children moved forward to touch it as soon as the snake was released; Doris, who had been afraid the day before, now showed no fear, crowding close and attempting to hit the snake's head with a wooden boat. The two oldest children in the group remained cautious; Lawrence, age five years seven months, climbed up on a table, and John, age five years ten months, retained hold of the experimenter's hand, and refused to come near. After a few minutes of play, the experimenter said, "Now everyone has touched it except John and Lawrence." Both of these now came forward and touched the snake's back, social pressure being evidently effective in encouraging a more positive response.

EXPERIMENTS WITH OLDER CHILDREN

The following results were obtained in a group of 36 school children, with an age range of from about six to ten years: The children were sitting on low chairs in a circle about 20 feet in diameter. The experimenter placed the suitcase containing the snake in the middle of the circle, asking, "Who wants to open the suitcase?" Harry, eight years of age, opened it, and took the snake out when requested. The snake glided about the floor, passing between the feet of the boys; no disturbance was shown. The experimenter now asked, "Who wants to touch the snake?" holding the snake's head so that children had to reach past it, and walking slowly around the inside of the circle. The first 11 children touched the snake with no hesitancy. Four boys about ten years of age hesitated, one withdrawing markedly, another falling over backward in his chair. (This was due to an emotional heightening, arising partly from fear and partly from a desire to show off.) Two girls refused to touch the snake, but jumped up and ran around behind the circle, following the experimenter and watching closely. An undercurrent of reassurance was constantly heard, "He won't let it hurt you. Go ahead, touch it, it won't bite."

Only nine of the 26 children showed definitely resistive behavior, and these were chiefly boys and chiefly the oldest in the group.

EXPERIMENTS WITH COLLEGE STUDENTS

How do adults behave, when presented with a similar situation?

In several classes of undergraduate and graduate students, the snake was introduced as "a perfectly harmless animal; the skin of this reptile has a smooth and pleasant feeling, and we guarantee that in touching him no one runs the slightest risk." In some classes the same reptile was used as in the preceding experiments; in others the snake was a boa constrictor, somewhat smaller and of a less "dangerous" appearance than the Spilotes. Of about 90 students nearly one-third refused to have the snake brought near; one-third touched him, with obvious hesitation and dislike, while the remainder (including as many women as men) reached forward with apparently complete freedom from any emotional disturbance. Several of the women obviously regarded the presence of a snake in the room as an almost unbearable ordeal, and several of the men solved the problem of emotional conflict by retiring to a neighboring room until the experiment was concluded.

RECOMMENDATIONS FOR FURTHER EXPERIMENTS

These studies exemplify a simple observational method, and can be readily repeated with other groups. It is desirable that the problem should be approached by cumulative records on the same children, presenting a series of animals (under standard conditions) to the *same* children at intervals of three months. It is also desirable that the observational data be checked by more rigorous laboratory methods, including the use of instruments, such as the galvanometer, which record the inner aspects of emotional stress. With some of our adult subjects, we noted that while they stroked the snake in an apparently composed fashion, the subject's face and palms were nevertheless covered with beads of perspiration, indicating a marked degree of emotional tension. With young children such repressions are less likely to occur: the emotion is more superficial, and expresses itself readily and frankly in external symptoms. In studying the elimination of a fear, however, we should bear in mind the possibility that an attitude of tolerance and self-assurance may be merely a mask for an internal emotional upset; methods of elimination which "cure" the external signs may sometimes fail to reduce, and may even increase, the actual emotional intensity. We are now collecting evidence on these points, by means of standard laboratory procedures.

It should be pointed out that our experiments of this character should not be attempted by workers who are not accustomed to handling both animals and children. A snake should not be used until he has been adequately tamed and has established a record of reacting well to handling. Some non-poisonous species are likely to be dangerous because of vicious and unpredictable tempers. The situation must always be kept in control, so that a nervous child is not over-frightened; a slight degree of fear, which he later recognizes as groundless, may be of hygienic value, but a marked emotional upset is never hygienic, and the experimenter must take care to avoid traumatic episodes. In regions where poisonous snakes are common, it may be undesirable to train young children in emotional tolerance. The subjects used in our experiments were city children who had never before seen a snake of any kind, and who would be unlikely to encounter a poisonous snake in the course of a lifetime. Even in infested districts, it would seem desirable to cultivate a reaction of intelligent caution, in place of the blinding and tumultuous fear which was shown in so many of our adult subjects.

THE NATURE OF FEAR

In our group of 51 children and about 90 adults, children up to the age of two years showed no fear of a snake; by three or three and a half, caution reactions were common; children of this age paid closer attention to the snake's movements, and were somewhat tentative in approaching and touching it. Definite fear behavior occurred more often after the age of four years, and was more pronounced in adults than in children. No sex differences were observed. This "maturing" of a specific fear may be interpreted in at least three ways: (a) as the result of conditioning, (b) as the result of the ripening of an innate fear of snakes, (c) as the result of a general maturation of behavior, which leads to greater sensitiveness and more discriminatory responses.

The first explanation, although it is current among present-day behaviorists, does not seem to be applicable to our group. Our children were developing in a common environment in an institution, and had no opportunity to be conditioned against snakes, either through pictures, stories, or from encounters with live specimens. When first seen in our experiments, the snake was as novel to them as a unicorn, and their response to it must be regarded as a novel and unpracticed adjustment. If the response changed from the age of two to the age of three years, this development cannot be interpreted in terms of *specific* training.

The second explanation we are also inclined to reject; it assumes an instinctive fear of snakes, a reaction which is latent and immature at birth, and which develops by a special process of innate growth; such a belief is related to the doctrine of innate ideas and the inheritance of acquired characters, and is not in keeping with present-day theory. It is possible to understand the inheritance and ripening of a general disposition, such as sex, for here we are dealing with a definite internal source of stimulation, and with a glandular basis which is subject to growth. It is possible to understand the inheritance and ripening of a specific simple pattern of response, such as a startle response to loss of support, which may be dependent upon a structural development in the semicircular canals or in the vestibular nerves. But the fear of a visual object, such as a snake, involves an emotional response to a complex and variable perception, differentiated out of a total situation. The perception will vary according to the size and other characteristics of the snake, according to its behavior and its distance from the perceiver. It appears very unlikely that such a complex and many-faceted perceptual-emotional disposition can be inherited, or that it can develop by innate ripening.

We are left, then, with the third interpretation, which is in agreement with the theory of fear discussed on an earlier page. Fear may be regarded as a response to certain changes in a total situation: changes requiring a sudden new adjustment which the individual is unprepared to make. The arousal of fear depends not only upon situational changes, but also upon the individual's *general* level of development. With a young infant, perhaps the only changes which are fear-producing are those which substitute loud sounds for quiet, pain for comfort, or loss of support for a previous state of bodily balance. As a child develops, his intelligence innately matures, and his perceptions become enriched through experience. New things startle him because of his keener perception of the fact that they *are* new and unusual. We have an old saying,

"They who know nothing fear nothing." It would be equally true to say, "They who know everything fear nothing." *Fear arises when we know enough to recognize the potential danger in a stimulus, but have not advanced to the point of a complete comprehension and control of the changing situation.*

ELIMINATING FEAR

One of the most striking results of our studies arises from the comparison of fear elimination in children and in adults. All of the preschool children readily became adapted to the snake and to other animals. With careful management, even those who were initially most distressed quickly lost their uncertainty under the influence of social example. This was not the case, however, among the adolescents and adults, for here we encountered many instances of sharp and persistent fear, which could not be counteracted except through a long course of training. Their fears had become "set" through the years, reinforced by many conditionings, and perhaps complicated with symbolic horrors of various sorts. In this we have concrete evidence of the impressionability of early childhood; a given amount of educational effort may be much more effective with preschool children than with the less plastic emotional organizations of adults. If we would shape the emotions, we must begin early.

Chapter 15

The tyranny of the future*

George A. Miller

What do people want? As regards Americans around the middle of the twentieth century, what they want is all too familiar. Listen to Rosser Reeves, a high-powered salesman whose business it is to know what people want:

> We know, for example, that we do not want to be fat. We do not want to smell bad. We want healthy children, and we want to be healthy ourselves. We want beautiful teeth. We want good clothes. We want people to like us. We do not want to be ugly. We seek love and affection. We want money. We like comfort. We yearn for more beautiful homes. We want honesty, self-respect, a place in the community. We want to own things in which we can take pride. We want to succeed in our jobs. We want to be secure in our old age.

These are proven demands of the market place. Never mind whether it is good to want such things, or whether we even have a right to want them. The point is that these are the things people in America work for, spend money on, devote their lives to. Surely here is where a psychologist should start to fashion his theory of human motivation.

This list, however, seems little better than our grandfather's lists of instincts. If one is to make scientific sense out of these human desires, one will first have to discover the underlying dimensions of similarity among them.

Notice first of all that these American demands are all perfectly explicit, conscious, and socially acceptable. One may suspect that beneath these manifest desires is concealed a less admirable core, but this is a difficult issue.

Next, notice how typically American the list is. Imagine collecting a similar catalogue from Neanderthal men or the Tartar hordes. Americans find it difficult to believe that their own longings for particular things are learned, that the American conception of the good life is not universal and inevitable, that human nature has its own dimensions in India, Brazil, Nigeria.

Consider the salesman's list in a broader context: In many parts of the world obesity is judged beautiful. In extremely cold regions where clothes are seldom removed, body odors are simply ignored. Concepts of health and disease, of normal and abnormal, vary widely from one culture to the next. Teeth we think beautiful do not look beautiful to everyone. And so on down the list. Each thing we think so desirable is desirable because we have learned to desire it. In another culture we would have learned to desire other things. Even within our own relatively homogeneous society different social groups have very different dreams of the future.

As a start, therefore, one asks how this learning takes place. Where and when in the life of a youngster does stern society sit him down and explain what to crave and what to despise?

One answer runs something like this. Homeostatic drives are primary, and all the environmental conditions that are consistently associated with the satisfaction of primary drives will thereby acquire a secondary power to satisfy us. Mother's smile becomes rewarding because it accompanies the satisfaction of so many of her child's primary motives. And by generalization the value of mother's smile extends to other smiles, to all smiles, to social approval in its broadest sense. Similarly, power over others becomes a social motive because it was first associated with the various biological satisfactions that others can provide. Avarice is a social motive because money is associated with the satisfaction of many other motives. And so on and on. It is apparently true that every social value can be traced back, in theory, at least, through some such hypothetical chain of associations, to primary, homeostatic drives. These biological primitives constitute—in theory—the latent core around which cluster these manifest desires that an advertiser can exploit.

There is little that is objectionable in such a theory until it is claimed that social action is *always* energized in this manner. No doubt it is true that some adult values are acquired by repeated association with eating, drinking, sexing. But many psychologists feel that the insistence—typified by orthodox Freudian theorists—that all human behavior, normal and abnormal alike, draws its energy either directly or indirectly from these life-preserving, species-preserving mechanisms imposes on us an unprofitable burden of explanation. According to this theory, the reasons for everything we do must somehow be traced back historically to our sex glands and to homeostatic changes in the chemistry of our blood.

It detracts little from the importance of homeostasis and the pleasure principle to argue that some important social motives are acquired and mediated by very different processes, symbolic processes that must take place in the central nervous system.

One objection to the borrowed-energy theory is that it encourages us to think of social motives as if they ran a course entirely parallel to homeostatic drives. For example, an organism works to reduce its primary drives, to bring its tensions to an absolute minimum, to return to homeostatic equilibrium. If social motives are learned by association with primary drives, it seems reasonable to assume that they will also manifest this self-terminating characteristic. When this pattern of tension-reduction is imposed on social motives, however, it leads to an odd distortion. The simple truth is that social action does not always reduce tensions. To imply that it must suggests that persistent diligence and hard work are symptoms of maladjustment, that exciting stories and martial music will never be popular, that sport, humor, and dancing are signs of insanity, in short, that nirvana is the only goal anyone could imagine in this life. But this is nonsense. No sane person would reduce all his motivation to a minimum. Emerson was wrong when he said that every man is as lazy as he dares to be. Instead—when homeostasis gives us a chance—we constantly seek out new tensions to keep us occupied and entertained.

If we slavishly follow an analogy to biological drives, we are likely to assume that social motives can be satiated, as hunger, thirst, and sex can be. And on that assumption we must be surprised to find that millionaires want to make money, that neurotics never seem to get all the love they desire, that famous people like to see their names in newspapers, and so on. Social motives grow by what they feed on; the more we succeed, the higher we set our level of aspiration.

The mistaken notion that social motives can be satiated has even confused some economists and led them to prophesy that when the market was saturated—when 80 per cent of the American families owned refrigerators, or 70 per cent owned automobiles—the economy would slump to a level set by the rate of replacement. They failed to include the wages of optimism. Families with a refrigerator wanted a better one; families with one car wanted two cars; families with both a refrigerator and a car wanted their own house. Homeostasis follows an entirely different course.

The orthodox notion that we must have motives to energize our social actions—just as homeostatic drives energize our search for food, drink, and a mate—has been losing adherents for many years. Probably it would by now be abandoned, except that the defectors have been unable to agree among themselves on any single theory to replace the simple homeostatic analogy. When we desert it, therefore, we set out upon an uncertain journey of exploration; what follows here is only one of several directions that we might have chosen.

Suppose one asks, not where the energy for social action comes from, but where it is going. A psychologist can take the biological source of our vitality for granted; given that we are alive, metabolism provides our energy. The psychological problem is how we organize and guide a flow that must inevitably continue until our final tension-reduction in the grave. What determines how we will use our brief gift of time?

Most human endeavors are guided not by learned motives, but by learned values. There are important differences. Motives are a source of energy, values a form of knowledge. Motives like to push us from the past, values try to draw us into the future. Many psychologists feel that these differences are purely verbal, that motive and value are two sides of the coin. Perhaps this is true. There is as much of philosophy as of science in these distinctions. Here, however, we shall try to keep separate our energies and our concepts.

Let us turn, therefore, to the question of how we acquire and use our conception of the values and cost of things.

Along with every name and every skill a child learns he also absorbs an evaluation. Along with "What is it?" goes "Is it dangerous? Do you like it? What good is it? How much does it cost?" These evaluations are different in every society, and a person who does not know them cannot function in a manner acceptable to the members of that society. In short, costs and values constitute a kind of personal and cultural knowledge that we have all acquired through many years of experience.

In our society there are several different realms of value corresponding to different social functions. Within any single realm it may be possible to develop a consistent system of values, but the demands from separate areas may conflict in ways that seem impossible to reconcile. Value systems can be classified as theoretical, economic, esthetic, religious, social, political; men can be classified according to the ways they assign priorities to one or another of these six realms.

Why do we have to learn these value systems? What purpose do they serve? The answer springs directly from the fact that we are constantly being put into situations where we must express a preference, must make a choice between two or more courses of action. If we believe in social motives, we say that we choose the course of action that mobilizes the greatest amount of energy. If we believe in values, we say that we choose the course of action that we expect will lead to the most valuable outcome. But whatever the explanation, the need to choose is inescapable.

The act of choice is often embedded in great conflict and uncertainty. We like to smoke; we value our good health; we are told the two are incompatible. What do we do? We have learned that freedom of speech is good, but we are convinced that someone is using it for evil ends. What do we do? We treasure all the human values that marriage represents, yet we chafe under its constraints and responsbilities. What do we do?

In these and in thousands of similar conflicts, what we must do is decide which values are greater, which are more important. And to facilitate the constantly recurring processes of choice, we try to organize our values into a coherent, usually hierarchical, system. It is a great help, of course, if the values involved are conscious, if we can make them explicit and talk about them. But even that is not enough to resolve all our problems, because our decisions are usually made in a complicated and idiosyncratic context of past achievements and future ambitions.

Since these comparisons must be made so frequently, it would be a wonderful simplification if we could always use a single, simple quantity as our measure of value. Money is the most obvious candidate, and we use it wherever we can. Indeed, Americans are often accused of putting too much faith in dollars and cents, of imposing a public rate of exchange where private opinion and personal conviction should be sovereign. But even for Americans, money is not always a meaningful measure of value. Psychological value depends upon the situation we find ourselves in and the way we expect the situation to develop. It is not a price tag fixed once and for all, the same for every customer, every day. There are times when a man would offer his kingdom for a horse.

If one tries to analyze conflicts of value, one finds that the simplest involve a triadic system of relations. There is the person himself and two other persons, things, or activities that are causing him trouble. Perhaps the easiest to sympathize with is a person who wants two things that are mutually exclusive; the child wants his dime but he wants the candy, too. A bit more special, perhaps, is a person who must choose between two things that are both unpleasant for him; the student who dislikes studying, but also dislikes failing is caught in this dilemma. In the third case, a person likes one thing and dislikes another, but cannot separate them; the hostess who wants to invite a friend to a dinner party, but cannot tolerate her friend's husband, knows what kind of conflicting evaluations must be settled in this situation.

In all these simple conflicts the person is faced with two alternatives. The child is comparing his situation when he has a dime and no candy with the alternative situation when he will have the candy but no dime. The student is weighing the advantages of leisurely failure against stressful (and uncertain) achievement. The hostess contemplates her dinner party with both Jane and John, or without either of them. The choice is between two situations, and the situations differ in only the two respects, X and Y.

Most choices, however, are a good deal more complicated. They can involve several alternatives that differ from one another in many aspects, where each aspect has several intermediate shades of value between all good and all bad, and where the choice may have consequences that will reverberate far into the unforeseeable future. Simply keeping track of the various possibilities and all their distinguishing features can be quite an intellectual feat; the additional task of deciding how to reconcile conflicting values may completely overload one's cognitive machinery. And on top of the cognitive problem, there may be important values that we refuse to formulate explicitly—that are banished into the limbo of unconsciousness.

It is scarcely surprising, therefore, that we adopt strategies for cutting through this complexity, for reducing the cognitive strain of making a rational decision. Probably the simplest strategy is to flip a coin; the reasoning here is that if you really cannot decide, the coin at least serves to get you back in action. A subtler variation on this scheme is to flip the coin and notice carefully whether you are relieved or disappointed by the way it falls; that bit of self-deception can sometimes help you to discover what you really want.

But random choices are too easy; they disregard all the relevant information. Less drastic is to disregard a part, but not all. A favorite strategy of this type is to ignore most of what one knows about the ways in which the alternatives differ from one another, to pretend that only one or two aspects of the situation are relevant. For example, when a group chooses a leader it should consider such values as power, ability, prestige, and the like; for each value the candidates may rank differently. But these several rankings are difficult to remember and think about. Instead of weighing Abel's skill against Baker's influence against our personal friendship for Charlie, we lump these different value scales into a single figure of merit that covers everything. Instead of deciding which candidate would be the best leader in given situations, we convince ourselves that the one we favor is the best for every conceivable situation. This phenomenon has been called the *halo effect;* because we know that a person is good in one important aspect, we put a halo of goodness over his other aspects as well. It makes the world a great deal simpler when the good guys are always smart, honest, beautiful, and brave, while the bad guys are always stupid, crooked, ugly cowards.

Out of thousands of inner battles we try to evolve a workable hierarchy of our own. Repeatedly, day after day, we face conflicts and make decisions that force us to search for rules, for strategies, for a structure that will reduce the complexity and ease of our burden of decision. Little wonder, therefore, that we prefer a single, simple ordering. We may even come to feel that there is a kind of inconsistency in multiple orderings, that all values *ought* to be measurable with a single yardstick.

The urge toward greater consistency among our various scales of value can itself assume the energizing properties of a social mother. When we find ourselves being inconsistent, it usually annoys us and we are likely to search for ways to eliminate the source of our inconsistency. Indeed, some psychologists have suggested that an effort toward consistency plays much the same role in our cognitive life that homeostasis plays in our biological drives.

When a person feels himself caught in an evaluative inconsistency, there are usually several avenues of escape open to him. He can revise his evaluation of one or the other objects involved. He can modify or deny the incompatibility or the inseparability of the two objects. He can withdraw entirely, or he can bring to bear additional factors that enrich or redefine the objects involved. Exactly what he will do in any particular situation cannot be predicted without an exact knowledge of his particular circumstances.

Consider the following situation: There is an object that you want, but you must work hard to earn it. You decide the cost is justified, and you go ahead. So far you have faced a conflict squarely and have resolved it reasonably. However, when you finally attain the thing you wanted, you discover that you were wrong. It is not valuable after all. Your effort has been wasted. Now you are faced with this inconsistency: The object is worthless, but you worked hard to get it. What do you do?

In this situation most people persuade themselves that the object really is valuable. Consider the alternatives. It is too late, of course, to separate the two conflicting aspects: to stop working for the object, or to try to redefine or withdraw from the situation. All that is over and done. The only consistent escape left is to overvalue your goal or to undervalue your work. To undervalue your work may have extended consequences for everything else you do; the possibility is too grim to face, hence you end up overvaluing the object. Otherwise said, when you find that your scale of values for labor and your scale of values for a commodity are badly out of line, you try to bring them into agreement so as to be consistent, to profit from the cognitive simplification that a single ordering implies.

What you should do, if you can, is to admit that you wasted your time, and face the inconsistent values squarely. If you don't, if you take the easier way of revising your values to make what you have done seem consistent and reasonable, you will increase your chances of making exactly the same mistake again on another occasion. A person who cannot cut his losses and get out may soon find himself totally unable to profit from experience; he will come to love the worthless things for which he has suffered. But facing one's conflicts squarely is usually easier to say than to do.

Sometimes people acquire values so deeply at odds with everything else they believe that no simple resolution of their conflict seems possible. In that case they may actually deny their disturbing values, may refuse to formulate them explicitly as part of their conscious picture of themselves. It was Freud who explored the depths of our capacity to deceive ourselves about what we value and what we fear. When these unconscious systems become involved, a whole new dimension of complexity is added to our problem.

Consider an example. Suppose you are told that a certain man is a trained athlete, that he has won prizes in several sports, and that he places the highest value on physical fitness and stamina. Under most conditions you would probably assume he was a thoroughly masculine type of person. But suppose you ask further and discover that he is thirty-five years old, without heterosexual experience, living with his mother, and sponsoring boys' clubs. Then the very same athletic values may take on exactly the opposite appearance; you may begin to wonder whether the man has a homosexual component, strong but latent, in his personality. You may begin to suspect that his interest in athletics is what Freud called reaction formation: perhaps the athletic activity conceals, yet simultaneously indulges, some deeply disturbing impulses he does not dare to admit consciously. If you are correct, the athlete has a conflict that he cannot face squarely. His tragedy is too large to play on the same mental stage he uses for his ordinary decisions. A reconstruction project of considerable magnitude would be required before he could even recognize, much less resolve his dilemma.

In short, it is not always easy to discover what you want, or to face what you discover. Only under the best possible conditions can you hope to resolve all claims in a reasonable and consistent way. Even if all your values can be stated explicitly, and even if you limit your attention to one decision at a time, the task is still formidable. But add the inescapable fact that each choice interacts with others now and in the future, that what you do presently determines the possibilities open to you later, and even the simplest decision will be seen to involve contingencies far too fine to contemplate. Who is wise enough to know what will be best for him in the long run? We can hope for little more than rude and abstract generalizations.

If we decide upon a particular course of action, it may be necessary to pursue it for long stretches of time—for days, months, even years. Some few decisions dedicate us to a particular path throughout an entire lifetime. Sticking to a long, elaborate program of activity is something we human beings can do—not as well as we would like perhaps, but far better than any other living organism. We manage it principally by using linguistic symbols to control our behavior, by constructing elaborate verbal plans that we remember and use to guide successive steps along the way.

That is not to say that man is the only planful animal. Anyone who has worked around monkeys or apes has observed them constructing and executing simple plans. The chimpanzee that hears a visitor approaching, and dashes quickly to the drinking fountain to fill its mouth with water, then runs back to its regular position where it waits patiently for an unsuspecting target to come within range—this chimp has conceived and carried out a plan just as surely as any human bureaucrat ever did. Even in lower animals there seem to be plans, although they are usually rather inflexible and are probably better regarded as instincts. Organisms that live entirely in the present, uninfluenced by the past and unprepared for the future, are low on the evolutionary scale.

Many animals can follow simple plans, but man has carried a planfulness to its most extreme form. Language is a critical element in this development, but language is not the sole reason for man's superiority.

When the gap between actuality and desirability grows so large that no simple reflex can repair it, we are forced to break up our task into a sequence of subtasks. In learning to perform such analysis man has been particularly favored, oddly enough, by his possession of an opposable thumb. The human hand is often praised as a marvelous tool and credited for much of man's success as an evolutionary experiment. Our ability to hold an object in front of our wonderful simian eyes, to carry things with us, to feed ourselves, to grasp tools—the significance of these skills for the evolution of modern man is by now a familiar story. But the development of the hand also had great psychological significance. The hand is our basic tool. As a tool, it intervenes between the man and his task. Instead of moving directly to the desired object, he reaches out, grasps, and hauls in; a series of steps is substituted for the immediate response. The way we use our hands introduces a sequential character into our behavior. In order to exploit this marvelous new tool, the human brain came under selective evolutionary pressure to develop new ways to organize the sequential aspects of behavior. Here, then, was the beginning of our unique ability to analyze problems and to coordinate long sequences of actions, to subject ourselves to the guiding influence of long-term plans.

Most plans are hierarchically organized. We hold some image of the state we hope to achieve. By comparing this image with perceived reality we notice the major discrepancies, we analyze our task into several main parts, and we decide on an order for doing them. We then begin to execute the first part of our plan; other parts are relegated to the status of intentions. But each subpart in turn is usually too complex for a simple reflex; again we must analyze and postpone some parts while we start to work on others. Thus it sometimes happens that we find ourselves working at unpleasant tasks, doing things we dislike or disapprove of, because they fit into a larger, hierarchically organized plan whose eventual value will, we assume, justify all our temporary discomforts. It is this ability to postpone gratification that distinguishes rational from sensory hedonism, that justifies Freud's reality principle as a supplement to his pleasure principle. Our willingness to renounce the pleasures of the moment and to submit to the tyranny of the future is one of the best measures of our humanity.

The capacity to postpone rewards has been studied in some detail. In rats, for example, delays longer than a few seconds considerably reduce the effectiveness of the reward to reinforce the animal's behavior. In children, the willingness to reject a small reward now on the promise of a larger reward later is known to develop with age; children are more likely to wait for a larger reward when parents are present than when they are absent; children who are socially responsible and reliable are more likely to postpone their rewards than are juvenile delinquents. The acceptance of delayed gratification can also be studied by survey research; many people plan far in advance for their large purchases—for houses, college education for their children, life insurance, cars, even for major appliances. Their plans and attitudes are often a more reliable indicator of future consumer buying than are such purely economic indicators as disposable personal income or savings.

There can be little doubt, therefore, of the psychological validity and importance of our expectations and the plans whereby we hope to achieve them, but they are so heterogeneous that only the most general and obvious comments can be made about them.

Suppose, for example, that we ask how much detail people include in their plans. There can be no universal answer, for this is one important way in which people differ. But one can point to variables that are probably involved. The amount of detail included in a plan will depend upon the importance of success; upon the amount of time available; upon the skill and competence of the person doing the planning. The first two are obvious enough, but the third merits further discussion.

There is little need to plan in detail an activity that you know you are competent to perform, that you have successfully performed many times before, that no longer holds any power to surprise you. If you are going to visit a friend, you need not decide in advance where to place your feet each step along the way. As one gets into more and more detail, the need for explicit planning declines correspondingly. Our most deliberate plans are constructed in terms of strategy, not tactics; in terms of molar acts, not molecular responses. One goes just far enough in elaborating a plan to reassure himself that he is competent to perform each subpart. Thus a person with considerable experience and competence in a particular area will not need to plan as carefully or in as much detail as would a novice. The old hand knows what he can do and how the parts must fit together; all of that must be painstakingly explored by the beginner.

A major component of our plans, therefore, must be our conception of our own competencies. As usual, the simplest example is an economic one. When we plan to buy something, the amount of money at our disposal sets a very clear, unambiguous limit on our ability to obtain the thing we want. Thus money serves as a kind of generalized competence, since it enables us to purchase the abilities of others and incorporate their extended competence into our own plans. People save money, often with no specific or immediate goal in view, but simply for a rainy day, for an emergency, for their old age, for any of a dozen vague reasons; but basically because it increases their potential competence to execute any of a variety of plans that they may someday formulate.

For most people there is a special kind of satisfaction and security associated with competence; in the absence of any very specific aim, they will work simply to increase their general level of skill and information. Reading, play, talking, going to school, traveling, hobbies, curiosity in general, all can contribute directly or indirectly to greater competence.

Professor R. W. White, the clinical psychologist, has referred to this urge for greater competence—the urge to be effective—as effectance motivation. He writes:

> Of all living creatures, it is man who takes the longest strides toward autonomy. This is not because of any unusual tendency toward bodily expansion at the expense of the environment. It is rather that man, with his mobile hands and abundantly developed brain, attains an extremely high level of competence in his transactions with his surroundings. The building of houses, roads and bridges, the making of tools and instruments, the domestication of plants and animals, all

qualify as planful changes made in the environment so that it comes more or less under control and serves our purposes rather than intruding upon them. We meet the fluctuations of outdoor temperature, for example, not only with our bodily homeostatic mechanisms, which alone would be painfully unequal to the task, but also with clothing, buildings, controlled fires, and such complicated devices as self-regulating central heating and air conditioning. Man as a species has developed a tremendous power of bringing the environment into his service, and each individual member of the species must attain what is really quite an impressive level of competence if he is to take part in the life around him.

White's description emphasizes how very important the development of competence is for young children. He does not mean that a child at play is grimly storing up skills for the rainy days ahead; the child plays, masters, and enjoys the efficacy that mastery brings. An organism that depends as heavily as we do upon flexibility and adaptability needs to be born with the kind of hunger for competence that White describes.

But a teacher is all too prone to exaggerate the importance of competence. Room for individual differences in these matters is enormous. A feeling of effectiveness can be valuable and rewarding, but it is more valuable to some than to others. And it is only one aspect of the vast and intricate structure we blandly call human nature. In an adult the child's urge for competence can become a need for achievement, for power, for security; it may even atrophy and disappear.

If there is one thing above all else we should learn from a study of human values, it is to respect their diversity. It is essential to leave one's ideas open to the great variety of possible motivations, to the endless subtle ways that people can project their past into a vision of the future. No single food delights every palate, no single slogan stirs every imagination, no single key unlocks every heart. The African does not share your dreams—and neither does your neighbor next door.

Part VI

Cognition

Chapter 16

Plans for remembering*

George A. Miller, Eugene Galanter, and Karl H. Pribram

Perhaps the most important aspect of human learning is not the number of times the material to be learned is repeated, or the number of pairings with a reinforcement, or the amount of transfer from previously learned material, but simply how the learner himself goes about organizing the material to be retained.

One evening we were entertaining a visiting colleague, a social psychologist of broad interests, and our discussion turned to Plans. "But exactly what is a Plan?" he asked. "How can you say that *memorizing* depends on Plans?"

"We'll show you," we replied. "Here is a Plan that you can use for memorizing. Remember first that:

> one is a bun,
> two is a shoe,
> three is a tree,
> four is a door,
> five is a hive,
> six are sticks,
> seven is heaven,
> eight is a gate,
> nine is a line, and
> ten is a hen."

"You know, even though it is only ten-thirty here, my watch says one-thirty. I'm really tired, and I'm sure I'll ruin your experiment."

"Don't worry, we have no real stake in it." We tightened our grip on his lapel. "Just relax and remember the rhyme. Now you have part of the Plan. The second part works like this: when we tell you a word, you must form a ludicrous or bizarre association with the first word in your list, and so on with the ten words we recite to you."

"Really, you know, it'll never work. I'm awfully tired," he replied.

---

*From Chapter 10 of *Plans and the Structure of Behavior,* by George A. Miller, Eugene Galanter, and Karl H. Pribram. Copyright © 1960 by Holt, Rinehart & Winston, Inc. Reprinted by permission of Holt, Rinehart & Winston, Inc.

"Have no fear," we answered, "just remember the rhyme and then form the association. Here are the words:

1. ashtray,
2. firewood,
3. picture,
4. cigarette,
5. table,
6. matchbook,
7. glass,
8. lamp,
9. shoe,
10. phonograph."

The words were read one at a time, and after reading the word, we waited until he announced that he had the association. It took about five seconds on the average to form the connection. After the seventh word he said that he was sure the first six were already forgotten. But we persevered.

After one trial through the list, we waited a minute or two so that he could collect himself and ask any questions that came to mind. Then we said, "What is number eight?"

He stared blankly, and then a smile crossed his face. "I'll be damned," he said. "It's 'lamp.' "

"And what number is cigarette?"

He laughed outright now, and then gave the correct answer.

"And there is no strain," he said, "absolutely no sweat."

We proceeded to demonstrate that he could in fact name every word correctly, and then asked, "Do you think that memorizing consists of piling up increments of response strength that accumulate as the words are repeated?" The question was lost in his amazement.

If so simple a Plan can reduce the difficulty of memorizing by a discriminable amount, is it not reasonable to suppose that subjects in a memorization experiment would also try to develop a Plan? Of course, they do not have a ready-made Plan of the kind just described. It takes subjects some time and some effort to construct Plans that will work for the sort of materials that we like to use in psychological experiments. In tests of immediate memory, for example, subjects seldom try any mnemonic tricks—with only one presentation of the material, there is little time to develop a Plan and little need for it, since the material will never be seen again. But without a Plan of some sort, the subject will never be able to recite a long list.

W. H. Wallace, S. H. Turner, and C. C. Perkins (1957) of the University of Pennsylvania have found that a person's capacity for forming associations is practically unlimited. They presented pairs of English words to their subjects, who, proceeding at their own pace, formed a visual image connecting the two words. The list of paired associates was given only once. Then the subjects were given one member of each pair and asked to write the other. Starting with lists of twenty-five pairs they worked up to lists of 700 pairs of words. Up to 500 pairs, the subjects were remembering about ninety-nine percent; at 700 pairs it dropped to ninety-five percent. Ordinarily the subjects used about twenty-five seconds to form the association, but when they had become more experienced they could work accurately with less than five seconds per pair. The subjects were not selected for their special abilities; they were ordinary people, conveniently available for the experiment. Freed of the necessity to translate the items into familiar form, freed of the necessity to organize them by a Plan into a fixed sequence, freed of the necessity to work at a mechanically fixed pace, the subjects had nothing to do but sit there and form connections—and they did it almost without error until both they and the experimenters ran out of patience. What is more, little had been forgotten two or three days later.[1]

But what of the traditional picture of an association as something to be constructed slowly through frequent contiguity and strengthened repeatedly by reinforcement? Slowly waxing and waning associations may be useful to characterize a conditioned salivary reflex, but they are not characteristic of human verbal learning. Irvin Rock (1957; Rock and Heimer, 1959) has succeeded in demonstrating that in learning paired associates there is an increment in associative strength until the first correct response occurs, and that thereafter the association remains fully available to the learner. Thus, the memorization of a list of paired associates is not delayed if, every time a pair is not recalled, a new pair is substituted in its place. In fact, subjects do not even notice that a substitution has been made. The association is not formed until the trial on which the learner has time to consider the pair of items; then it is formed and remembered throughout the remainder of the learning.

Observations such as these suggest that it is not storage, but retrieval, that is the real bottleneck in verbal learning. Building the connections seems to be far simpler than finding them later. A new association leading from A to B becomes merely one of many associations leading from A to something else. The time and effort that goes into a job of memorization is devoted to ensuring that there will be some way to get access to the particular association we want when the time comes to revive it. In this view of the problem, the memorizer's task is quite similar to a librarian's. In a large library it is essential to have books labeled by a code. If a book is moved accidentally to another shelf, it may remain lost for years. The librarian must mark the volumes, place them on the shelves in the correct places, enter cards into the central directory under two or three different schemes of reference—all that labor adds nothing to the information or entertainment contained in the book, but merely ensures that it may be possible to locate the book when its contents are relevant.

Memorizing is much too complex to lie open to such a simple analogy. The memorizer is more like a librarian who writes all his own books and is his own reading public. The point of the metaphor is simply that there is a great deal more to a memory—either in a library or a cranium—than the simple hooking of things together two at a time. Let us imagine that this hooking operation is available and that it is as cheap and easy as it would have to be to support the discursive human intellect. What do we do with it? Given that we can nail two boards together, how do we build a house?

---

[1]Students might wish to try such a procedure with foreign language vocabulary. Other types of Plans could, of course, be constructed for other subjects—*eds.*

Chapter 17

A cognitive theory of dreams*

Calvin S. Hall

What kinds of conceptions are found in dreams? One is tempted to reply all kinds but this is not correct since many ideas seem to be excluded from dreams. Dreams are relatively silent regarding political and economic questions: they have little or nothing to say about current events in the world of affairs. I was collecting dreams daily from students during the last days of the war with Japan when the first atomic bomb was exploded, yet this catastrophe did not register in a single dream. Presidential elections, declarations of war, the diplomatic struggles of great powers, major athletic contests, local happenings that make the headlines, all are pretty largely ignored in dreams. A count of characters in a large sample of dreams reveals that the number of prominent people appearing in dreams is very small. Nor are intellectual, scientific, cultural and professional topics or the affairs of finance, business, and industry the subject matter of dreams.

What then is left? The whole world of the personal, the intimate, the emotional, and the conflictual remain. These are the ideas which register in dreams. For the sake of discussion, we shall present a classification of some common conceptions found in dreams.

Conceptions of self. A dream is a mirror that reflects the self-conceptions of the dreamer. Ideas of self are revealed by the repertoire of parts taken by the dreamer in a series of dreams. The repertoire may consist of a few roles, or it may be extensive and varied. In one dream series, for example, the dreamer is pictured as a great general, a rich and influential man, and an important steel manufacturer. In each case, however, he loses his power by being disabled in vigorous combat with a superior force. Here we see that a self-conception of strength and potency cannot be maintained. A typical dream of strength turning into weakness is the following one.

> "I was sitting knee deep in quarters in my room. People kept rushing into my room and stealing handfuls of money. I chased after them, grasping them violently and retrieving my money. But after a while so many people kept grabbing my money at once that I couldn't chase them all so I just sat there and cried."

*From *Journal of General Psychology* 49:273-282, 1953. By permission of the author and The Journal Press.

This young man's conceptions of himself are disjunctive; he is both strong and weak, with weakness winning out over strength.

Perhaps no other medium gives us a more candid picture of what a person thinks about himself than do dreams. It was Ralph Waldo Emerson who wrote: "A skillful man reads his dreams for his self-knowledge."

Conceptions of other people. Dreams reveal what the dreamer thinks about his mother and father, his brothers and sisters, his spouse and children, and diverse other classes of people. These conceptions, like those of self, are embodied in the roles played by the various characters. If the dreamer conceives of his father as a stern, demanding, autocratic person, the father is assigned a part that is in keeping with this conception. If he thinks of his mother as a nurturant person, she will perform some service in the dream to depict her nurturance. Young men commonly dream about being attacked by other men, thereby displaying a conception of enmity that exists in males for other males. Less commonly, young men are friendly with other men. Women also conceive of men as attackers but their dreams reveal many other conceptions. In a single dream series, multiple conceptions of the same person or class of persons are the rule rather than the exception, which suggests that the average person has a network of conceptions regarding his mother, father, siblings, and various other individuals and classes with whom he interacts during his waking life. These ideational or cognitive networks are conceptual systems, and it is one of the aims of dream analysis to delineate these conceptual systems.

Conceptions of the world. By the world is meant the totality of the environment, that which is not-self. In dreams as in poetic fancy the world may be invested with animistic qualities which reflect the dreamer's conceptions of the world. It may be viewed as benign, hostile, turbulent, sorrowful, lonely, or degraded, depending upon the mood of the dreamer. These world-conceptions are often conveyed by the character of the dream setting. If the dreamer feels that the world presents a cold, bleak face, he may materialize this conception in the form of a cold climate and a bleak, rocky setting. A dreamer who feels that his world is one of turbulence and agitation may dream of thunderstorms, raging seas, battles, milling crowds, and traffic jams. A feeling that the world is benign and peaceful can be scenically represented in dreams by serene natural settings.

Conceptions of impulses, prohibitions, and penalties. Since dreams are filled with impulse gratification, in particular those of sex and aggression, it is not surprising that Freud came to the conclusion that wish-fulfillment is the essence of dreams, and that the objective of dream analysis is the discovery of the wish which is fulfilled. It is hardly necessary, however, to consult dreams in order to learn that man seeks gratification of his urges. What dreams can tell us more profitably is how the dreamer conceives of his impulses, for it is these conceptions, not the impulses directly, that ordinarily elicit specific ways of behaving. Most people experience a sex drive, but they differ in respect to their conceptions of the sex drive. The sex impulse may be regarded variously as wicked, as unclean, as a mechanical pressure needing periodic release, as a natural force serving reproduction, as a way of expressing love and tenderness, or as a primitive and uncontrollable form of energy against which one wages a losing battle. Among our collection of nocturnal emission dreams, these and many other conceptions of this biological force appear. The following dream reveals a purely mechanical conception of sex.

> "I got out of bed and went into the bathroom and attempted to turn on the water faucet. I turned and turned but no water came out. I then decided to call a plumber. Soon afterwards the door opened and an individual dressed in coveralls approached me. Upon closer examination I discovered that the plumber was a female. I scoffed at the idea of a lady plumber, but unruffled she went to the basin, turned the faucet, and water immediately flowed. An emission occurred."

Dreams also show the person's conceptions of the obstacles that stand in the way of the gratification of his impulses. These obstacles are often prohibitions emanating from his conscience and may be represented in dreams by such obstacles as walls, curbs, and locked doors, by acts of restraint such as putting on the brakes of a car, or by the appearance of authority figures who interrupt the dreamer's pleasure. If an impulse is gratified, the dreamer may express his conception of the punishment that will be visited upon him for his transgression. He may be punished directly by another person, or he may be the victim of misfortune. In any event, the kinds of obstacles and the kinds of penalties which appear in dreams are interpreted in order to throw light upon the nature of the conceptual system which is called the superego. This conceptual system which is assumed to be detached from the ego contains the moral ideology of the person.

Conceptions of problems and conflicts. Perhaps the most important information provided by dreams is the way in which they illuminate the basic predicaments of a person as that person sees them. Dreams give one an inside view of the person's problems, a personal formulation that is not so likely to be as distorted or as superficial as are the reports made in waking life. Since it is the way in which a person conceives of his conflicts that determines his behavior, the inside view is a prerequisite for clear understanding of human conduct. As we have shown in another place, the delineation of a person's conflicts may be made by analyzing a dream series.

Of what value is it to know the conceptions of a person as expressed in his dreams? How does it help the psychologist to understand the person and thereby to predict and control his behavior? Of one thing we can be quite certain, namely that these conceptions are not dependable guides to objective reality: what one conceives to be true and what is actually true do not invariably coincide. A person may conceive of his father as a stern, autocratic, unreasonable person when, in fact, his father does not possess these characteristics in the eyes of impartial observers. Dreams should not be read for the purpose of constructing a picture of objective reality.

Our thesis is that dreams are one dependable source of information regarding subjective reality, and that knowledge of subjective reality is useful precisely because it does have effects in the conduct of a person. If a boy sees his father as an autocratic authority, he will react toward his father as though he really is that way. In other words, these personal cognitions are the real antecedents of behavior.

Parenthetically, we would like to observe that psychology may have been hampered in its development because it has tended to ignore subjective cognitions in favor of objective stimulus variables. Stimulus conditions are varied and the effects in behavior are noted, often without taking into consideration that the person's conception of the stimulus may be the decisive factor. People may react differently to the same stimulus because they have different conceptions of the stimulus or they may react in the same way to different stimuli because they have similar conceptions. This is a truism whose truth is too often forgotten in psychological experiments, although there are indications that the pendulum is swinging back in the direction of cognition variables.

Although this is not the place to develop fully our theory of *conceptual systems*, it is not inappropriate to mention briefly our view that the conceptions of a person are organized into interconnected networks. One network may consist of the conceptions that a person has of his family, and this network in turn may be interconnected with a network of ideas about government, or religion, or education. A recent study has demonstrated in a convincing manner how ideas about minority groups are intimately related with ideas about family, religion, government and economics. It is the task of psychology, as we see it, to explore these conceptual systems or personal ideologies, to show how they are interrelated, to learn how they are developed, to demonstrate how they control and regulate conduct, and to discover how they may be changed. In order to do all of these things, it is necessary to devise methods of finding out what a person's conceptions are. Attitude-opinion questionnaire methods have reached a high level of development and are employed on a large scale to determine people's beliefs about everything under the sun. The value of such methods, although great, is nonetheless limited by several factors inherent in the methods. The respondent may not answer a question either because he does not want to or because he does not know the answer, or he may answer it untruthfully either intentionally or unintentionally. Moreover, the wording of the question is an important variable. At best, questionnaires get at the conscious and verbalizable conceptions of a person.

If one assumes, as the writer does, that the contents of personal ideologies are pretty largely unconscious or preconscious, then methods have to be used which will reveal these unconscious conceptions. Projective methods, especially of the picture-story type, lend themselves to the exploration of conceptual systems, although they have not been employed to any great extent for this purpose. Picture-story tests do have one drawback, however, and that is that the person's conceptions may not be fully laid bare by the collection of pictures used. Since the material obtained will be a function of the kind of pictures shown to the person, it is possible that those conceptions which are of greatest significance for him may not be tapped. This limitation does not apply to dreams. The dreamer makes his own pictures of those conceptions that are of greatest importance to him currently. Over a period of time, his dreams will depict the essential features of his conceptual systems. Moreover, dreams tap the unconscious and bring to the surface those prototypic conceptions around which conceptual systems are formed. It is our view that prototypic conceptions have their origin in early life and that they are more likely to express themselves in dreams than through any other medium. For these reasons, we feel that dreams constitute the best material for studying the conceptual systems of a person and that such knowledge is absolutely essential if we are to understand why people behave as they do.

We shall conclude by demonstrating how the views presented in this paper may be utilized in analyzing a dream. The following dream was reported by a young man.

"I was at the blackboard in a school room doing a trig problem but I was having trouble with it because I could not remember the valence of nitrogen. I was about to give up on it when a girl came up to me and asked if I would like to dance. The music was good but very erratic, being very fast one instant and very slow the next; however, we were always exactly in step. She was an excellent dancer. When the music stopped we were both in the school shower but we still had our clothes on. I wanted to take hers off and make love to her but I had never done anything like that before so we just laughed and splashed water.

"Then I was outside the school. It was night and lights shone in all the windows silhouetting a wild orgy of a party. I felt very lonely. I wanted to go inside but something seemed to hold me back. I heard chimes ringing in the church."

In the opening scene, we see the dreamer hard at work on a mathematical problem with which he is having difficulty. His self-conception is that of an industrious student engaged in a purely intellectual task for which he does not have the requisite knowledge. A girl appears and invites him to dance; that is, he conceives of the girl as a temptress and of himself as her victim. At her bidding, he leaves the hardships of intellectual activity for the pleasures of sensuality. Their sensuality stops short of complete fulfillment because he cannot conceive of himself as consummating the sexual act. The scene changes in line with a new conception. The dreamer now sees himself as a lonely outsider looking in on a wild orgy. He would like to go in, but he is held back by an unidentified force. The church bells, embodying as they do ideas of virtue and morality, suggest that the unknown force is his own conception of moral conduct.

This dream, then, reveals two opposing conceptual systems, one which contains the young man's conception of himself as a moral, industrious, and intellectual person, the other which contains his conception of himself as being either moral or sensual. When he is doing the "right" thing, he is lured away by sexuality; when he is doing the "wrong" thing he is pulled away by morality. A self-conception of inadequacy for either role is portrayed by his inability to solve the intellectual task or to fulfill his sexual wish. In this dream we see that it is not the sex drive per se that is of significance, but rather his conception of it as being forbidden to him.

Other dreams collected from this young man help to fill out the contents of his conceptual systems. In one dream, he does consummate the sex act, but only because the girl actively seduces him. This suggests that his conception of morality can be subordinated when he sees himself as the victim of external forces. Even in this dream, however, the dreamer feels ashamed because he is so easily excited. His personal ideology regarding women is an interesting yet not uncommon one. Women are of two types: aggressively sexual women who seduce men and pure women who are to be loved in a respectful manner but with whom sexual relations are forbidden prior to marriage.

We have spoken of the disjunctive nature of the dreamer's moral and immoral self-conceptions. In one dream he makes a partial fusion of these opposed views.

> "I was studying for a test with my girl. We were lying on the bed in her room reviewing our notes and asking each other questions about them. As each topic would come up, instead of discussing the text, I would demonstrate a different point in making love to her. Although each type of love making seemed different, it never got beyond the kissing stage."

Work and sex are integrated, although the sex impulse is kept within bounds. The girl in the dream is one of the "nice" girls in the dreamer's life toward whom he would not be likely to have unrestrained sexual feelings.

Chapter 18

When prophecy fails*

Leon Festinger, Henry W. Riecken, and Stanley Schachter

A man with conviction is a hard man to change. Tell him you disagree and he turns away. Show him facts or figures and he questions your sources. Appeal to logic and he fails to see your point.

We have all experienced the futility of trying to change a strong conviction, especially if the convinced person has some investment in his belief. We are familiar with the variety of ingenious defenses with which people protect their convictions, managing to keep them unscathed through the most devastating attacks.

But man's resourcefulness goes beyond simply protecting a belief. Suppose an individual believes something with his whole heart; suppose further that he has a commitment to this belief, that he has taken irrevocable actions because of it; finally, suppose that he is presented with evidence, unequivocal and undeniable evidence, that his belief is wrong: what will happen? The individual will frequently emerge, not only unshaken, but even more convinced of the truth of his beliefs than ever before. Indeed, he may even show a new fervor about convincing and converting other people to his point of view.

How and why does such a response to contradictory evidence come about? Let us begin by stating the conditions under which we would expect to observe increased fervor following the disconfirmation of a belief. There are five such conditions.

1. A belief must be held with deep conviction and it must have some relevance to action, that is, to what the believer does or how he behaves.

2. The person holding the belief must have committed himself to it; that is, for the sake of his belief, he must have taken some important action that is difficult to undo. In general, the more important such actions are, and the more difficult they are to undo, the greater is the individual's commitment to the belief.

3. The belief must be sufficiently specific and sufficiently concerned with the real world so that events may unequivocally refute the belief.

4. Such undeniable disconfirmatory evidence must occur and must be recognized by the individual holding the belief.

*Abridged from Leon Festinger, Henry W. Riecken, and Stanley Schachter, *When Prophecy Fails*, University of Minnesota Press, Minneapolis. Copyright © 1956 by University of Minnesota.

122

The first two of these conditions specify the circumstances that will make the belief resistant to change. The third and fourth conditions together, on the other hand, point to factors that would exert powerful pressure on a believer to discard his belief. It is, of course, possible that an individual, even though deeply convinced of a belief, may discard it in the face of unequivocal disconfirmation. We must, therefore, state a fifth condition specifying the circumstances under which the belief will be discarded and those under which it will be maintained with new fervor.

5. The individual believer must have social support. It is unlikely that one isolated believer could withstand the kind of disconfirming evidence we have specified. If, however, the believer is a member of a group of convinced persons who can support one another, we would expect the belief to be maintained and the believers to attempt to proselyte or to persuade nonmembers that the belief is correct.

Since our explanation will rest upon one derivation from a general theory, we will first state the bare essentials of the theory which are necessary for this derivation. The full theory has wide implications and a variety of experiments have already been conducted to test derivations concerning such things as the consequences of decisions, the effects of producing forced compliance, and some patterns of voluntary exposure to new information. At this point, we shall draw out in detail only those implications that are relevant to the phenomenon of increased proselyting following disconfirmation of a prediction. For this purpose we shall introduce the concepts of consonance and dissonance.

Dissonance and consonance are relations among cognitions—that is, among opinions, beliefs, knowledge of the environment, and knowledge of one's own actions and feelings. Two opinions, or beliefs, or items of knowledge are *dissonant* with each other if they do not fit together—that is, if they are inconsistent, or if, considering only the particular two items, one does not follow from the other. For example, a cigarette smoker who believes that smoking is bad for his health has an opinion that is dissonant with the knowledge that he is continuing to smoke. He may have many other opinions, beliefs, or items of knowledge that are consonant with continuing to smoke but the dissonance nevertheless exists too.

Dissonance produces discomfort and, correspondingly, there will arise pressures to reduce or eliminate the dissonance. Attempts to reduce dissonance represent the observable manifestations that dissonance exists. Such attempts may take any or all of three forms. The person may try to change one or more of the beliefs, opinions, or behaviors involved in the dissonance; to acquire new information or beliefs that will increase the existing consonance and thus cause the total dissonance to be reduced; or to forget or reduce the importance of those cognitions that are in a dissonant relationship.

If any of the above attempts are to be successful, they must meet with support from either the physical or the social environment. In the absence of such support, the most determined efforts to reduce dissonance may be unsuccessful.

• • •

One day in late September the Lake City *Herald* carried a two-column story, on a back page, headlined: PROPHECY FROM PLANET. CLARION

CALL TO CITY: FLEE THAT FLOOD. IT'LL SWAMP US ON DEC. 21, OUTER SPACE TELLS SUBURBANITE. The body of the story expanded somewhat on these bare facts:

"Lake City will be destroyed by a flood from Great Lake just before dawn, Dec. 21, according to a suburban housewife. Mrs. Marian Keech, of 847 West School street, says the prophecy is not her own. It is the purport of many messages she has received by automatic writing, she says. . . . The messages, according to Mrs. Keech, are sent to her by superior beings from a planet called 'Clarion.' These beings have been visiting the earth, she says, in what we call flying saucers. During their visits, she says, they have observed fault lines in the earth's crust that foretoken the deluge. Mrs. Keech reports she was told the flood will spread to form an inland sea stretching from the Arctic Circle to the Gulf of Mexico. At the same time, she says, a cataclysm will submerge the West Coast from Seattle, Wash., to Chile in South America."

The story went on to report briefly the origin of Mrs. Keech's experiences and to quote several messages that seemed to indicate she had been chosen as a person to learn and transmit teachings from the "superior beings." A photograph of Mrs. Keech accompanied the story. She appeared to be about fifty years of age, and she sat poised with pad and pencil in her lap, a slight, wiry woman with dark hair and intense, bright eyes. The story was not derogatory, nor did the reporter comment upon or interpret any of the information he had gathered.

Since Mrs. Keech's pronouncement made a specific prediction of a specific event, since she, at least, was publicly committed to belief in it, and since she apparently was interested to some extent in informing a wider public about it, this seemed to be an opportunity to conduct a "field" test of the theoretical ideas to which the reader has been introduced.

In early October two of the authors called on Mrs. Keech and tried to learn whether there were other convinced persons in her orbit of influence, whether they too believed in the specific prediction, and what commitments of time, energy, reputation, or material possessions they might be making in connection with the prediction. The results of this first visit encouraged us to go on. The three of us and some hired observers joined the group and, as participants, gathered data about the conviction, commitment, and proselyting activity of the individuals who were actively interested in Mrs. Keech's ideas. We tried to learn as much as possible about the events that had preceded the news story, and, of course, kept records of subsequent developments. The information collected about events before early October is retrospective. It comes primarily from documents and from conversations with the people concerned in the events. From October to early January almost all the data are first-hand observations, with an occasional report of an event we did not cover directly but heard about later through someone in the group of believers who had been there at the time.

Columnists and editorial writers tried invariably to be funny at the expense of the group. One gossip columnist began his piece: "Had any messages from outer space lately?" while another wrote: "When that story first broke about Dr. Thomas Armstrong predicting the 'end of the world on Dec. 21' (later changed to a tidal wave engulfing Lake City), comedian Jimmy Edmonson put in a hurry-up call: 'Anybody want to buy two on the 50-yard line for the Rose Bowl cheap?' " An editorial writer, commenting on Mrs. Keech's method of communicating with outer space, took the opportunity to ask for a prediction: "For a starter (are you listening, Venus?) who is going to be the next mayor of Lake City? P.S. If the answer has fins on it, don't bother."

In succeeding days, the ridicule mounted. Dr. Armstrong and Mrs. Keech were both hurt and angry at the press notices that belittled them, and became even more reluctant to talk to reporters. They frequently referred to the "unfair" and "distorted" accounts of their beliefs.

Late on Friday morning, December 17, as the newspaper publicity began to have its effect, a trickle of callers, both in person and on the phone, asked for more information and explanation. High school students predominated, but there were several adults, too, mostly women. There were a small number of practical jokers, but a substantial proportion of the callers were sincere, although sometimes skeptical.

The treatment accorded these inquiring souls seemed confused, though it was consistent with the established policy of selective proselyting. Only the chosen were eligible for instruction, and mere curiosity seekers or those who came to jeer were to be turned away. How to discriminate between chosen and heathen was a matter for one's inner knowing. Whoever answered the telephone or the doorbell (usually Mark Post or Dr. Armstrong) made a preliminary judgment as to the visitor's sincerity. If they "passed" they were sometimes brought in and treated to a brief lecture or had their questions answered. Whoever happened to be on deck handled the case, and, if the only available instructor was busy with a previous caller, the potential proselytes were often left to twiddle their thumbs. There was no plan, no systematic indoctrination, but simply huge, indifferent chaos. Toward the middle of the afternoon, when all hands were fatigued, even sincere inquirers were sometimes turned away, especially over the phone, and told there was nothing to say beyond what had appeared in the newspapers.*

By 11:30 all was in readiness and there was nothing to do but wait and think of things that had been overlooked. The few details that did come up were disposed of hurriedly, for everything had to be in order by midnight. When Arthur Bergen suddenly remembered that his shoes had metal toecaps, it was too late to cut them out. From the ensuing excitement emerged the suggestion that he should simply loosen the laces and step out of his shoes before entering the saucer. At about 11:35, one of the authors let it be known that he had not removed the zipper from his trousers. This knowledge produced a near panic reaction. He was rushed into the bedroom where Dr. Armstrong, his hands trembling and his eyes darting to the clock every few seconds, slashed out the zipper with a razor blade and wrenched its clasps free with wire cutters. By the time the operation was complete it was 11:50, too late to do more than sew up the rent with a few rough stitches. Midnight was almost at hand and everyone must be ready on the dot.

The last ten minutes were tense ones for the group in the living room.

---

*Actually, the group did have another piece of information: before the anticipated flood, they were to be "rescued" by the flying saucer people.—*eds.*

They had nothing to do but sit and wait, their coats in their laps. In the tense silence two clocks ticked loudly, one about ten minutes faster than the other. When the faster of the two pointed to 12:05, one of the observers remarked aloud on the fact. A chorus of people replied that midnight had not yet come. Bob Eastman affirmed that the slower clock was correct; he had set it himself only that afternoon. It showed only four minutes before midnight.

These four minutes passed in complete silence except for a single utterance. When the (slower) clock on the mantel showed only one minute remaining before the guide to the saucer was due, Marian exclaimed in a strained, high-pitched voice: "And not a plan has gone astray!" The clock chimed twelve, each stroke painfully clear in the expectant hush. The believers sat motionless. One might have expected some visible reaction. Midnight had passed and nothing had happened. The cataclysm itself was less than seven hours away. But there was little to see in the reactions of the people in that room. There was no talking, no sound. People sat stock still, their faces seemingly frozen and expressionless. Mark Post was the only person who even moved. He lay down on the sofa and closed his eyes, but did not sleep. Later, when spoken to, he answered monosyllabically, but otherwise lay immobile. The others showed nothing on the surface, although it became clear later that they had been hit hard. The next morning both Bertha Blatsky and Dr. Armstrong, for example, admitted that the shock had been overwhelming. Having lived through that trial, Dr. Armstrong felt, he could now stand anything.

One of the authors walked out the front door to get some air and Dr. Armstrong, thinking he was becoming disaffected and needed bolstering, dashed out after him. The doctor proceeded to deliver an inspirational talk, an important part of which was a statement about his own situation and his own belief. This is presented below as nearly verbatim as his listener could record it immediately after Dr. Armstrong left him alone "to meditate":

"I've had to go a long way. I've given up just about everything. I've cut every tie: I've burned every bridge. I've turned my back on the world. I can't afford to doubt. I have to believe. And there isn't any other truth. The preachers and priests don't have it and you have to look closely to find it even in the Bible. I've taken an awful beating in the last few months, just an awful beating. But I do know who I am and I know what I've got to do. I know I've got to teach just as Jesus knew, and I don't care what happens tonight. I can't afford to doubt. I don't doubt even if we have to make an announcement to the press tomorrow and admit we were wrong. You're having your period of doubt now, but hang on, boy, hang on. This is a tough time but we know that the boys upstairs are taking care of us. They've given us their promise. These are tough times and the way is not easy. We all have to take a beating. I've taken a terrific one, but I have no doubt."

While Dr. Armstrong was outdoors counseling the observer, Mrs. Keech broke down and cried bitterly. She knew, she sobbed, there were some who were beginning to doubt but we must beam light on those who needed it most and we must hold the group together. The rest of the group lost their composure too. They were all, now, visibly shaken and many were close to tears. It was a bad quarter of an hour.

Soon afterward, however, the observer re-entered the house and announced that Dr. Armstrong had helped him a lot. His return cheered the group considerably and brought visible relief to Mrs. Keech. But the fundamental problem of the group remained; it was now almost 4:30 A.M. and still no way of handling the disconfirmation had been found. By now, too, most of the group were talking openly about the failure of the man to come at midnight. They milled about the living room or stood in small groups discussing their feelings. Both Edna and Mark Post, for example, compared the events of this night to the disappointment they had suffered three days earlier when they stood for hours in the icy back yard waiting for a saucer to land.

But this atmosphere did not remain long. At about 4:45 A.M. Marian once more summoned everyone to the living room, announcing that she had just received a message which she read aloud. She then read these momentous words:

> "For this day is it established that there is but one God of Earth, and He is in thy midst, and from his hand thou hast written these words. And mighty is the word of God—and by his word have ye been saved—for from the mouth of death have ye been delivered and at no time has there been such a force loosed upon the Earth. Not since the beginning of time upon this Earth has there been such a force of Good and light as now floods this room and that which has been loosed within this room now floods the entire Earth. As thy God has spoken through the two who sit within these walls has he manifested that which he has given thee to do"

This message was received with enthusiasm by the group. It was an adequate, even an elegant, explanation of the disconfirmation. The cataclysm had been called off. The little group, sitting all night long, had spread so much light that God had saved the world from destruction. As soon as the full acceptability of the message was clear, Marian had two more messages in rapid succession, the first of which was to be used as an introduction to the main message: It read: "Such are the facts as stated that the group has sat for the Father's message the night through and God has spoken and that is every word to be said." The second message and the introduction were to be headed "The Christmas Message to the People of Earth"; this "Christmas Message" together with the fact that it had been received at 4:45 A.M. was to be released immediately to the newspapers.

. . . the rest of the believers were jubilant, for they had a satisfying explanation of the disconfirmation. The whole atmosphere of the group changed abruptly and, with it, their behavior changed too. From this point on their behavior toward the newspapers showed an almost violent contrast to what it had been. Instead of avoiding newspaper reporters and feeling that the attention they were getting in the press was painful, they almost instantly became avid seekers of publicity.

Early in December, Dr. Armstrong had instructed the student members* of the Seekers simply to go about their own affairs and wait for whatever might happen on the day of the cataclysm. If they were among the chosen, they would be picked up wherever they were. Consequently most of the members

---

*Believers from "Collegeville" whose dispersion denied them the social support available to the Lake City group.—*eds.*

scattered to their homes for the Christmas vacation. This dispersion, though fortunate in that it allowed us to test the importance of the isolation factor, did enormously complicate the problems of observation.

In summary, the effect of disconfirmation on the individuals from Collegeville about whom we have data was . . . to decrease conviction and either to have no effect on proselyting or to inhibit it. This result is quite the opposite of the general pattern in Lake City, where proselyting surged up and there were only two defectors and two whose doubts increased. Thus, most of the Collegeville group reduced the dissonance created by disconfirmation through giving up belief, whereas in Lake City the members held fast and tried to create a supportive circle of believers.

Part VII

Psychological testing

Chapter 19

How to cheat on personality tests*

William H. Whyte, Jr.

Psychological tests are extremely useful devices for screening out groups of people who have more of the attribute for which they are being tested—intelligence, musical talent, potential flying ability, and the like—than do groups who have been selected in other ways. When it comes to judgments about a particular individual, however, psychological tests, although improving all the time, are far from perfect. . . .

The important thing to recognize is that you don't win a good score: you avoid a bad one. What a bad score would be depends upon the particular profile the company in question intends to measure you against, and this varies according to companies and according to the type of work. Your score is usually rendered in terms of your percentile rating—that is, how you answer questions in relation to how other people have answered them. Sometimes it is perfectly all right for you to score in the 80th or 90th percentile; if you are being tested, for example, to see if you would make a good chemist, a score indicating that you are likely to be more reflective than ninety out of a hundred adults might not harm you and might even do you some good.

By and large, however, your safety lies in getting a score somewhere between the 40th and 60th percentiles, which is to say, you should try to answer as if you were like everybody else is supposed to be. This is not always too easy to figure out, of course, and this is one of the reasons why I will go into some detail in the following paragraphs on the principal types of questions. When in doubt, however, there are two general rules you can follow: (1) When asked for word associations or comments about the world, give the most conventional, run-of-the-mill, pedestrian answer possible. (2) To settle on the most beneficial answer to any question, repeat to yourself:

a) I loved my father and my mother, but my father a little bit more.

b) I like things pretty well the way they are.

c) I never worry much about anything.

---

d) I don't care for books or music much.

e) I love my wife and children.

f) I don't let them get in the way of company work.

Now to specifics. The first five questions in the composite test are examples of the ordinary, garden variety of self-report questions.[1] Generally speaking, they are designed to reveal your degree of introversion or extroversion, your stability, and such. While it is true that in these "inventory" types of tests there is not a right or wrong answer to any *one* question, cumulatively you can get yourself into a lot of trouble if you are not wary. "Have you enjoyed reading books as much as having company in?" "Do you sometimes feel self-conscious?"—You can easily see what is being asked for here.

Stay in character. The trick is to mediate yourself a score as near the norm as possible without departing too far from your own true self. It won't necessarily hurt you, for example, to say that you have enjoyed reading books as much as having company in. It will hurt you, however, to answer every such question in that vein if you are, in fact, the kind that does enjoy books and a measure of solitude. Strive for the happy mean; on one hand, recognize that a display of too much introversion, a desire for reflection, or sensitivity is to be avoided. On the other hand, don't overcompensate. If you try too hard to deny these qualities in yourself, you'll end so far on the other end of the scale as to be rated excessively insensitive or extroverted. If you are somewhat introverted, then, don't strive to get yourself in the 70th or 80th percentile for extroversion, but merely try to get up into the 40th percentile.

---

[1] Leading Tests of this type include:

The Personality Inventory by Robert G. Bernreuter. Published by the Stanford University Press, Stanford, California. Copyright 1935 by The Board of Trustees of Leland Stanford Junior University. All rights reserved.

125 questions; measures several different things at once; scoring keys available for neurotic tendency; self-sufficiency; introversion-extroversion; dominance-submission; self-confidence; sociability.

Thurstone Temperament Schedule by L. L. Thurstone. Copyright 1949 by L. L. Thurstone. Published by Science Research Associates, Chicago, Ill. 140 questions. Measures, at once, seven areas of temperament: to wit, degree to which one is active, vigorous, impulsive, dominant, stable, sociable, reflective. "The primary aim of the Thurstone Temperament Schedule . . . is to evaluate an individual in terms of his relatively permanent temperament traits. One of the values of the schedule is that it helps provide an objective pattern, or profile, of personal traits which you can use to predict probable success or failure in a particular situation."

Minesota T-S-E Inventory by M. Catherine Evans and T. R. McConnell. Copyright 1942 by Science Research Associates, Chicago, Illinois.

150 questions. Measures three types of introversion-extroversion—thinking, social and emotional.

The Personal Audit by Clifford R. Adams and William M. Lepley, Psycho-Educational Clinic, Pennsylvania State College. Published by Science Research Associates, Chicago, Ill. Copyright 1945 by Clifford R. Adams. All rights reserved.

450 questions. Nine parts, of 50 questions each. Each part measures "a relatively independent component of personality." Extremes of each trait listed thus: seriousness-impulsiveness; firmness-indecision; tranquility-irritability; frankness-evasion; stability-instability; tolerance-intolerance; steadiness-emotionality; persistence-fluctuation; contentment-worry.

Since you will probably be taking not one, but a battery of tests, you must be consistent. The tester will be comparing your extroversion score on one test with, say, your sociability score on another, and if these don't correlate the way the tables say they should, suspicion will be aroused. Even when you are taking only one test, consistency is important. Many contain built-in L ("lie") scores, and woe betide you if you answer some questions as if you were a life of the party type and others as if you were an excellent follower. Another pitfall to avoid is giving yourself the benefit of the doubt on all questions in which one answer is clearly preferable to another, viz.: "Do you frequently daydream?" In some tests ways have been worked out to penalize you for this. (By the same token, occasionally you are given credit for excessive frankness. But you'd better not count on it.)

Be emphatic to the values of the test maker. Question five asks*:

"Do you prefer serious motion pictures about famous historical personalities to musical comedies?" If you answer this question honestly you are quite likely to get a good score for the wrong reasons. If you vote for the musical comedies, you are given a credit for extroversion. It might be, of course, that you are a very thoughtful person who dislikes the kind of pretentious, self-consciously arty "prestige" pictures which Hollywood does badly, and rather enjoy the musical comedies which it does well. The point illustrated here is that, before answering such questions, you must ask yourself which of the alternatives the test maker, not yourself, would regard as the more artistic.

Choose your neurosis. When you come across questions that are like the ones from 6 to 11—"I often get pink spots all over"—be very much on your guard. Such questions were originally a by-product of efforts to screen mentally disturbed people; they measure degrees of neurotic tendency and were meant mainly for use in mental institutions and psychiatric clinics.[2] The Organization has no business at all to throw these questions at you, but its curiosity is powerful and some companies have been adopting these tests as standard. Should you find yourself being asked about spiders, Oedipus complexes, and such, you must, even more than in the previous type of test, remain consistent and as much in character as possible—these tests almost always have lie scores built into them. A few mild neuroses conceded here and there won't give you too bad a score, and in conceding neuroses you should know that more often than not you have the best margin for error if you err on the side of being "hypermanic"—that is, too energetic and active.

Don't be too dominant. Question 12, which asks you what you would do if somebody barged in ahead of you in a store, is fairly typical of the kind of

---

*The composite personality test discussed in this selection has been reprinted in the instructor's manual.—*eds.*

[2] Outstanding example is the *Minnesota Multiphasic Personality Inventory,* Revised Edition, by Starke R. Hathaway and J. Charnley McKinley. Published by The Psychological Corporation, N.Y. 495 questions. This yields scores on hypochondriasis, depression, hysteria, psychopathic deviation, masculinity and femininity, paranoia, psychoasthenia, schizophrenia, hypomania. It also yields a score on the subject's "test-taking attitude," with a score for his degree of "defensiveness-frankness." If the subject consistently gives himself the benefit of the doubt, or vice versa, the scoring reveals the fact. This is not a test for the amateur to trifle with.

questions designed to find out how passive or dominant you may be. As always, the middle course is best. Resist the temptation to show yourself as trying to control each situation. You might think companies would prefer that characteristic to passivity, but they often regard it as a sign that you wouldn't be a permissive kind of leader. To err slightly on the side of acquiescence will rarely give you a bad score.

Incline to conservatism. Questions 13 through 17, which ask you to comment on a variety of propositions, yield a measure of how conservative or radical your views are.[3] To go to either extreme earns you a bad score, but in most situations you should resolve any doubts you have on a particular question by deciding in favor of the accepted.

Similarly with word associations. In questions 18 through 23, each word in capitals is followed by four words, ranging from the conventional to the somewhat unusual. The trouble here is that if you are not a totally conventional person you may be somewhat puzzled as to what the conventional response is. Here is one tip: before examining any one question closely and reading it from left to right, read vertically through the whole list of questions and you may well see a definite pattern. In making up tests, testers are thinking of ease in scoring, and on some test forms the most conventional responses will be found in one column, the next most conventional in the next, and so on. All you have to do then is go down the list and pick, alternately, the most conventional, and the second most conventional. Instead of a high score for emotionalism, which you might easily get were you to proceed on your own, you earn a stability score that will indicate "normal ways of thinking."

Don't split hairs. When you come to hypothetical situations designed to test your judgment, you have come to the toughest of all questions.[4] In this kind there are correct answers, and the testers make no bones about it. Restricted as the choice is, however, determining which are the correct ones is extremely difficult, and the more intelligent you are the more difficult. One tester, indeed, states that the measurement of practical judgment is "unique and statistically independent of such factors as intelligence, and academic and social background." He has a point. Consider the question about the woman

---

[3] An example of this kind of testing is the *Conservatism-Radicalism Opinionaire* by Theodore F. Lentz and Colleagues of The Attitude Research Laboratory. Published by Character Research Association, Washington University, St. Louis, Mo., Dept. of Education. Copyright 1935. 60 statements are given; the subject indicates whether he tends to agree or disagree. His score is obtained by checking the number of times he sides with the conservative statement side *vs.* the radical one.

[4] Two tests of this type are:

Test of Practical Judgement by Alfred J. Cardall, N.B.A., Ed.D. Published by Science Research Associates, Inc., Chicago, Ill. Copyright 1942, 1950 by Science Research Associates, Inc. All rights reserved. 48 Forced-choice questions "designed to measure the element of practical judgment as it operates in everyday business and social situations." How were the "best" answers chosen? "Rigorous statistical analysis was supplemented by consensus of authority. . . ."

Practical Social Judgment by Thomas N. Jenkins, Ph.D. Copyright 1947. All rights reserved. Executive Analysis Corporation, N.Y. 52 questions about hypothetical situations; subject must choose the "best" and the "poorest" of given answers.

and the baby at the window of the burning house. It is impossible to decide which is the best course of action unless you know how big the fire is, whether she is on the first floor or the second, whether there is a ladder handy, how near the fire department is, plus a number of other considerations.

On this type of question, let me confess that I can be of very little help to the reader. I have made a very thorough study of these tests, have administered them to many people of unquestioned judgment, and invariably the results have been baffling. But there does seem to be one moral: don't think too much. The searching mind is severely handicapped by such forced choices and may easily miss what is meant to be the obviously right answer. Suppress this quality in yourself by answering these questions as quickly as you possibly can, with practically no pause for reflection.

The judgment questions from 25 through 28 are much easier to answer.[5] The right answers here are, simply, those which represent sound personnel policy, and this is not hard to figure out. Again, don't quibble. It is true enough that it is virtually impossible to tell the worker why he didn't get promoted unless you know whether he was a good worker, or a poor one, or whether Jones's uncle did in fact own the plant (in which case, candor could be eminently sensible). The mealy-mouthed answer d)—"Let's figure out how you can improve"—is the "right" answer. Similarly with questions about the worker's home life. It isn't the concern of the company, but it is modern personnel dogma that it should be, and therefore "agree" is the right answer. So with the question about whether good supervisors are born or made. To say that a good supervisor is born deprecates the whole apparatus of modern organization training, and that kind of attitude won't get you anywhere.

Know your company. Questions 29 and 30 are characteristic of the kind of test that attempts to measure the relative emphasis you attach to certain values—such as aesthetic, economic, religious, social.[6] The profile of you it produces is matched against the profile that the company thinks is desirable. To be considered as a potential executive, you will probably do best when you emphasize economic motivation the most; aesthetic and religious, the least. In question 29, accordingly, you should say the skyscraper makes you think of industrial growth. Theoretical motivation is also a good thing; if you were trying out for the research department, for example, you might wish to say that you think Sir Isaac Newton helped mankind more than Shakespeare and thereby increase your rating for theoretical learning. Were you trying out for a public

---

[5] An example of this kind of test is *How Supervise?* by Quentin W. File, edited by H. H. Remmers. Published by The Psychological Corporation, N.Y. Copyright 1948, by Purdue Research Foundation, Lafayette, Indiana. 100 questions on management policy and attitudes.

[6] *A Study of Values,* Revised Edition, by Gordon W. Allport, Philip E. Vernon, and Gardner Lindzey. Copyright 1951, by Gordon W. Allport, Philip E. Vernon, and Gardner Lindzey. Copyright 1931 by Gordon W. Allport and Philip E. Vernon. Published by Houghton, Mifflin Co.

45 forced-choice questions. Answers are scored to give a measure of the relative prominence of six motives in a person: theoretical, economic, aesthetic, social, political, and religious. A profile is charted to show how he varies from the norm on each of the six.

relations job, however, you might wish to vote for Shakespeare, for a somewhat higher aesthetic score would not be amiss in this case.

There are many more kinds of tests and there is no telling what surprises the testers will come up with in the future. But the principles will probably change little, and by obeying a few simple precepts and getting yourself in the right frame of mind, you have the wherewithal to adapt to any new testing situation. In all of us there is a streak of normalcy.

Chapter 20

Student acceptance of generalized personality interpretations*

R. Ulrich, T. Stachnik, and R. Stainton

One reason for the continuing popularity of astrology, palmistry, and other pseudoscientific methods is probably the fact that they help people to find order and direction within the often confusing conditions of modern life. But why is the credibility of these procedures maintained despite their lack of objective support? The following article may provide an answer to this question, as well as help us to understand the "denominationalism" that has characterized the adherents of various schools of therapy within psychology itself.

Previous investigators have been concerned with how individuals react to personality interpretations which are based on information obtained from personality tests. Since "virtually every psychological trait can be observed to some degree in everyone" (Forer, 1949), it is possible that such interpretations may be given in terms so general that they could apply to almost anyone. The following study was conducted in an attempt to discover the degree of acceptance of vague, generalized personality interpretations, presumably derived from personality tests, and to determine whether the "prestige" of the person making the interpretation is related to acceptance.

Procedure. Two experiments were performed involving 136 students from three educational psychology classes plus 79 other Ss. In the first experiment (N = 57), the instructor of the class administered both the Bell Adjustment Inventory and the House-Tree-Person (HTP) test. The students were told by the instructor that he would score and interpret each of their tests and return the interpretations to them at a later date. About a week later each student was given an interpretation with his or her name on it. All interpretations returned were identical, but the statements were arranged in a different order.

*From *Psychological Reports* 13:831-834, 1963. Reprinted with permission of author and publisher.

The students were then asked to read and think about the interpretations carefully and to rate them as follows:

> A. Rate the interpretation of your personality according to the following scale:
> I feel that the interpretation was:
> >   Excellent   Good   Average   Poor   Very Poor
> B. Please make any additional comments about the interpretation that you feel would be appropriate.

In the second experiment members of two classes (total N = 79) were given instructions for administering the tests to one other person, *e.g.*, a roommate, neighbor, etc. Both the tests and the personality interpretations were the same as those used in Exp. I. The students were not to reveal to their Ss that they were part of an experiment. They were simply to state that they were studying personality testing and needed an S for practice. Ss were to be given the tests, and several days later they were to be given the interpretation. Ss were then to be instructed to rate the interpretation. The method of rating was similar to that of the first experiment.

The following interpretation, adapted from Forer, was used in both experiments.

> "You have a strong need for other people to like you and for them to admire you. You have a tendency to be critical of yourself. You have a great deal of unused capacity which you have not turned to your advantage. While you have some personality weaknesses, you are generally able to compensate for them. Your sexual adjustment has presented problems for you. Disciplined and controlled on the outside, you tend to be worrisome and insecure inside. At times you have serious doubts as to whether you have made the right decision or done the right thing. You prefer a certain amount of change and variety and become dissatisfied when hemmed in by restrictions and limitations. You pride yourself as being an independent thinker and do not accept others' opinions without satisfactory proof. You have found it unwise to be too frank in revealing yourself to others. At times you are extroverted, affable, sociable, while at other times you are introverted, wary, and reserved. Some of your aspirations tend to be pretty unrealistic."

Results. It is evident from the data that Ss for the most part accepted the interpretations. Table 10 shows the students' ratings of the test interpretation for the first experiment. Fifty-three of the 57 students rated the interpretation as good or excellent. Row 2 gives the students' ratings of the test interpretations for the second experiment. Fifty-nine of the 79 students rated the interpretation as good or excellent in spite of the fact that these interpretations

Table 10. Ratings of personality interpretations

Total	Excellent	Good	Average	Poor	Very poor
Psychologist's interpretations					
57	27	26	3	1	0
Student's interpretations					
79	29	30	15	5	0

were given by admittedly inexperienced students! Chi-square tests significant at the .001 level indicate that in both experiments the ratings given the interpretations were higher than chance expectancy.

Other data obtained were the comments of Ss concerning the validity as well as the helpfulness of the interpretation. Several examples were chosen which are indicative of the opinions and reactions of the majority of the Ss. The following statements were taken directly from the students' papers.

"I feel that you have done a fine job with the material which you had to work with. I agree with almost all your statements and think they answer the problems I may have."

"On the nose! Very good. I wish you had said more, but what you did mention is all true without a doubt. I wish you could go further into this personality sometime."

"The results have brought out several points which have worried me because I was not sure if I had imagined these to be personality traits of mine. Tests like this could be valuable to an individual in helping him to solve some of his own problems."

"I believe this interpretation applies to me individually, as there are too many facets which fit me too well to be a generalization."

"The interpretation is surprisingly accurate and specific in description. I shall take note of many of the things said."

"I feel that the interpretation does apply to me individually. For the first time things that I have been vaguely aware of have been put into concise and constructive statements which I would like to use as a plan for improving myself."

"It appears to me that the results of this test are unbelievably close to the truth. For a short test of this type, I was expecting large generalizations for results, but this was not the case; and I give all of the credit to the examiner whose conclusions were well calculated."

The first three statements were written by the group of Ss who were given the test and interpretation by a professional psychologist. The last four statements were written by those Ss given the test and interpretation by students. These results indicate not only that Ss were "taken in" by the interpretation, but also that Ss were very likely to praise highly the examiner on his conclusions.

Discussion. The principal finding is that the majority of the people tested accepted personality interpretation stated in general terms as an accurate description of their own personalities without being aware that the same interpretation could be applied to almost anyone.

A previous study demonstrated the same phenomenon and suggested that the probability of acceptance of the interpretation was increased when it was made by a prestigeful person, *i.e.,* a psychologist. However, in the present study the interpretations made by inexperienced students were as readily accepted as those made by a professional psychologist. The mean ratings given the student and psychologist interpretations were 4.05 and 4.38, respectively ($t = 21$, n.s.). This in part indicates the awe with which personality tests *per se* are viewed by the naive student or others of comparable test sophistication.

Furthermore, the fact that some of the students did praise the interpretation demonstrates that individuals accepting a general interpretation as an accurate description of their personality are very likely to praise the examiner. It has been noted that approval can serve as a reinforcement, thereby increasing the probability that the approved behavior will recur. It thus follows that in a counseling setting such reinforcement might cause the examiner to continue to make this type of vague, general interpretation. When the counselor has given a test and is interpreting the results, general statements used by him are perhaps reinforced by statements of praise similar to those observed in the present experiment, although neither the client nor the counselor is capable of verbalizing the contingency which has caused such a situation to occur.

Part VIII

Personality

Chapter 21

The unconscious in everyday life*

Sigmund Freud

According to Freud, the operation of the unconscious mind, pursuing its own goals and employing its own methods to do so, can be seen in the most trivial of everyday acts—especially those that appear to be merely accidental. Other psychologists are inclined to explain such acts in terms of competing responses that are called out by the same stimulus situation. But the central point for yet a third group of psychologists seems to be that, in human beings at least, stimulus associations frequently tend to be made on the basis of their meaningfulness rather than in terms of their physical similarity to one another.

Among the examples of the mistakes in speech collected by me, I can scarcely find one in which I would be obliged to attribute the speech disturbance simply and solely to what Wundt calls "contact effect of sound." Almost invariably I discover besides this a disturbing influence of something *outside* of the intended speech. The disturbing element is either a single unconscious thought, which comes to light through the speech-blunder and can only be brought to consciousness through a searching analysis, or it is a more general psychic motive, which directs itself against the entire speech.

Example (a) Seeing my daughter make an unpleasant face while biting into an apple, I wished to quote the following couplet:

> "The ape he is a funny sight,
> When in the apple he takes a bite."

But I began: *"The apel . . ."* This seems to be a contamination of *"ape"* and *"apple"* (compromise formation), or it may be also conceived as an anticipation of the prepared "apple." The true state of affairs, however, was this: I began the quotation once before, and made no mistake the first time. I made the mistake only during the repetition, which was necessary because my daughter, having been distracted from another side, did not listen to me. This repetition with the added impatience to disburden myself of the sentence I must

*Abridged from Freud, S.: *Psychopathology of Everyday Life (Psychopathologie des Alltagslebens)*, New York, 1938, Random House, Inc., pp. 73-80.

include in the motivation of the speech-blunder, which represented itself as a function of condensation.

(b) My daughter said, "I wrote to Mrs. Schresinger." The woman's name was Schlesinger. This speech-blunder may depend on the tendency to facilitate articulation. I must state, however, that this mistake was made by my daughter a few moments after I had said *apel* instead of *ape*. Mistakes in speech are in a great measure contagious; a similar peculiarity was noticed by Meringer and Mayer in the forgetting of names. I know of no reason for this psychic contagiousness.

(c) "I *sut* up like a pocket knife," said a patient in the beginning of treatment, instead of "I *shut up*." This suggests a difficulty of articulation which may serve as an excuse for the interchanging of sounds. When her attention was called to the speech-blunder, she promptly replied, "Yes, that happened because you said 'earnesht' instead of 'earnest'." As a matter of fact, I received her with the remark, "Today we shall be in earnest" (because it was the last hour before her discharge from treatment), and I jokingly changed the word into *earnesht*. In the course of the hour, she repeatedly made mistakes in speech, and I finally observed that it was not only because she imitated me but because she had a special reason in her unconscious to linger at the word earnest (Ernst) as a name.[1]

(d) A woman, speaking about a game invented by her children and called by them "the man in the box," said "the manx in the boc." I could readily understand her mistake. It was while analyzing her dream, in which her husband is depicted as very generous in money matters—just the reverse of reality —that she made this speech-blunder. The day before she had asked for a new set of furs, which her husband denied her, claiming that he could not afford to spend so much money. She upbraided him for his stinginess, "for putting away so much into the strongbox," and mentioned a friend whose husband has not nearly his income, and yet he presented his wife with a *mink* coat for her birthday. The mistake is now comprehensible. The word *manx (manks)* reduces itself to the "minks" which she longs for, and the *box* refers to her husband's stinginess.[2]

(e) A similar mechanism is shown in the mistake of another patient whose memory deserted her in the midst of a long-forgotten childish reminiscence. Her memory failed to inform her of what part of the body the prying and lustful hand of another had touched her. Soon thereafter she visited one of her friends, with whom she discussed summer homes. Asked where her cottage in M. was located, she answered, "Near the *mountain loin*" instead of "*mountain lane*."

(f) Another patient, whom I asked at the end of her visit how her uncle was, answered: "I don't know, I only see him now *in flagrante*."

---

[1] It turned out that she was under the influence of unconscious thoughts concerning pregnancy and prevention of conception. With the words "shut up like a pocket knife," which she uttered consciously as a complaint, she meant to describe the position of the child in the womb. The word "earnest" in my remark recalled to her the name (S. Ernst) of the well-known Vienna business firm in Kärthner Strasse, which used to advertise the sale of articles for the prevention of conception.

[2] Given by Editor.

The following day she said: "I am really ashamed of myself for having given you such a stupid answer yesterday. Naturally, you must have thought me a very uneducated person who always mistakes the meaning of foreign words. I wished to say *en passant*." We did not know at the time where she got the incorrectly used foreign words, but during the same session, she reproduced a reminiscence as a continuation of the theme from the previous day, in which being caught *in flagrante* played the principal part. The mistake of the previous day had therefore anticipated the recollection, which, at that time, had not yet become conscious.

(g) In discussing her summer plans, a patient said, "I shall remain most of the summer in *Elberlon*." She noted her mistake, and asked me to analyze it. The associations to *Elberlon* elicited: seashore on the Jersey coast—summer resort—vacation travelling. This recalled travelling in Europe with her cousin, a topic which we had discussed the day before during the analysis of a dream. The dream dealt with her dislike for this cousin, and she admitted that it was mainly due to the fact that the latter was the favorite of the man whom they met together while travelling abroad. During the dream analysis, she could not recall the name of the city in which they met this man, and I did not make any effort at the time to bring it to her consciousness, as we were engrossed in a totally different problem. When asked to focus her attention again on Elberlon and reproduce her associations, she said, "It brings to mind *Elberlawn—lawn—field—and Elberfield*." Elberfield was the lost name of the city in Germany. Here the mistake served to bring to consciousness in a concealed manner a memory which was connected with a painful feeling.

• • •

(i) Before calling on me, a patient telephoned for an appointment and also wished to be informed about my consultation fee. He was told that the first consultation was ten dollars; after the examination was over, he again asked what he was to pay and added: "I don't like to owe money to anyone, especially to doctors; I prefer to pay right away." Instead of *pay* he said *play*. His last voluntary remarks and his mistake put me on my guard, but after a few more uncalled-for remarks, he set me at ease by taking money from his pocket. He counted four paper dollars and was very chagrined and surprised because he had no more money with him and promised to send me a cheque for the balance. I was sure that his mistake betrayed him, that he was only *playing* with me, but there was nothing to be done. At the end of a few weeks, I sent him a bill for the balance, and the letter was returned to me by the post office authorities marked "Not found."

(j) Miss X. spoke very warmly of Mr. Y., which was rather strange, as before this, she had always expressed her indifference, not to say her contempt, for him. On being asked about this sudden change of heart, she said: "I really never had anything against him; he was always nice to me, but I never gave him the chance to cultivate my acquaintance." She said "cuptivate." This neologism was a contamination of *cultivate* and *captivate,* and foretold the coming betrothal.

(k) An illustration of the mechanisms of contamination and condensation will be found in the following *lapsus linguae*. Speaking of Miss Z., Miss W.

depicted her as a very "straitlaced" person who was not given to levity, etc. Miss X. thereupon remarked: "Yes, that is a very characteristic description, she always appealed to me as very *straicet-brazed.*" Here the mistake resolved itself into *straitlaced* and *brazenfaced,* which corresponded to Miss W.'s opinion of Miss Z.

(1) I was to give a lecture to a woman. Her husband, upon whose request this was done, stood behind the door listening. At the end of my sermonizing, which had made a visible impression, I said: "Goodbye, Sir!" To the experienced person, I thus betrayed the fact that the words were directed toward the husband, that I had spoken to oblige him.

(m) Two women stopped in front of a drugstore, and one said to her companion, "If you will wait a few *moments*, I'll soon be back," but she said *movements* instead. She was on her way to buy some castoria for her child.

(n) Mr. L., who is fonder of being called on than of calling, spoke to me through the telephone from a nearby summer resort. He wanted to know when I would pay him a visit. I reminded him that it was his turn to visit me, and called his attention to the fact that, as he was the happy possessor of an automobile, it would be easier for him to call on me. (We were at different summer resorts, separated by about one half-hour's railway trip.) He gladly promised to call and asked: "How about Labor Day (September 1st), will it be convenient for you?" When I answered in the affirmative, he said, "Very well, then, put me down for *Election* Day" (November). His mistake was quite plain. He likes to visit me, but it was inconvenient to travel so far. In November, we would both be in the city. My analysis proved correct.

(o) A friend described to me a nervous patient and wished to know whether I could benefit him. I remarked: "I believe that in time I can remove all his symptoms by psychoanalysis, because it is a durable case," wishing to say "curable"!

(p) I repeatedly addressed my patient as "Mrs. Smith," her married daughter's name, when her real name is "Mrs. James." My attention having been called to it, I soon discovered that I had another patient of the same name who refused to pay for the treatment. Mrs. Smith was also my patient and paid her bills promptly.

(q) A *lapsus linguae* sometimes stands for a particular characteristic. A young woman, who is the dominating spirit in her home, said of her ailing husband, that he had consulted the doctor about a wholesome diet for himself, and then added: "The doctor said that diet has nothing to do with his ailments, and that he can eat and drink what *I* want."

(r) I cannot omit this excellent and instructive example, although according to my authority, it is about twenty years old. A lady once expressed herself in society—the very words show that they were uttered with fervor and under the pressure of a great many secret emotions: "Yes, a woman must be pretty if she is to please the men. A man is much better off. As long as he has *five* straight limbs, he needs no more!"

This example affords us a good insight into the intimate mechanisms of a mistake in speech by means of condensation and contamination. It is quite obvious that we have here a fusion of two similar modes of expression:

"As long as he has his four *straight limbs.*"
"As long as he has all his *five senses.*"

Or the term "straight" may be the common element of the two intended expressions:

"As long as he has his *straight* limbs."
"All five should be *straight.*"

It may also be assumed that both modes of expression—viz., those of the five senses and those of the straight five—have cooperated to introduce into the sentence about the straight limbs first a number and then the mysterious five instead of the simple four. But this fusion surely would not have succeeded if it had not expressed good sense in the form resulting from the mistake; if it had not expressed a cynical truth which, naturally, could not be uttered unconcealed, coming as it did from a woman.

Finally, we shall not hesitate to call attention to the fact that the woman's saying, following its wording, would just as well be an excellent witticism as a jocose speech-blunder. It is simply a question whether she uttered these words with conscious or unconscious intention. The behavior of the speaker in this case certainly speaks against the conscious intention, and thus excludes wit.

(s) Owing to similarity of material, I add here another case of speech-blunder, the interpretation of which requires less skill. A professor of anatomy strove to explain the nostril, which, as is known, is a very difficult anatomical structure. To his question whether his audience grasped his ideas, he received an affirmative reply. The professor, known for his self-esteem, thereupon remarked: "I can hardly believe this, for the number of people who understand the nostril, even in a city of millions like Vienna, can be counted *on a finger*— pardon me, I meant to say *on the fingers* of a hand."

In the psychotherapeutic procedure which I employ in the solution and removal of neurotic symptoms, I am often confronted with the task of discovering from the accidental utterances and fancies of the patient the thought contents, which, though striving for concealment, nevertheless unintentionally betray themselves. In doing this, the mistakes often perform the most valuable service, as I can show through most convincing and still most singular examples.

For example, patients speak of an aunt and later, without noting the mistake, call her "my mother," or designate a husband as a "brother." In this way, they attract my attention to the fact that they have "identified" these persons with each other, that they have placed them in the same category, which for their emotional life signifies the recurrence of the same type. Or, a young man of twenty years presents himself during my office hours with these words: "I am the father of N. N., whom you have treated—pardon me, I mean the brother; why, he is four years older than I." I understand through this mistake that he wishes to express that, like the brother, he, too, is ill through the fault of the father; like his brother he wishes to be cured, but that the father is the one most in need of treatment. At other times, an unusual arrangement of words, or a forced expression, is sufficient to disclose in the speech of a patient the participation of a repressed thought having a different motive.

Hence, in coarse as well as in finer speech disturbances, which may, nevertheless, be subsumed as "speech-blunders," I find that it is not the contact effects of the sound, but the thoughts outside the intended speech, which determine the origin of the speech-blunder, and also suffice to explain the newly formed mistakes in speech. I do not doubt the laws whereby the sounds produce changes upon one another; but they alone do not appear to me sufficiently forcible to mar the correct execution of speech. In those cases which I have studied and investigated more closely, they merely represent the preformed mechanism, which is conveniently utilized by a more remote psychic motive. The latter does not, however, form a part of the sphere of influence of these sound relations. *In a large number of substitutions caused by mistakes in talking, there is an entire absence of such phonetic laws.* In this respect, I am in full accord with Wundt, who likewise assumes that the conditions underlying speech-blunders are complex and go far beyond the contact effect of the sounds.

If I accept as certain "these more remote psychic influences," following Wundt's expression, there is still nothing to detain me from conceding also that in accelerated speech, with a certain amount of diverted attention, the causes of speech-blunder may be easily limited to the definite law of Meringer and Mayer. However, in a number of examples gathered by these authors, a more complicated solution is quite apparent.

In some forms of speech-blunders we may assume that the disturbing factor is the result of striking against obscene words and meanings. The purposive disfigurement and distortion of words and phrases, which is so popular with vulgar persons, aims at nothing else but the employing of a harmless motive as a reminder of the obscene, and this sport is so frequent that it would not be at all remarkable if it appeared unintentionally and contrary to the will.

I trust that the readers will not depreciate the value of these interpretations, for which there is no proof, and of these examples which I have myself collected and explained by means of analysis. But, if secretly I still cherish the expectation that even the apparently simple cases of speech-blunder will be traced to a disturbance caused by a half-repressed idea outside of the intended context, I am tempted to it by a noteworthy observation of Meringer. This author asserts that it is remarkable that nobody wishes to admit having made a mistake in speaking. There are many intelligent and honest people who are offended if we tell them that they made a mistake in speaking. I would not risk making this assertion as general as does Meringer, using the term "nobody." But the emotional trace which clings to the demonstration of the mistake, which manifestly belongs to the nature of shame, has its significance. It may be classed with the anger displayed at the inability to recall a forgotten name, and with the surprise at the tenaciousness of an apparently indifferent memory, and it invaribly points to the participation of a motive in the formation of the disturbance.

The distorting of names amounts to an insult when done intentionally, and could have the same significance in a whole series of cases where it appears as unintentional speech-blunders. The person who, according to Mayer's report, once said "Freuder" instead of "Freud," because shortly before he pronounced the name "Breuer," and what at another time, spoke of the "Freuer-Breudian" method, was certainly not particularly enthusiastic over this method. Later, under the mistakes in writing, I shall report a case of name disfigurement which certainly admits of no other explanation.[3]

As a disturbing element in these cases, there is an intermingling of a criticism which must be omitted, because at the time being, it does not correspond to the intention of the speaker.

---

[3]It may be observed that aristocrats in particular very frequently distort the names of the physicians they consult, from which we may conclude that inwardly they slight them, in spite of the politeness with which they are wont to greet them. I shall cite here some excellent observations concerning the forgetting of names from the works of Dr. Ernest Jones: *Papers on Psychoanalysis,* Chap. iii., p. 49:

"Few people can avoid feeling a twinge of resentment when they find that their name has been forgotten, particularly if it is by someone with whom they had hoped or expected it would be remembered. They instinctively realize that if they had made a greater impression on the person's mind, he would certainly have remembered them again, for the name is an integral part of the personality. Similarly, few things are more flattering to most people than to find themselves addressed by name by a great personage where they could hardly have anticipated it. Napoleon, like most leaders of men, was a master of this art. In the midst of the disastrous campaign of France in 1814, he gave an amazing proof of his memory in this direction. When in a town near Craonne, he recollected that he had met the mayor, De Bussy, over twenty years ago in the La Fère Regiment. The delighted De Bussy at once threw himself into his service with extraordinary zeal. Conversely, there is no surer way of affronting someone than by pretending to forget his name; the insinuation is thus conveyed that the person is so unimportant in our eyes that we cannot be bothered to remember his name. This device is often exploited in literature. In Turgeniev's *Smoke* (p. 255) the following passage occurs: ' "So you still find Baden entertaining, M'sieur—Litvinov." Ratmirov always uttered Litvinov's surname with hesitation, every time, as though he had forgotten it, and could not at once recall it. In this way, as well as by the lofty flourish of his hat in saluting him, he meant to insult his pride.' The same author, in his *Fathers and Children* (p. 107), writes: 'The Governor invited Kirsanov and Bazarov to his ball, and within a few minutes invited them a second time, regarding them as brothers, and calling them Kisarov.' Here the forgetting that he had spoken to them, the mistake in the names and the inability to distinguish between the two young men, constitute a culmination of disparagement. Falsification of a name has the same signification as forgetting it; it is only a step towards complete amnesia."

Chapter 22

Some hypotheses regarding the facilitation of personal growth*

Carl R. Rogers

To be faced by a troubled, conflicted person who is seeking and expecting help, has always constituted a great challenge to me. Do I have the knowledge, the resources, the psychological strength, the skill—do I have whatever it takes to be of help to such an individual?

For more than twenty-five years I have been trying to meet this kind of challenge. It has caused me to draw upon every element of my professional background: the rigorous methods of personality measurement which I first learned at Teachers' College, Columbia; the Freudian psychoanalytic insights and methods of the Institute for Child Guidance where I worked as interne; the continuing developments in the field of clinical psychology, with which I have been closely associated; the briefer exposure to the work of Otto Rank, to the methods of psychiatric social work, and other resources too numerous to mention. But most of all it has meant a continual learning from my own experience and that of my colleagues at the Counseling Center as we have endeavored to discover for ourselves effective means of working with people in distress. Gradually I have developed a way of working which grows out of that experience, and which can be tested, refined, and reshaped by further experience and by research.

A GENERAL HYPOTHESIS

One brief way of describing the change which has taken place in me is to say that in my early professional years I was asking the question, How can I treat, or cure, or change this person? Now I would phrase the question in this way: How can I provide a relationship which this person may use for his own personal growth?

It is as I have come to put the question in this second way that I realize that whatever I have learned is applicable to all of my human relationships, not just working with clients with problems. It is for this reason that I feel

---

*From *On Becoming a Person: A Therapist's View of Psychotherapy*, New York, 1961, Houghton Mifflin Co., pp. 31-38.

it is possible that the learnings which have had meaning for me in my experience may have some meaning for you in your experience, since all of us are involved in human relationships.

Perhaps I should start with a negative learning. It has gradually been driven home to me that I cannot be of help to this troubled person by means of any intellectual or training procedure. No approach which relies upon knowledge, upon training, upon the acceptance of something that is *taught,* is of any use. These approaches seem so tempting and direct that I have, in the past, tried a great many of them. It is possible to explain a person to himself, to prescribe steps which should lead him forward, to train him in knowledge about a more satisfying mode of life. But such methods are, in my experience, futile and inconsequential. The most they can accomplish is some temporary change, which soon disappears, leaving the individual more than ever convinced of his inadequacy.

The failure of any such approach through the intellect has forced me to recognize that change appears to come about through experience in a relationship. So I am going to try to state very briefly and informally, some of the essential hypotheses regarding a helping relationship which have seemed to gain increasing confirmation both from experience and research.

I can state the overall hypothesis in one sentence, as follows. If I can provide a certain type of relationship, the other person will discover within himself the capacity to use that relationship for growth, and change and personal development will occur.

THE RELATIONSHIP

But what meaning do these terms have? Let me take separately the three major phrases in this sentence and indicate something of the meaning they have for me. What is this certain type of relationship I would like to provide?

I have found that the more that I can be genuine in the relationship, the more helpful it will be. This means that I need to be aware of my own feelings, in so far as possible, rather than presenting an outward façade of one attitude, while actually holding another attitude at a deeper or unconscious level. Being genuine also involves the willingness to be and to express, in my words and my behavior, the various feelings and attitudes which exist in me. It is only in this way that the relationship can have *reality,* and reality seems deeply important as a first condition. It is only by providing the genuine reality which is in me, that the other person can successfully seek for the reality in him. I have found this to be true even when the attitudes I feel are not attitudes with which I am pleased, or attitudes which seem conducive to a good relationship. It seems extremely important to be *real.*

As a second condition, I find that the more acceptance and liking I feel toward this individual, the more I will be creating a relationship which he can use. By acceptance I mean a warm regard for him as a person of unconditional self-worth—of value no matter what his condition, his behavior, or his feelings. It means a respect and liking for him as a separate person, a willingness for him to possess his own feelings in his own way. It means an acceptance of and regard for his attitudes of the moment, no matter how negative or positive, no matter how much they may contradict other attitudes he has held in the past. This acceptance of each fluctuating aspect of this other person makes it for him a relationship of warmth and safety, and the safety of being liked and prized as a person seems a highly important element in a helping relationship.

I also find that the relationship is significant to the extent that I feel a continuing desire to understand—a sensitive empathy with each of the client's feelings and communications as they seem to him at that moment. Acceptance does not mean much until it involves understanding. It is only as I *understand* the feelings and thoughts which seem so horrible to you, or so weak, or so sentimental, or so bizarre—it is only as I see them as you see them, and accept them and you, that you feel really free to explore all the hidden nooks and frightening crannies of your inner and often buried experience. This *freedom* is an important condition of the relationship. There is implied here a freedom to explore oneself at both conscious and unconscious levels, as rapidly as one can dare to embark on this dangerous quest. There is also a complete freedom from any type of moral or diagnostic evaluation, since all such evaluations are, I believe, always threatening.

Thus the relationship which I have found helpful is characterized by a sort of transparency on my part, in which my real feelings are evident; by an acceptance of this other person as a separate person with value in his own right; and by a deep empathic understanding which enables me to see his private world through his eyes. When these conditions are achieved, I become a companion to my client, accompanying him in the frightening search for himself, which he now feels free to undertake.

I am by no means always able to achieve this kind of relationship with another, and sometimes, even when I feel I have achieved it in myself, he may be too frightened to perceive what is being offered to him. But I would say that when I hold in myself the kind of attitudes I have described, and when the other person can to some degree experience these attitudes, then I believe that change and constructive personal development will *invariably* occur—and I include the word "invariably" only after long and careful consideration.

THE MOTIVATION FOR CHANGE

So much for the relationship. The second phrase in my overall hypothesis was that the individual will discover within himself the capacity to use this relationship for growth. I will try to indicate something of the meaning which that phrase has for me. Gradually my experience has forced me to conclude that the individual has within himself the capacity and the tendency, latent if not evident, to move forward toward maturity. In a suitable psychological climate this tendency is released, and becomes actual rather than potential. It is evident in the capacity of the individual to understand those aspects of his life and of himself which are causing him pain and dissatisfaction, an understanding which probes beneath his conscious knowledge of himself into those experiences which he has hidden from himself because of their threatening nature. It shows itself in the tendency to reorganize his personality and his relationship to life in ways which are regarded as more mature. Whether one calls it a growth tendency, a drive toward self-actualization, or a forward-moving directional tendency, it is the mainspring of life, and is, in the last analysis, the tendency upon which all psychotherapy depends. It is the urge which is evident in all organic and human life—to expand, extend, become autonomous, develop, mature—the tendency to express and activate all the capacities of the organism, to the extent that such activation enhances the organism or the self. This tendency may become deeply buried under layer after layer of encrusted psychological defenses; it may be hidden behind elaborate façades which deny its existence; but it is my belief that it exists in every individual, and awaits only the proper conditions to be released and expressed.

THE OUTCOMES

I have attempted to describe the relationship which is basic to constructive personality change. I have tried to put into words the type of capacity which the individual brings to such a relationship. The third phrase of my general statement was that change and personal development would occur. It is my hypothesis that in such a relationship the individual will reorganize himself at both the conscious and deeper levels of his personality in such a manner as to cope with life more constructively, more intelligently, and in a more socialized as well as a more satisfying way.

Here I can depart from speculation and bring in the steadily increasing body of solid research knowledge which is accumulating. We know now that individuals who live in such a relationship even for a relatively limited number of hours show profound and significant changes in personality, attitudes, and behavior, changes that do not occur in matched control groups. In such a relationship the individual becomes more integrated, more effective. He shows fewer of the characteristics which are usually termed neurotic or psychotic, and more of the characteristics of the healthy, well-functioning person. He changes his perception of himself, becoming more realistic in his views of self. He becomes more like the person he wishes to be. He values himself more highly. He is more self-confident and self-directing. He has a better understanding of himself, becomes more open to his experience, denies or represses less of his experience. He becomes more accepting in his attitudes toward others, seeing others as more similar to himself.

In his behavior he shows similar changes. He is less frustrated by stress, and recovers from stress more quickly. He becomes more mature in his everyday behavior as this is observed by friends. He is less defensive, more adaptive, more able to meet situations creatively.

These are some of the changes which we now know come about in individuals who have completed a series of counseling interviews in which the psychological atmosphere approximates the relationship I described. Each of the statements made is based upon objective evidence. Much more research needs to be done, but there can no longer be any doubt as to the effectiveness of such a relationship in producing personality change.

A BROAD HYPOTHESIS OF HUMAN RELATIONSHIPS

To me, the exciting thing about these research findings is not simply the fact that they give evidence of the efficacy of one form of psychotherapy, though that is by no means unimportant. The excitement comes from the fact that these findings justify an even broader hypothesis regarding all human relationships. There seems every reason to suppose that the therapeutic relationship is only one instance of interpersonal relations, and that the same lawfulness governs all such relationships. Thus it seems reasonable to hypothesize that if the parent creates with his child a psychological climate such as we have described, then the child will become more self-directing, socialized, and mature. To the extent that the teacher creates such a relationship with his class, the student will become a self-initiated learner, more original, more self-disciplined, less anxious and other-directed. If the administrator, or military or industrial leader, creates such a climate within his organization, then his staff will become more self-responsible, more creative, better able to adapt to new problems, more basically cooperative. It appears possible to me that we are seeing the emergence of a new field of human relationships, in which we may specify that if certain attitudinal conditions exist, then certain definable changes will occur.

CONCLUSION

Let me conclude by returning to a personal statement. I have tried to share with you something of what I have learned in trying to be of help to troubled, unhappy, maladjusted individuals. I have formulated the hypothesis which has gradually come to have meaning for me—not only in my relationship to clients in distress, but in all my human relationships. I have indicated that such research knowledge as we have supports this hypothesis, but that there is much more investigation needed. I should like now to pull together into one statement the conditions of this general hypothesis, and the effects which are specified.

If I can create a relationship characterized on my part:

by a genuineness and transparency, in which I am my real feelings;

by a warm acceptance of and prizing of the other person as a separate individual;

by a sensitive ability to see his world and himself as he sees them;

Then the other individual in the relationship:

will experience and understand aspects of himself which previously he has repressed;

will find himself becoming better integrated, more able to function effectively;

will become more similar to the person he would like to be;

will be more self-directing and self-confident;

will become more of a person, more unique and more self-expressive;

will be more understanding, more acceptant of others;

will be able to cope with the problems of life more adequately and more comfortably.

I believe that this statement holds whether I am speaking of my relationship with a client, with a group of students or staff members, with my family or children. It seems to me that we have here a general hypothesis which offers exciting possibilities for the development of creative, adaptive, autonomous persons.

Chapter 23

Psychological aspects of spirit possession*

Walter Mischel and Frances Mischel

In attempting to understand the reasons why people engage in practices that might appear to be bizarre or subscribe to one particular
ideology in preference to another, it is essential to examine the reinforcing aspects of the situation and the personality needs of the individuals concerned instead of searching for explanations in terms of the
logical appeal of a closely reasoned ideology.

Of the numerous factors most immediately and directly involved in the induction of possession, the categorization into "falling with or without the
drums" is most commonly made by the participants. "Falling with (or to) the
drums" refers to possession in response to, or in the presence of, drumming.
Drumming is an integral part of formal ceremonials. In combination with the
crowd excitement, singing, darkness, candles, circular rhythmic dancing, and
other ceremonial aspects, drumming engenders an atmosphere in which possession has become the expected, desired, and usual behavior. This is by far the
most common immediate stimulus for possession. "Falling to the drums" occurs
at the regularly scheduled "feasts" or "sacrifices," and it is here that the less
active followers as well as the more dominant leaders and "old heads" have the
opportunity to "manifest the powers."

In addition to individual responses to the drumming, the power may be
"passed on" from person to person. Thus, those already in possession may approach bystanders and rub their heads, faces, chests, and arms, pour oil on
them, pick them up, and hold them in the air, or the possessed person may
spin onlookers by the waist. Such behavior is the final inducement to possession.

Possession without the stimulation of drumming and formal ceremony is
much more rare and almost completely restricted to the *Orisha* leaders and
dominant followers. Within this prestigeful group, possession may take place
at any time and in almost any setting, but the following are examples of the
more usual settings.

Dreams and visions may serve as the immediate stimulus. The individual

*Reproduced by permission of American Anthropological Association from *American
Anthropologist* **60**:249-260, 1958.

may report such dreams or their interpretation through the power possessing him shortly after his dream or vision experience. The transition is often extremely short, the one following so quickly from the other that it is apparently an extension or expansion of it.

Leaders occasionally undergo possession to give medication, advice, aid in recovering lost objects, and other such functions outside the context of formal ceremonies. Virtually all leaders have regularly scheduled times when they perform such functions for the multitudes who seek their help. On such occasions the leaders are sometimes said to be "in power," at least for brief periods. However, the behavior involved in such manifestation of power is quite different from that observed in connection with possession in response to drumming. There is less motor activity and less dramatic facial and behavioral change. Usually there is some dilation of the eyes. Changes in speech are less marked; the utterances are mostly in English, and primarily coherent. Persons who are "in power" are said to have a "special gift," but all the "old heads" and leaders are credited with this gift. A much higher value is attributed to this kind of possession. Leaders are said to be able to "get power" at any time because of their constant close association and communication with the powers. They "just concentrate" or "look for a time at the (statue of the) saint." Cult followers express different views on the nature of this kind of power. Some appear to interpret the leader as actually being in power or possessed; others appear to feel that the leader is "still himself" but by virtue of his "gift" is "always close to the powers," and thus able to communicate with them and interpret their wishes (by means of readings of the *obi* seeds and similar devices) without undergoing possession.

Another important stimulus is a crisis. The individual is apt to experience possession when confronted by serious marital or other interpersonal problems, by difficult decisions, by involvement in court cases, or by other severely frustrating or conflict-producing events. At such times, particular emphasis is placed on the messages and advice delivered by the power through the horse, as reported and reconstructed by the audience to the manifestation.

Finally, a form of possession known as "weré" occurs with some frequency. Individuals in this state are considered "messengers of the powers." Weré possession is a half-way state between full possession and normal behavior, and a high degree of consciousness is retained. It is marked by disobeying ceremonial regulations by such acts as smoking, swearing, or mocking sacred places by spitting on the *tombs* of the powers. The behavior becomes extremely childish; the possessed may speak with a marked lisp, wet or soil himself, and use vulgar language and gestures. He is treated tolerantly by onlookers, as one might treat a naughty but loved child. One person in this state maintained that he had just landed from "New York Thity" and that his plane was parked outside the gate. He cordially invited all available females to examine the inside of the plane with him (invoking gales of hysterical laughter from all present). Weré possession may or may not follow actual possession. Most often, an individual who has just been strongly possessed will manifest a weré, but many cases were also observed where the weré persons had not undergone a previous possession.

Although the weré is termed a messenger, he delivers no actual messages. The term indicates that a power sent the weré in his place, since the former was "too busy to stay." Most were possessions occur at the end of a feast after the drumming and dancing have ceased, and promote a gay and light-hearted atmosphere.

Levels of possession

The level of possession (the depth, involvement, loss of control and consciousness, and intensity of behavior) is by no means constant, either among individuals or at different times with the same person. At times it appears to consist merely of a brief "overshadowing" or momentary loss of control, dizziness, and a partial and temporary loss of consciousness. On other occasions, it involves an almost total and prolonged loss of consciousness and of many controls over motor behavior. However, even in the most extreme examples observed, the individual seemed to retain sufficient consciousness and control to permit him to behave without injury to self or others; that is, without stumbling over objects or mishandling implements. Further, the possessed individual appears to recognize those about him and may refer to them by name and make reference to known past experiences. He may also refer to himself by his secular name and allude to aspects of his daily life. On occasion, things that were expressed privately in the normal state are publicly reiterated or rephrased under possession. It should be emphasized that possession does not appear to be an all-or-none process, utterly separated from the individual's usual state. Rather, an extension and distortion of everyday behavior seems to be involved, and possession behavior cannot be rigidly dichotomized from the person's secular roles. It would appear more useful to deal with different levels of involvement in possession behavior rather than "possession" versus "normality."

Recovery from possession

The manner of ending possession varies. Most often, a possessed person spins rapidly while standing in one place and suddenly falls to the ground. Onlookers immediately rush to his assistance, help him to a seat, and place water to his lips. In a few moments he regains command of himself and possession is over. At times, a very gradual cessation of activity, accompanied by shaking of the head or holding the head in the hands, indicates the end of possession. Although recovery occurs most often in the *palais*, some individuals, either alone or aided by others, run to the chapelle where they lie down on the floor and await the "power's going back." Occasionally an individual leaves the palais in order not to hear the drums, or he may signal the drums to stop so that the power will leave. In such instances, this is interpreted as the power's refusal to stay at the feast because of activities which disturb him, or he is said to be "too busy" to remain.

We turn now to an examination of some of the reinforcement consequences of possession behavior.

REINFORCEMENT CONSEQUENCES

In accord with learning theory, it will be assumed that behavior during spirit possession, like any other behavior, is perpetuated only if it is in some way reinforcing or rewarding to those who exhibit it (Miller and Dollard 1950; Rotter 1954). This assumption by no means excludes the possibility that the same behavior may also have negatively reinforcing consequences, as is dramatically illustrated in the learning of "abnormal" or socially unacceptable patterns. Despite their ultimately negative consequences for the individual, these patterns still appear to have sufficient positive reinforcement (e.g. via their temporary alleviation of anxiety) to be maintained tenaciously.

We hypothesize that the practice of spirit possession permits the sanctioned expression of behaviors[1] which are otherwise socially unacceptable or unavailable. In a learning theory interpretation the sanctioned expression or release of otherwise unacceptable behavior is not in itself reinforcing: rather, the consequences of the behavior—for example, other people's reactions of praise or reproof—are the reinforcements and the determinants of whether or not the behavior will be repeated. We shall examine some of the behavioral patterns enacted during spirit possession and indicate what their positive and negative reinforcement consequences appear to be.[2] The methods used to infer these consequences were participant observation and intensive clinical interviews and testing with twenty of the most active participants. It is hoped that isolation of behavior patterns, in terms of the kinds of reinforcements which appear to be gained through them, will help to clarify a phenomenon which has heretofore been presented largely in an essentially global and undifferentiated manner.

Perhaps the most striking pattern of behavior during possession is that in which the possessed controls the activities of those around him. Both the degree and temporal duration of this control vary greatly between individuals and situations; a relatively limited number of individuals, primarily cult leaders, exert the greatest and most consistent control. In the most extreme examples, the possessed is virtually in absolute control of those around him. His slightest wish is immediately carried out; the onlookers are utterly at his disposal and ready to advance, retreat, sing, or keep silent at his command. Oil, rum, implements such as axes, swords, food, and candles, are quickly brought in response to his signals. The attitude of the Shango followers when the power is exerting his control over them tends to be one of awe and respect, frequently mingled with fear. The Shango followers flock close to the power, attentive to every word, alert to any advice, warning, or recommendation that may issue. This kind of behavior on the part of the group, with its inferred gratification to the horse, is in striking contrast to the secular role of the horse (generally of the lowest social status). The domestic who thirty minutes earlier was submissive to the whims of her British mistress is, under possession, transformed into a god; the unemployed laborer is master of an audience of several hundred people. The transition is often an almost direct role reversal—from passive impotence to central importance, dominance, power, and recognition, which appear to be the major reinforcements obtained through this behavior pattern. However, these reinforcements are not available to all, for some who attempt to gain such stature under possession are met by ridicule and rejection.[3]

---

[1]"Behavior," as used throughout this paper, includes not only explicit behaviors or overt acts, but also such "implicit" behaviors as are commonly subsumed under terms such as "wishes," "feelings," "thoughts."

[2]We shall not be concerned here with the "social" reinforcements of possession behavior, e.g., with the ways in which particular behaviors during possession may influence the individual's position in the group and his relationships to other group members.

[3]This problem will be discussed in a paper now being prepared.

A much less frequently observed pattern is that in which the possessed may tear his clothing, beat himself, roll on the ground for prolonged periods, aim dangerous implements in his own direction, and so forth. This behavior seems to be directed at self-inflicted violence or harm, but self-injury is quite rare and was never observed. The overall impression gained from this behavior (an impression shared by many Shango followers) is that the individual is doing penance. The interpretation of cult members is that such activity is a reflection of the unworthiness of the horse, and that, due to infractions or evil deeds (primarily "uncleanliness"), the power is angry with the horse and punishing it. The reaction of onlookers to this behavior appears to be quiet noninterference, or acceptance with occasional intervention, e.g., efforts to pacify the power when behavior becomes extremely violent. Public expression or confession of guilt may also take place in this essentially nonpunitive setting. The reinforcement obtained by the possessed through this behavior may be the reduction of guilt and anxiety, both of which are interpreted here as socially learned drives. The individual who has learned to expect negative reinforcement, e.g. punishment for certain overt or contemplated behavior, obtains a measure of relief or drive reduction through punitive acts. Further, by taking the punishment into his own hands he may avert more severe expected punishment from outside, unknown, and dreaded sources over which he has no control.

Close physical interaction between the possessed and his audience distinguishes another pattern. The possessed may crawl through the spread legs of other participants of either sex or squat on the prostrate form of another, massaging his chest, breasts, thighs, and shoulders, and bouncing up and down on the body. Particularly when female horses manifest male powers, the implement used (usually an axe, cutlass, or sword) is frequently flourished near the genitals of other participants, with both a menacing and sexual effect. The possessed may lift persons and let them ride on his back or shoulders, bouncing the rider. Or the possessed may kneel in front of a standing figure (most often the male leader) and rub his face on or around the groin. The variations in this pattern are numerous. Closely intermingled with this appear to be seemingly hostile and aggressive activities, as when extremely rough or threatening behavior is directed at the person whom the possessed is straddling and rubbing. For example, the possessed may push, crush, or lash persons with whom he has a much more restricted relationship in his normal state.

It is inferred that the reinforcements derived from such behavior are primarily the attainment of intimate, though often fleeting, interpersonal relationships which are desired by the horse but which are too prohibited socially to be permitted gratification in the nonpossessed state. The content (e.g., sexual, hostile) and the objects vary considerably but share the characteristics of being desired by the horse but unattainable in the normal state.

A striking pattern which is prohibited in the nonpossessed state involves the reversal of sex roles. Many females manifest male powers and, to a lesser degree, males manifest female powers. In such cases the female, under possession by a male power, is free to enact typically masculine behavior, and the male is free to enact typically feminine behavior. Individuals who have not learned clear sex roles, or who do not accept their roles, and whose goals partially involve those traditionally prescribed for members of the opposite sex, have a particularly appealing opportunity to assume temporarily the behavior usually considered appropriate only for the opposite sex. For example, the woman who resents a passive role can behave in a dominating, aggressive, belligerent manner; the man who finds the aggressive role difficult can behave in a passive, submissive manner.

The childish behavior which occurs in weré possession, found also in Brazil, has been discussed (Herskovits 1943) and considered as a period of relaxation in which to bridge the gulf between the ecstatic condition of possession and normalcy. An alternative, and not necessarily contradictory, interpretation is that childish, regressive behaviors—such as soiling, baby talk, and auto-eroticism—are still pleasurable to the individual, both directly and for their possible symbolic meanings. Within weré possession, behaviors which are still gratifying, but which have long since become unacceptable and which the individual has been forced to abandon, can again be enacted without inhibition.

Thus far we have been discussing the potentially reinforcing consequences of specific behavior patterns. Apart from these specific behavioral enactments, the practice of spirit possession in Trinidad appears to have two other major positively reinforcing general functions. First, it supplies an available, socially sanctioned (at least within the practicing group) framework for the interpretation and acceptance of otherwise threatening and disturbing phenomena, such as unusual ("abnormal") psychological or physical symptoms. For example, where hysterical (i.e., apparently nonorganic) symptoms develop, the afflicted person himself or those around him, while under possession, interpret these as the first "signs" of the special "gift." This not only prevents the deviation from becoming a source of social stigma but, on the contrary, makes it a valued behavior, regardless of the ultimate personal consequences. The belief system which can render behavior which would otherwise be considered a malignant symptom into one that is prized and reinforced is itself reinforced by the process.

Second, the practice of spirit possession is also rewarding since it permits reference of virtually all serious problems to the "powers" for solution. Thereby, the individual is to some degree freed of responsibility for controlling and directing his own life. This not only gives aid in difficult decisions but also alleviates anxiety about such choices. The horse assumes a relatively passive role; it is the powers who handle the problems confronting him. Except for rather flexible adherence to a few vaguely interpreted general rules for "clean living," the participant surrenders control for ordering his life and bearing the consequences. This passivity is implied by use of the word "horse" to describe the possessed, who is said to be "ridden" by the power, directed by the power, and a tool or plastic medium controlled by forces from which he disassociates himself. The individual is thought of and considers himself a horse, not only prior to or during possession, but at other times as well. His identity, his self-concept, and his social roles are influenced to a considerable degree by the kind of horse he is, by the powers who most habitually possess him, and by his behavior at such times.

This personal passivity must not be over-emphasized. Although the individual does remove most major decisions from his own conscious and immediate jurisdiction, they are not surrendered to an abstract or remote power. The power to which they are transferred is directly and personally experienced within the participant's own body and, although not credited as such by the possessed, is an extension, as it were, of the individual's conscious behavior. That is, the power is an aspect of the individual himself, presumably without his awareness, which emerges during possession. Thus, the solutions reached by the power are not actually foreign or external to the individual but rather reflections of his own personality, under disguise. Within this condition, the kinds of behaviors which have been indicated can be enacted in both symbolic and overt form during possession, supplying the individual with gratifications and yet freeing him from personal responsibility for any negative consequences.

We have been emphasizing only the positively reinforcing aspects of possession. However, it must be recognized that, for some individuals, possession is also associated with negative values or is negatively reinforcing. This is reflected in the considerable number of participants who make seemingly intense and elaborate efforts to avoid possession. For the most part, this avoidance pattern is not complete since the individual continues to return not only to the ceremonies but also to the center of activities within which the chances for becoming possessed are greatest. In these instances one may infer an approach-avoidance type of conflict in relation to possession. Such conflict is seen in the individuals who hover and sway at the edge of the palais, attracted to the drums, "overshadowed," and at the same time slapping themselves or throwing water on their faces in the attempt to avoid possession. In other cases, the anticipated negative consequences of possession are so strong that the individual avoids the ceremonies altogether or, more commonly, joins that large proportion of people who constitute an interested but relatively uninvolved audience, carefully maintaining their distance, and intent on the feasting and entertainment aspects of ceremonies rather than on personal involvement with the drumming and dancing.

In Trinidad, some of the major negative reinforcements of possession include the following: On a cultural level, and perhaps of major import, is the perceived conflict between this kind of "African" activity and the increasingly sought values and activities of the more middle class segments of the population, particularly of the European groups. As acculturation continues and upward mobility develops, this conflict may well become intensified. Perhaps associated with this, at least in part, is the aversion to the complete abandon—rolling on the ground, dirtying oneself, and the like—displayed in possession. This, and the fear of loss of self control, may in turn be related to fears and conflicts, with varying degrees of awareness, about expressing potentially undesirable behaviors publicly or even partially admitting them to oneself. Further detrimental to possession is the widespread belief that aspects of behavior under possession reflect on the quality and worth of the horse; for example, a violent possession in which the horse may be hurt indicates that he has not been living a good life. It would not be surprising, then, for certain self-doubting individuals to be particularly wary about possession. In addition, some individuals expressed fear both of self injury and of injury by, or retribution from the powers while under possession. All of these factors may be involved in the embarrassment, fear, and avoidance expressed by numerous

Shango participants both overtly and in the form of ambivalent and conflicting attitudes in relation to possession.

It seems apparent that the specifics of each aspect of possession discussed may potentially apply only to possession behavior in Trinidad's Shango group. Particular physical manifestations and psychological goals or reinforcements obviously vary with the culture in which they are operative.

Although our approach has been to infer reinforcements on a rational and primarily external basis, it is important to keep in mind that for the participants, "possession by the god [is] the supreme religious experience" (Herskovits 1941:215). For those actively involved, the experience of possession is the supreme life experience as well. Daily behavior is directly and indirectly influenced by the powers; they are always there, ready to be called on for advice and guidance in every stress situation experienced by the horse. Dreams and visions play a major role within the culture, and their content is generally interpreted as containing messages from the powers. Before major trips or before undertaking some special task, a dream containing advice from the powers is frequently experienced; such advice is rigidly adhered to, and serves to orient and guide behavior. Meaning and direction are given to the life of the participating individual; as one leader put it, "being a Shango woman is my life."

Part IX

Developmental psychology

Chapter 24

The effect of rearing conditions
on behavior*

Harry F. Harlow and Margaret K. Harlow

A wealth of clinical evidence shows that human children who have never had adequate maternal care or who have been separated from adequate maternal care within some critical stage, suffer disturbance and delay or even irreparable damage in terms of subsequent personal-social development. The importance of maternal ministrations in the child's development is further supported by many clinical investigations and by some limited experimental data.

Personality malfunctions that have been attributed to maternal inadequacy include such syndromes as marasmus, hospitalism, infantile autism, feeble-mindedness, inadequate maternal responsiveness, and deviant or depressed heterosexuality. If these disorders are the results of maternal inadequacy, only research with human subjects can establish the conditions and kinds of maternal behavior that produce them. Unfortunately, experiments critical to the resolution of these problems cannot be done with human subjects. We cannot rear babies in illuminated black boxes during the first half-year, year, or two years of their lives. We cannot have mothers rear their children in isolation from other children and from adults for the first two, four, or eight years. We dare not have human children reared with either no mothers or inadequate mothers while providing them with maximal opportunity to interact with age-mates, either identically reared or differentially reared. Yet these are the kinds of experiments which are required if we are to assess the effects of maternal variables unconfounded with other experiential variables on the child's personal-social development.

Most clinical investigations have given primary attention to the effects of maternal privation, defined as infant separation after the infant has established profound, or at least adequate, maternal attachments. Relatively little attention has been given to the effects of the absence or inadequacy of opportunity for the child to interact with other children and to form adequate affectional pat-

---

*Reprinted with permission from *Bulletin of the Menninger Clinic* 26:213-224, copyright 1962 by the Menninger Foundation.

terns with and for them. We know that it is important for the child to form effective infant-mother affectional patterns, but it also is likely that he must form effective child-child affectional patterns if he is to attain normal personal-social, sexual, and parental patterns. Obviously these affectional systems are not independent. It is possible, but by no means a certainty, that at the human level, normal child-child affection requires previous affectional bonds between mother or mother-figure and child. It is certain that the mother plays an important role in the formation of peer affections by providing for and encouraging associations between infants or children, or by preventing or discouraging such associations. Human mothers may also markedly influence the nature and course of child-child relationships.

Psychoanalytic theory, which looks for temporal reduction and temporal primacy, will ascribe primary importance to the earliest causes and conditions whether or not these are of greatest importance. Initial traumas have a false clarity as causative agents since they are not confounded by preceding events, whereas the role of all subsequent events is confounded by the role of these events operating during previous experience. Yet primacy in time need not, and often should not, be equated with primacy in importance.

EFFECTS OF TOTAL SOCIAL DEPRIVATION ON MONKEYS

Six years ago we took two newborn rhesus monkeys, one male and one female, and subjected them to total social deprivation for the first two years of life. Each was placed in a solid, illuminated cage such that it never saw any other animal—monkey or human—even though it was tested for food responsiveness and learning by remote-control techniques. During isolation these monkeys adapted to solid food slowly and learned with great difficulty, but they were found to have normal weight and good coats when removed—there were no signs of marasmus. At the conclusion of the two years' isolation, they were tested for social responsiveness to each other and to normal monkeys smaller and younger than themselves. They did not respond to each other and either froze or huddled in a corner when abused by the younger animals. Placed together in a cage in a room with many caged monkeys, they showed withdrawal from this new external world, and in the more than two years they lived together, they remained abnormally frightened, showed minimal interaction, and engaged in no sex activities. In follow-up social tests at four years of age with smaller and weaker monkeys, they made no effort to defend themselves except for one brief episode with one of the pair, after which it curled into a ball and passively accepted abuse. The potential for social behaviors in these animals had apparently been obliterated.

We have preliminary, incomplete data on the effects of such total social deprivation confined to a six-month period and are obtaining other data on the effects of such deprivation over a twelve-month period. The results to date indicate severe but not complete withdrawal from external environmental stimulation. Repeated testing in our playroom situation reveals that one of these monkeys is almost totally unresponsive socially and the other only occasionally engages in brief, infantile-type social interactions. Normally, the playroom is a highly stimulating situation for monkeys. It is 8 feet high with 36 square feet of floor space, and it contains multiple stationary and mobile toys and tools, flying rings, a rotating wheel, an artificial tree, a wire-mesh climbing ramp, and a high, wide ledge, offering opportunities to explore and play in a three-dimensional world.

We also have data on eight monkeys subjected to total social isolation from other monkeys during the first 80 days of life. Although they neither saw nor contacted nor heard other monkeys, they did see and contact human experimenters, who removed them from their isolation boxes and tested them repeatedly on learning problems after the second week of life. A year later these animals appear to be normally responsive to external environmental stimulation and they are socially responsive to each other when tested in the playroom. This social responsiveness as measured by the appearance of increasingly complex play patterns has become qualitatively normal, but probably it is depressed somewhat quantitatively. Whether there will be subsequent effects on heterosexual and maternal behavior remains for future observation.

If we assume a rough developmental ratio of four to one for monkey to man, the results on these eight monkeys are not completely in accord with human clinical data, which at best are only roughly comparable to our experimental situation. Social isolation up to eight or ten months of age is reported to endanger or impair the personal-social development of human infants. It may be that the stimulation and handling of the monkeys in the learning experiments played a positive role in preparing them for subsequent exposure to a monkey environment, thus minimizing the isolation effects. It is also possible that the human infant is more susceptible than the monkey infant to damage from social isolation.

EFFECTS OF EARLY PARTIAL SOCIAL DEPRIVATION

We have data on various groups of monkeys raised from the day of their birth without their mothers and without any monkey companionship at least through the first half-year. One group of 56, now ranging in age from five to eight years, was raised in individual bare wire cages where they could see and hear other monkeys, but not touch them. A group of four was similarly housed for up to five years, but had access to a single wire surrogate[1] during the first half-year of life. A third group of over 100 monkeys was raised identically except for access to a cloth surrogate[2] or to both a cloth surrogate and a wire surrogate[1] during at least six months of the first year. Approximately half of these animals have been housed after six months or one year of age with another monkey of like age and like or unlike sex for part or all the time since.

Although there may be differences in the personal-social behaviors of the monkeys comprising these groups, we cannot be sure at the present time, and for this reason we group them together. Many members of all three groups have developed what appear to be abnormal behaviors, including sitting and staring fixedly into space, repetitive stereotyped circling movements about the cage, clasping the head in the hands and arms while engaging in rocking,

---

[1] A wire surrogate mother is a bare, welded wire cylindrical form surmounted by a wooden head with a crude face and supported semiupright in a wooden frame.

[2] A cloth surrogate differs from the wire surrogate in that the wire cylinder is cushioned with a sheathing of terrycloth.

autistic-type movements and intrapunitive responses of grasping a foot, hand, arm, or leg and chewing or tearing at it with the teeth to the point of injury.

The sex behavior of the six oldest wire-cage-raised monkeys was first measured by Mason in 1960 and compared with that of rhesus monkeys of equal age which had lived in the wild during most of the first year of life. All the wild-raised monkeys, male and female, showed normal sex behavior, characterized in the male by dorsoventral mounting, clasping the legs of the female by the feet, and holding the buttocks by the hands. The females in turn sexually presented themselves by elevating their buttocks and tails, lowering their heads, and frequently looking backward without threatening. No laboratory-raised male or female showed normal sex behavior. Attempted mounting by the male was random in regard to body part, and the most frequent pattern was grasping a side of the female's body and thrusting laterally. The female's patterns were totally disordered and often involved sitting down and staring aimlessly into space. Although none of these animals was sexually mature, heterosexual positioning in both male and female normally develops during the second year.

Attempt to breed the cage-raised monkeys approximately two years later also ended in complete failure. When the oldest wire-cage-raised females were between five and seven years of age and the oldest surrogate-raised females were between three and five years, repeated attempts were made to breed 11 of the wire-cage-raised females and four of the cloth-surrogate-raised females with highly selected males from our breeding colony. The females were placed in the large breeding cages during estrus, and if no fighting ensued within 15 minutes, they were left overnight. Eventually one wire-cage-raised female and three cloth-surrogate females became pregnant. Although observation did not reveal clear-cut differences in the behavior of these two groups, the differences in pregnancy approach significance in spite of—or possibly because of—the greater immaturity of the cloth-surrogate-raised females. Actually, no female, impregnated or not, demonstrated a normal pattern of sexual behavior. Many females tried to avoid the males; some actually threatened the males and would probably have been injured had our males not been carefully screened. When the males approached and positioned the females, the females usually collapsed and fell flat on the floor. Impregnation of the four females was achieved only through the patience, persistence, knowledgeability, and motor skill of the breeding males.

We have subsequently tested many wire-cage- and surrogate-mother-raised males and females with experienced breeding females and experienced breeding males, respectively, in a large 8-foot by 8-foot by 8-foot room especially designed for breeding studies. All the males have continued to show the disorganized and inappropriately oriented sexual responsiveness which we have already described, and no male has ever appropriately mounted our experienced and cooperative breeding-stock females, let alone achieved intromission.

With a single exception we have never seen normal, appropriate sexual posturing in our wire-cage- or surrogate-raised females. The females do not approach the males, nor do they groom or present. One cloth-surrogate-raised female was not impregnated throughout six mating sessions, and during this time she began to respond positively and appropriately to the males and eventually developed a normal, full-blown pattern of sexual presentation and sexual posturing during copulation.

EFFECTS OF MATERNAL CONDITIONS

Direct comparison of the effects of being raised by real monkey mothers and cloth-surrogate mothers on subsequent personal-social development has been measured by the use of our playpen test situation. In two playpen situations babies were housed with their real mothers, and in a third setup the babies were housed with cloth mothers. The playpen consists of large living cages, each housing a mother and an infant and adjoining a compartment of the playpen. A small opening in each living cage restrains the mother, but gives the infant continuous access to the adjoining playpen compartment. During two daily test sessions, each an hour in length, the screens between playpen compartments were raised, permitting the infant monkeys to interact as pairs during the first six months and as both pairs and groups of four during the second six months. Two experimenters independently observed and recorded the behavior exhibited during test sessions.

The infants raised by real monkey mothers were more socially responsive to each other than were the infants raised by the cloth surrogates. They showed a wider range of facial expressions, and, probably of paramount importance, they developed simple interactive play patterns earlier than the surrogate-raised monkeys and achieved a level of complex play patterns not achieved by the surrogate-raised monkeys during an 18-month test period.

All the male, mother-raised infants have at one time or another responded sexually toward the mother with pelvic thrusting and in at least two cases by dorsoventral mounting. In three cases pelvic thrusting to a female was observed before 50 days of age and in fourth case, before 100 days of age. Only two (one male and one female) cloth-surrogate-raised monkeys were observed to show pelvic thrusting to the surrogate, and this occurred initially at approximately 100 days of age. Frequency of this sexual play was much higher toward real mothers than toward surrogates. In both situations maximal frequency occurred at about five months and then declined, apparently being superseded by thrusting directed toward other infants.

Surrogate babies and mothered babies showed no significant differences in first-observed, infant-directed thrusting, but the actual mean score of the surrogate group was lower. The frequency of sexual play was higher for the real-mothered babies than for the surrogate babies. Finally, seven of eight mother-raised monkeys showed appropriate adult-form sex behaviors during the first 18 months, including ankle clasp by the males, whereas adult-oriented sex behavior was not observed in the cloth-surrogate-raised babies.

There is every reason to believe that normal mothering facilitates the development of heterosexual behavior in rhesus monkeys. This may be in part the result of direct contacts with the mother growing out of the intimate bonds between mother and child. One must not, however, underestimate the importance of the role which the real mother apparently plays, indirect though it is, in stimulating the infants to associate with other infants. This is accomplished from the third month on by discouraging the infant from constant clinging as it matures. From time to time the mother restrains the infant's approaches or cuffs it if it nips her or pulls her hair. The chastised infant seeks the companionship of other babies until the storm subsides—the other mothers by this time generally reject all but their own babies—and in the infant-infant interchanges, strong affectional bonds develop along with behaviors, sexual and nonsexual, appropriate to the sexes.

In the present study, as in all ordinary human situations, there is confounding in the roles played by the mother-infant affectional systems and the infant-infant and peer-peer affectional systems in determining later behavior. We expect to resolve this in part by raising two groups of monkey babies with real mothers, but denying them any opportunity to interact with other infants for six months in the one group and 12 months in the other before subjecting them to social testing.

Some information is supplied by another experiment involving eight rhesus babies raised on cloth-surrogate mothers, but tested 20 minutes a day in the playroom, which is a more stimulating environment than that afforded by the relatively cramped and bare confines of the play compartments of the playpen situation. These surrogate-mothered babies showed excellent and appropriately timed play behaviors and very early came to assume both sexual and nonsexual behaviors appropriate to males and females. The males threatened, the females did not; the males initiated rough-and-tumble play, but not the females. Males chased males and males chased females, but females practically never chased males and seldom chased females. By a year of age considerable appropriate male and female sex behavior had occurred, and full and complete copulation, other than insemination, was repeatedly observed in the two males and two females on which observations were continued during the second year of life.

It is obvious that we must not underestimate the importance and role of the infant-infant affectional system as a determiner of adolescent and adult adjustments. It is more than possible that this system is essential if the animal is to respond positively to sheer physical contact with a peer, and it is through the operation of this system, probably both in monkey and man, that sexual roles become identified and, usually, acceptable.

The role of the mother in the formation of the adult personality is obviously important, but the exact mechanics are open for experimentation. The most tender and intimate associations occur at a stage in which the monkey infant and human infant can to a considerable extent be molded. Monkey and human mother both have the obligation of gradually dissolving the intense physical bonds which characterize the early mother-child relationship. For the monkey mother it is easy and natural—when the infant becomes mature enough and strong enough to become bothersome, she rejects or punishes it and the baby retreats for a time. Subsequently, she welcomes the baby back. Independence is gradually established. For the human mother, with her more complicated motivational systems and her complex culture, it may be difficult to achieve this gradual separation. The overprotective mother is a well-known clinical extreme in the human problem of weaning the infant and child emotionally. Probably the surrogate monkey mother is a parallel of the overprotective human mother, failing usually to equal the normal mother in rearing socially and sexually adjusted monkeys because, at least in part, she is ever available to provide comfort and security. She never discourages contact and thereby never encourages independence in her infant and affectional relationships with other infants and children. The normal state of complete dependency necessary in early infancy is prolonged until it hinders normal personal-social development.

As we have already pointed out, four of our laboratory-raised females never had real mothers of their own, one being raised in a bare wire cage and three with cloth surrogates. The first week after the birth of the baby to the wire-cage-raised female, the mother sat fixedly at one side of the cage staring into space, almost unaware of her infant or of human beings, even when they barked at and threatened the baby. There was no sign of maternal responses, and when the infant approached and attempted contact, the mother rebuffed it, often with vigor. . . .

The next two unmothered mothers constantly rebuffed the approaches of their infants, but, in addition, frequently engaged in cruel and unprovoked attacks. They struck and beat their babies, mouthed them roughly, and pushed their faces into the wire-mesh floor. These attacks seemed to be exaggerated in the presence of human beings, and for this reason all formal testing was abandoned for three days for the third unmothered mother because we feared for the life of the infant. The fourth unmothered mother ignored and rejected her infant but did not exhibit excessive cruelty.

In strong contrast to the frailty of the maternal affectional system was the vigor and persistence of the infants' bondage to the mother—time after time, hour after hour, the infants returned, contacted, and clasped the mother in spite of being hit, kicked, and scraped unceremoniously off the mother's body. . . . The physical punishment which these infants took or sought for the privilege of brief contact even to the back or side of the mother's body testified to the fact that, even in infants, attachment to the mother may be prepotent over pain and suffering. One could not help but be reminded of children, removed from indifferent or cruel, indigent, and alcoholic parents, whose primary insistent wish is to return home.

The degree to which monkey data are generalizable to the human being will remain an unsolved dilemma. Nevertheless, we are so struck by the many apparent analogies that we are tempted to say the monkey experiments give us faith in the human clinical observations.

SUMMARY

Starting on the first day of life, infant rhesus monkeys have been reared in a variety of situations, including total isolation; partial isolation, either in individual bare wire cages in a colony room for two years or longer, or in individual wire cages with access to one or two mother surrogates for at least the first six months; and in situations with real or surrogate mothers plus contact with other infants for the first year or two of life.

Total isolation for two years resulted in failure to display social or sexual behavior in the next two years, spent in a joint living cage. Results on six months of such isolation are still being gathered and suggest severe, but not complete, social deficits. Only mild effects have been observed thus far in monkeys isolated through the first 80 days of life.

Partial isolation has produced behavioral aberrations in many monkeys and sexual inadequacy in all males and in all but one female. Four females were impregnated, in spite of inadequate posturing, and proved to be completely inadequate mothers.

Infants raised by live mothers were more advanced in social and sexual behavior than infants raised by surrogate mothers in a controlled playpen situation. The mother's role is not entirely clear, however, because in a more stimulating playroom situation, surrogate-mothered babies have shown normal social and sexual behavior.

Over all, it appears that the longer and the more complete the social deprivation, the more devastating are the behavioral effects. Further research is needed to evaluate the relative contributions of live mothers and infant companions to later adjustment.

Chapter 25

The ape in our house*

Cathy Hayes

Probably no other psychologists have employed the case study approach in a manner as intriguing as have the Hayeses, who attempted to provide an environment that was as nearly "human" as possible for a baby chimpanzee in order to investigate the effect of this type of enriched experience on the animal's development.

August 28, 1950, was Viki's third birthday. A detailed account of that day may serve as a summary of the troubles and triumphs of Viki's daily life.

At 8:00 A.M. Keith unlatched her crib and raised the top. Out sprang Viki, like a large furry ball. She dashed to the bathroom and onto the diaper-changing board. Keith unpinned her and she leaped to her potty, just in time.

Next Keith gave Viki her toothbrush and she brushed her teeth, making little pleasure barks over the appetizing tooth powder. Finally, she washed her face. Most of it received only a swipe of the cloth, but she stood on the rim of the washbasin and peered into the mirror, to give her eyebrow ridges an exaggerated share of attention. Her toilet completed, she was put into her room until breakfast was ready.

At 8:30 A.M. I came downstairs. Viki greeted me with a soft "uh uh uh uh" through her screen door. She watched me getting breakfast with mounting interest, until, by the time I set the tray on the coffee table, she was hopping up and down and banging on her door.

I opened it and out she burst with a rush. She bounded to the top of the radio, ricocheted off the couch and onto the desk, where she stood hooting her hello to the new day.

I held out a glass of orange juice and she took it daintily between her thumb and forefinger. I poured the coffee and handed a cup to Keith. Viki put down her glass, which was now empty, climbed to the arm of Keith's chair, said "Cup!" and then helped herself. I gave her a cup of coffee of her own. Drinking all the while, she wandered about the room, over chair rungs,

---

*From *The Ape in Our House,* Chapter 23, copyright © 1951 by Catherine Hayes, reprinted by permission of McIntosh & Otis, Inc., New York.

under tables, up and down door jambs. When her cup was empty, she asked me for a refill by holding the cup under the spout of the coffee pot and saying, "Mama!" and then, "Cup!"

She carried her second cup of coffee to the desk, where she lay on one elbow and blew at her coffee to cool it. I passed a plate of doughnuts. Viki took one in each hand and dunked them.

At 9:00 A.M. the phone rang. While Keith talked, Viki stood on the table, one hand on his shoulder, glancing first at him and then at the phone. As he finished his conversation and started to hang up, she claimed the receiver and put it to her ear. She listened for a minute with a faraway look in her eyes. Then she made a Bronx cheer and hung up.

Jumping lightly from the table, she picked up her red wooden box and put it over her head. Since it covers her whole face, this box makes good blindman's buff equipment. She ambled about the room, bumping into things and chuckling. Unfortunately, she bumped into her juice glass, and it fell to the floor with a crash.

She snatched the box from her head and clung to me, looking shamefaced. I put her into her room while I gathered up the broken glass, and in the confusion, Keith escaped to the quiet of the Laboratory.

At 9:15 A.M. Viki and I went to the garage to do the washing. She stood beside the tub, watching my every movement, and "helping" by dousing the clothes up and down, and rubbing them on the washboard. But when she lifted them high in the air to suck out the soapy water, I cried, "No! No!" She hooted at me and climbed up the wall. Straddling a rafter, she lay silently, staring at me.

When I started the rinsing process, she scrambled down. She is a real help here, since her strong hands can wring the laundry drier than mine are able to. However, when we had finished wringing, and I was ready to hang up the clothes, she wiped her sandy feet on them. "Oh, Viki, look what you've done!" I wailed, apparently sounding more distressed than I had intended, for she put her arms around me and kissed me thoroughly.

Then she ran off, and returned a second later with the spray gun. She took the cap off, held the sprayer under the faucet to fill it with water, screwed the cap back on, and sprayed the garage floor.

By 10:00 A.M. we were finished with the washing, and went inside to do our housework. To cheer us along, I turned on the radio. As I squatted before the dial, Viki jumped to the top of the cabinet, placed her hands on my head, and leapfrogged over me. When I started to get up, she pushed me down again, so that she could have one more leap. Then, as I walked away, she tuned out the station, and when I stooped down to adjust it, she took still another jump.

Viki helped me carry the trash to the garbage pit for burning, she pushed a dust mop around her own room, and when I started to wash her bed and its waterproof mattress, she took the cloth away from me, and climbed in to do the job right. Finally she performed her one regular chore: she washed the bathroom mirror and soap dish, rubbing so vigorously that the paper toweling disintegrated.

At 11:00 A.M. it was time for Viki to "go to school." As I took the equipment from the hall cabinet, she grinned and guided me to our work table with eager little barks.

First we worked on our six-piece jigsaw puzzle. Viki assembled it correctly without much trouble.

Next I put paper and crayons before her. She scribbled enthusiastically enough, but made no effort to copy my marks, although she had been imitating my housework all morning. She paid no attention either when I drew a border and told her to keep her scribble inside of the line. (I'm sure that she could do these things, if she knew what I wanted, but I cannot figure out how to get this idea across to her. It would be so simple with language! Her little friend Chrissie recently visited her older brother's school. There the children taunted her about being "too little to stay inside the line." Chrissie worked feverishly until she had mastered the idea.)

Next I gave Viki some tasks aimed at improving her dexterity. At "school" on her third birthday she built towers and bridges of tiny dice. She also threaded a needle, worked a spring paper clip, and scribbled with a pencil the size of a match in a miniature notebook.

12:00 noon was Viki's lunchtime. (She now eats breakfast and dinner with us, as a child would, but at lunch she is still working for food.) On her third birthday, we built matching towers. She imitated my selection of blocks without error. When instead of a tower I built a train of three dissimilar blocks, she selected three matching ones from the jumble before her and assembled them in the same order as mine. Finally I built a three-block tower without letting her see my construction work. When I showed it to her, she immediately selected the correct blocks, and stacked them to match my finished model.

At 12:15 P.M. we were ready to go out into the yard. (This play space now serves its purpose well, since Viki seems to have given up her ambition to break out of The Fence—at least temporarily.) Viki made a dash for her swing, which we have recently suspended from the only tree in the yard. She chinned herself on the elevated bar, and climbed the ropes; then she came to me, and taking me by the hand, led me to it. There she climbed to the bar and sat waiting to be pushed.

After I had pushed her for a while, she ran to a nearby lawn chair and climbed up on it. She waited expectantly, eight feet from the swing, until I fulfilled my part of this popular game by swinging the bar toward her. She leaped off into space, and with perfect timing grabbed the approaching bar and flew through the air on it.

Bored with the swing, Viki went to the sandbox. The first thing she did was to "plant" a weed. I was very impressed with the way she carefully pressed the sand around it until I remembered that she had recently seen Mrs. Clarke planting some young seedlings.

Now Viki began an entirely new activity. Bending over from the waist, she made an impression of her hand in the sand, and then deepened the print with her finger. She made a print of her foot, too, and while so doing she seemed to notice for the first time that her toes wiggle all as one while her fingers can move independently. She plunked down on the sand and studied this phenomenon. She found that she could grasp the toes and move one at a time, but on their own, they would act only as a team. But this seemed to be pretty deep stuff for a three-year-old chimpanzee; she jumped up from the sand all of a sudden, and raced madly around the yard.

She was interrupted by a car driving up to Mrs. Clarke's house. She sat on the edge of her sandbox, clapping her hands and calling to the people. They waved to her, but did not come over. She went back to the sand. Scooping up a handful, she stirred it into the rain water which had collected in her coaster. She then brought a handful of this mixture and lovingly patted it onto the top of my head. We hurried indoors.

While I cleaned the mud out of my hair, Viki washed her hands vigorously.

At 1:00 P.M. we returned to the yard to play with balloons. (Viki is very destructive of rubber balls. Therefore, in the interests of economy and habit formation, I am giving her several balloons every day. She plays with them as she does with balls, but when she bites a balloon, she loses her gay and lively companion in one bang. Perhaps in time she will thus be shown what we cannot tell her, and we can resume our various games with the more expensive balls.)

On her birthday, when Viki had broken the last of the balloons, she looked forlorn. Picking up the fragments of one, she put the mouthpiece to my lips. I showed her that it was no good, and tossed it away. It landed on the wires of The Fence. Viki approached it cautiously. Then she took my hand and led me to the place. She tried to make me touch the balloon, although she herself avoided The Fence.

At 1:30 P.M. I brought out the typewriter to bring Viki's diary up to date. She immediately planted herself between me and the machine. It was a very hot day, but I have grown used to her furry little self against me. I did not even mind when she bit hunks out of my carbon paper; but when she began snatching each type arm as it flew up, I chased her away. She hooted at me sassily and took it out on her sand bucket. Laying it on its side, she stomped it flat. Then, with a grin, she came back to me, to help some more with the typing.

By 2:30 P.M. I had finished the notes and lay back in a lawn chair to rest. Viki sat on the arm of my chair and we gazed out toward the highway together. Suddenly she startled and said, "Boo!"

Following her gaze, I saw that beyond the Grove, across the road, in the middle of the town's cemetery, a golden spot of sunshine was falling through a gap in the overcast sky. As we watched, the break in the cloud came toward us, leaving the cemetery clearing a black hole, while the trees between the clearing and the road were suddenly a shining curtain of Spanish moss. Next the road became a silver ribbon with the trees as a somber backdrop. Viki's "boo" became higher, almost shrill. The sunny spot came slowly toward us, and one by one the pecan trees were flecked with sunshine. Viki's arm gently circled my neck, and when a second later we were warmed by the dazzling sun, her "boo" had dropped to an awestruck murmur.

At 3:00 P.M. we took our bath. Viki submitted bravely to the soaping process, but her real pleasure came afterward, as she played in the water and rinsed herself with the spray.

At 3:30 P.M. we went to Viki's room to play. I proposed our old game "Go get the dog!" without noticing that the toy was not in sight. Nevertheless she went in search of it. For five busy minutes, she dug through her box of blocks, looked under the couch, and even under the rug. Finally, she emerged dusty and triumphant from behind her crib, holding up her toy dog.

After a session of this game, I tried to interest her in block construction. She ignored me until I incorporated some toy cars into my elevated highway structure. Then she pushed the cars back and forth for about ten minutes.

At 4:00 P.M. I told Viki that she must play by herself now, while I prepared the birthday cake and the dinner. As I closed her screen door, she galloped off to her mirror, where she sat examining her teeth and making play sounds like "ahhh," "tsk," and "kkkkkk."

Next I heard her pounding at her toy workbench, where she has mastered the hammer and nail, the claw hammer, the screw driver, and the nut and bolt. (The other toys available to her at all times in her room include a tricycle, stuffed animals, a toy telephone, blocks, and various educational toys. Only these are rugged enough to withstand her vigorous play. Things like clay, painting and sewing equipment, jigsaw puzzles, and the plastic animals of her toy farm are given to her only when we can observe and supervise her play.)

At 4:15 P.M. I went to her room again, to let her come and beat the cake batter, one of her favorite chores. But I found her asleep on top of her crib, lying on her stomach, with the dog clutched in her arms. (Short naps before or after dinner are her only daytime sleeping.)

I glanced about her room and noticed an odd structure in one corner. She had built a tall arch with two blocks on each side and a fifth block across the top. Later, we saw her making sounds into her toy phone and then holding it toward this structure. Keith hypothesized that she was hanging up the phone. I thought it might be her "baby" whom she was letting "listen." But she never told us what it really was.

At 5:00 P.M. I heard a commotion in Viki's room. She was pounding at the windows, and hooting. Papa was home!

I let her out and she jumped up and down as he opened the door. Then, in a wink, she was onto his shoulders and ready for a piggyback ride.

When I called them to the table, Viki slipped into her chair. She drank some milk, ate a forkful of asparagus, bit the buttered top off her roll, and then ran off, munching on a frankfurter. She ran to her room, where she got her dog, placed it upon her shoulders, and paraded past us—giving it a piggyback ride.

When Keith and I pushed back our chairs to leave the table, Viki leaped to her place and polished off her plate quickly.

6:00 P.M. Enter the birthday cake! Viki went wild at the sight of it, jumping around the room and sputtering food barks. (To her this was probably just another cake—as this whole day had lacked special significance. On the other hand, Chrissie had anticipated her recent third birthday for weeks. Chrissie can also give a rather explicit account of what the birthday celebrates. Viki may never know about birth until she herself witnesses it or experiences it.)

By 6:30 P.M. Viki was full of cake. She gently returned her empty plate to the coffee table and went to the telephone. She held the receiver to her ear for a while, and then frantically dialed several numbers. (Her dialing is completely random, but occasionally she does call an actual number.) Suddenly, now, she stopped dialing and said "Boo!" At the same time we heard a faraway voice calling, "Hello! Hello!" I murmured apologies and hung up.

By 7:00 P.M. I had cleared away the dishes and was ready for the evening's entertainment. I gathered up a supply of clean diapers and Viki's blanket. Viki began making pleasure barks of anticipation. And when Keith asked, "Viki, do you want to go to the show?" she raced to the door, all gay and ready to go. In the car she bounded from the front seat, to the back seat, to the place behind the wheel, which she energetically turned back and forth.

At the drive-in theater, she made excited little yelps as her beloved public peeked in the windows and laughed at her antics. The little boy in the next car saw her sitting a-straddle my open window and insisted that he be allowed to sit in the window of his car. His father complied with small enthusiasm.

First came the color cartoon, always fascinating, and then a newsreel, which featured a gymnastic contest. Viki commented freely on the performance of the athletes who did many of her best tricks.

When the main feature started, she turned her attention to the adjacent cars. To our right were two middle-aged ladies who stared at her silently. She found the car on the left more rewarding. This carful of children and grownups whispered "Psst!" to get her attention. She obliged by blowing spit bubbles at them.

At 8:00 P.M. the screen resounded with a duel, complete with clashing swords. Viki attended carefully to this part. When the hero raised a glass of wine, to toast his fallen foe, Viki said, "Cup!" I decided that it was time for refreshments.

At the refreshment stand, a little girl, about Viki's age, told me a very unlikely story: "I saw a little furry baby," she said. "Back there, the man had a furry baby in a pink dress."

Her mother looked embarrassed and said, "As we passed one of the cars, she saw a monkey inside and she was simply fascinated. Calls it a 'furry baby.' I can't imagine why she singled you out to tell this tale to. I'm sorry."

"Guess I look like the gullible type," I said.

Returning to the car, I found Keith in a stew. "Will you please hold her a minute? I'm trying to light a cigarette and she keeps blowing out my lighter."

Viki drank her soda pop, helping herself to handfuls of popcorn from our family box. Then she went to the back seat and became very quiet.

At 8:30 P.M. I glanced back, expecting to see her asleep. Instead, she was at the window, making faces. Her audience was five little children who sat crosslegged on the ground, silent as Indians as they looked at her.

Now Viki climbed into my lap and put my hand on her ribs. I tickled her. She chuckled. I stopped, and she put my hand back on her ribs, pushing it suggestively until I tickled some more. Then, all of a sudden, she was asleep.

At 9:30 P.M. we prepared to leave. The intermission lights had gone on, causing Viki to jump up and look about. Now, for the first time, the two ladies in the car to our right spoke, "She's very beautiful, isn't she?"

I agreed that by chimpanzee standards, she is indeed a fine specimen. "But her eyes!" one of the women said, "Those eyes would be beautiful in any species."

It was 10:30 P.M. when we arrived home, and Viki was too sleepy to wait for her bedtime cocoa. She curled up on the couch and closed her eyes. When I asked, "Don't you want to say goodnight to Papa?" she flipped her hand a few times and let it fall to her side. I picked her up then, and took her to her crib.

Viki's third birthday was a very ordinary day in her life, and her activities were quite typical of this period. We have seen that, except for language, she is still quite similar in abilities to the child of this age. We realize, however, that her interests are a little different, more athletic, less verbal.

We have seen also that the advantage of language is much more than a mere chattering of words. Even at this early age of three years, the child, through language, is gaining more information, inspiration, and direction from adults than we could hope to give Viki.

We may consider intelligence as made up of three components:

1. The individual is born with a certain amount of *innate capacity,* and our experiment establishes this one fact at least: Until three years of age, the only obvious and important deficit in the ape's innate intelligence, as compared with man's, is a missing facility for using and understanding language.

2. The *personal experience* component of intelligence is what the individual learns for himself, motor and manipulatory skills, basic perceptions, social interplay, the elementary stunts of getting along in our civilized jungle. Viki has done very well in this respect. Exposed to the life of a child, she has absorbed about as much, through personal experience alone, as a child could.

3. But there is a third element of intelligence—*group intelligence.* Through language, the individual at a very early age begins to acquire knowledge secondhand from teachers, books, and daily communication with other people, infinitely more knowledge than he could ever gain through personal experience. Language conveys not only information, but ideals, traditions, and abstract philosophy. It fosters that cumulative thing—invention. It enables the mechanic and the mathematician to make use of each other's skills. And this has been going on for thousands of years in man.

This aspect of our intellectual life is so characteristic of our species that we take it very much for granted, and seldom appreciate how mentally ineffective each of us would be if we had to function strictly as individuals. Much has been made of the human brain's ability to cope with any change in our environment. But no one man, isolated from birth, could do this very well. It is man's collective brain, working over the centuries, which has made us increasingly versatile. It is man's unique ability to communicate knowledge which has led to that peculiarly human product, civilization.

Since apes do not acquire language to any significant extent—not even privileged apes like Viki, who are coached intensively on it, and who could profit a great deal by it—it seems unlikely that apes ever have or ever will develop a civilization.

Our Viki has tapped our cultural store of knowledge to an impressive degree, but the child of three has greater access to it. Year by year, Viki will continue to learn as much as we can communicate to her, but without language, communication will be difficult.

Upon man's innate capacity for using language depends not only the growth of civilization, but perhaps its very survival. For instance, if my lamp were to go out at this moment, I would first of all replace the bulb. If my lamp remained dark, but the other lamps in the room were on, I would examine the switch or the socket. If I saw any irregularities, I would repair them—after consulting a more informed human or a book, in all probability, for while I am very ignorant personally, almost every accomplishment of the human race is available to me in the world's massive accumulation of literature.

If all the lights in the room went out, I would replace a fuse, and if this did not remedy the matter, I would assume the trouble to be a power failure. The idea of trouble-shooting in a power plant appalls me, but if it suddenly became my responsibility, I'm sure I could find some books which would tell me what to do.

Now what would happen if the world were to be populated only by apes, each as educated as Viki is likely to be by adulthood? What would Viki do if her lamp went out? Being a bulb-snatcher of long standing, she might (accidentally or with some insight) remove a defective bulb and replace it with a sound one. This is as far as her training now goes. We could show her how to replace a fuse, by imitation, or how to repair a plug, or a socket, or a switch. We might even set up an elaborate training program, showing her how to test all these trouble spots in a logical order. But there is not time enough to teach her, in this way, even a small portion of what the child is simply *told*.

And some things cannot be communicated by any amount of demonstration or personal experience. If the trouble with Viki's light lay in the power plant, there would be no hope of her resolving it. How could she be given the idea of electricity, of its being generated, and coming from a distant place? Left in the hands of the most supereducated apes imaginable, our civilization would fall to pieces. One by one, the lights of the world would go out.

Chapter 26

The elimination of tantrum behavior by extinction procedures*

Carl D. Williams

Many of the behavior problems exhibited by young children have developed because their parents have unknowingly trained them to behave in a manner that the parents view as produced by stubbornness, willfulness, etc. on the part of the child. By determining what type of "payoff" is maintaining an undesirable pattern of behavior and by taking steps to ensure that this payoff is never forthcoming, the source of a great many behavior problems may be shown to lie not within the child himself, but within the child's experience.

This paper reports the successful treatment of tyrant-like tantrum behavior in a male child by the removal of reinforcement. The subject (S) was approximately 21 months old. He had been seriously ill much of the first 18 months of his life. His health then improved considerably, and he gained weight and vigor.

S now demanded the special care and attention that had been given him over the many critical months. He enforced some of his wishes, especially at bedtime, by unleashing tantrum behavior to control the actions of his parents.

The parents and an aunt took turns in putting him to bed both at night and for S's afternoon nap. If the parent left the bedroom after putting S in his bed, S would scream and fuss until the parent returned to the room. As a result, the parent was unable to leave the bedroom until after S went to sleep. If the parent began to read while in the bedroom, S would cry until the reading material was put down. The parents felt that S enjoyed his control over them and that he fought off going to sleep as long as he could. In any event, a parent was spending from one-half to two hours each bedtime just waiting in the bedroom until S went to sleep.

Following medical reassurance regarding S's physical condition, it was de-

*From *Journal of Abnormal and Social Psychology* 59:269, 1959. Reprinted by permission of the author and American Psychological Association.

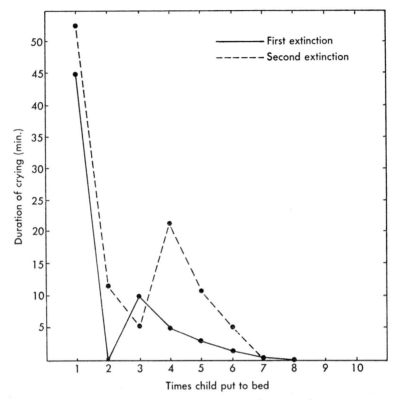

Fig. 1. Length of crying in two extinction series as a function of successive occasions of being put to bed.

cided to remove the reinforcement of this tyrant-like tantrum behavior. Consistent with the learning principle that, in general, behavior that is not reinforced will be extinguished, a parent or the aunt put *S* to bed in a leisurely and relaxed fashion. After bedtime pleasantries, the parent left the bedroom and closed the door. *S* screamed and raged, but the parent did not re-enter the room. The duration of screaming and crying was obtained from the time the door was closed.

The results are shown in Fig. 1. It can be seen that *S* continued screaming for 45 min. the first time he was put to bed in the first extinction series. *S* did not cry at all the second time he was put to bed. This is perhaps attributable to his fatigue from the crying of Occasion 1. By the tenth occasion, *S* no longer whimpered, fussed, or cried when the parent left the room. Rather, he smiled as they left. The parents felt that he made happy sounds until he dropped off to sleep.

About a week later, *S* screamed and fussed after the aunt put him to bed, probably reflecting spontaneous recovery of the tantrum behavior. The aunt then reinforced the tantrum behavior by returning to *S*'s bedroom and remaining there until he went to sleep. It was then necessary to extinguish this behavior a second time.

Fig. 1 shows that the second extinction curve is similar to the first. Both curves are generally similar to extinction curves obtained with subhuman subjects. The second extinction series reached zero by the ninth occasion. No further tantrums at bedtime were reported during the next two years.

It should be emphasized that the treatment in this case did not involve aversive punishment. All that was done was to remove the reinforcement. Extinction of the tyrant-like tantrum behavior then occurred.

No unfortunate side- or aftereffects of this treatment were observed. At three and three-quarters years of age, *S* appeared to be a friendly, expressive, outgoing child.

Part X

Frustration and conflict

Chapter 27

What is a neurosis?*

John Dollard and Neal Miller

Neurotic misery is real—not imaginary. Observers, not understanding the neurotic conflict, often belittle the suffering of neurotics and confuse neurosis with malingering. Neurotic habits are forced upon an individual by peculiar conditions of life and are not cheap attempts to escape duty and responsibility. In most cases the misery is attested by many specific complaints. These complaints or symptoms differ with each category of neurosis but sleeplessness, restlessness, irritability, sexual inhibitions, distaste for life, lack of clear personal goals, phobias, headaches, and irrational fears are among the more common ones.

At times the depth of the misery of the neurotic is concealed by his symptoms. Only when they are withdrawn does his true anguish appear. Occasionally the misery will be private, not easily visible to outside observers because friends and relatives are ringed around the neurotic person and prevent observation of his pain. In still other cases, the neurotic person is miserable but apathetic. He has lost even the hope that complaining and attracting attention will be helpful. However this may be, *if the neurotic takes the usual risks of life* he is miserable. He suffers if he attempts to love, marry, and be a parent. He fails if he tries to work responsibly and independently. His social relations tend to be invaded by peculiar demands and conditions. Neurotic misery is thus often masked by the protective conditions of life (as in childhood) and appears only when the individual has to "go it on his own."

Conflict produces misery. Suffering so intense as that shown by neurotics must have powerful causes, and it does. The neurotic is miserable because he is in conflict. As a usual thing two or more strong drives are operating in him and producing incompatible responses. Strongly driven to approach and as strongly to flee, he is not able to act to reduce either of the conflicting drives. These drives therefore remain dammed up, active, and nagging.

Where such a drive conflict is conscious there is no problem in convincing anyone why it should produce misery. If we picture a very hungry man confronting food which he knows to be poisoned, we can understand that he is driven on the one hand by hunger and on the other by fear. He oscillates at some distance from the tempting food, fearing to grasp but unable to leave.

Everyone understands immediately the turmoil produced by such a conflict of hunger and fear.

Many people remember from their adolescence the tension of a strong sex conflict. Primary sex responses heightened by imaginative elaboration are met by intense fear. Though usually not allowed to talk about such matters, children sometimes can, and the misery they reveal is one of the most serious prices exacted of adolescents in our culture. That this conflict is acquired and not innate was shown by Margaret Mead in her brilliant book, "Coming of Age in Samoa" (1928). It is also agonizingly depicted in a novel by Vardis Fisher (1932).

Our third example of conscious conflict shows anger pitted against fear. In the early part of the war, an officer, newly commissioned from civilian life and without the habits of the professional soldier, was sent to an Army post. There he met a superior officer who decided to make an example of some minor mistake. The ranking officer lectured and berated the subordinate, refusing to let him speak and explain his behavior. He made him stand at attention against the wall for half an hour while this lecture was going on. The new-made officer quaked in fearful conflict. He detected the sadistic satisfaction which his superior got in dressing him down. He had never so much wanted to kill anyone. On the other hand, the junior officer felt the strong pressure of his own conscience to be a competent soldier and some real fear about what the consequence of assault might be. We met him shortly after this episode, and he still shook with rage when he described the experience. There was no doubt in his mind but that bearing strong, conflicting drives is one of the most severe causes of misery.

Repression causes stupidity. In each of the above cases, however, the individual could eventually solve his conflict. The hungry man could find nourishing food; the sex-tortured adolescent could eventually marry; the new officer could and did avoid his punishing superior.

With the neurotic this is not the case. He is not able to solve his conflict even with the passage of time. Though obviously intelligent in some ways, he is stupid in-so-far as his neurotic conflict is concerned. This stupidity is not an over-all affair, however. It is really a stupid area in the mind of a person who is quite intelligent in other respects. For some reason he cannot use his head on his neurotic conflicts.

Though the neurotic is sure he is miserable and is vocal about his symptoms, he is vague about what it is within him that could produce such painful effects. The fact that the neurotic cannot describe his own conflicts has been the source of great confusion in dealing with him either in terms of scientific theory or in terms of clinical practice. Nor can the therapist immediately spot these areas of stupidity. Only after extensive study of the patient's life can the areas of repression be clearly identified. Then the surprising fact emerges that the competing drives which afflict the neurotic person are not labeled. He has no language to describe the conflicting forces within him.

Without language and adequate labeling the higher mental processes cannot function. When these processes are knocked out by repression, the person cannot guide himself by mental means to a resolution of his conflict. Since the neurotic cannot help himself, he must have the help of others if he is to be helped at all—though millions today live out their lives in strong neurotic pain and never get help. The neurotic, therefore, is, or appears to be, stupid because he is unable to use his mind in dealing with certain of his problems. He feels that someone should help him, but he does not know how to ask for help since he does not know what his problem is. He may feel aggrieved that he is suffering but he cannot explain his case.

Symptoms slightly reduce conflict. Although in many ways superficial, the symptoms of the neurotic are the most obvious aspect of his problems. These are what the patient is familiar with and feels he should be rid of. The phobias, inhibitions, avoidances, compulsions, rationalizations, and psychosomatic symptoms of the neurotic are experienced as a nuisance by him and by all who have to deal with him. The symptoms cannot be integrated into the texture of sensible social relations. The patient, however, believes that the symptoms *are* his disorder. It is these he wishes to be rid of and, not knowing that a serious conflict underlies them, he would like to confine the therapeutic discussion to getting rid of the symptoms.

The symptoms do not solve the basic conflict in which the neurotic person is plunged, but they mitigate it. They are responses which tend to reduce the conflict, and in part they succeed. When a successful symptom occurs it is reinforced because it reduces neurotic misery. The symptom is thus learned as a habit. One very common function of symptoms is to keep the neurotic person away from those stimuli which would activate and intensify his neurotic conflict. Thus, the combat pilot with a harrowing military disaster behind him may "walk away" from the sight of any airplane. As he walks toward the plane his anxiety goes up; as he walks away it goes down. "Walking away" is thus reinforced. It is this phobic walking away which constitutes his symptom. If the whole situation is not understood, such behavior seems bizarre to the casual witness.

THE CASE OF MRS. A.

We are presenting the facts about Mrs. A. for two reasons: (1) as background material on a case from which we will draw many concrete examples throughout the book; (2) as a set of facts from which we can illustrate the relationships between misery and conflict, stupidity and repression, symptoms and reinforcement. The reader will understand, of course, that the sole function of this case material is to give a clear exposition of principles by means of concrete illustrations; it is *not* presented as evidence or proof.

The facts. Mrs. A was an unusually pretty twenty-three-year-old married woman. Her husband worked in the offices of an insurance company. When she came to the therapist she was exceedingly upset. She had a number of fears. One of the strongest of these was that her heart would stop beating if she did not concentrate on counting the beats.

The therapist, who saw Mrs. A twice a week over a three-month period, took careful notes. The life-history data that we present were pieced together from the patient's statements during a total of 26 hours. The scope of the material is necessarily limited by the brevity of the treatment. The treatment had to end when a change in the husband's work forced her to move to another city.

Her first neurotic symptoms had appeared five months before she came to the psychiatrist. While she was shopping in a New York store, she felt faint and became afraid that something would happen to her and "no one would know where I was." She telephoned her husband's office and asked him to come and get her. Thereafter she was afraid to go out alone. Shortly after this time, she talked with an aunt who had a neurotic fear of heart trouble. After a conversation with this aunt, Mrs. A's fears changed from a fear of fainting to a concern about her heart.

Mrs. A. was an orphan, born of unknown parents in a city in the upper South. She spent the first few months of life in an orphanage, then was placed in a foster home, where she lived, except for a year when she was doing war work in Washington, until her marriage at the age of twenty.

The foster parents belonged to the working class, had three children of their own, two girls and a boy, all of them older than the patient. The foster mother, who dominated the family, was cruel, strict, and miserly toward all the children. She had a coarse and vulgar demeanor, swore continually, and punished the foster child for the least offense. Mrs. A. recalls: "She whipped me all the time—whether I'd done anything or not."

The foster mother had imposed a very repressive sex training on the patient, making her feel that sex was dirty and wrong. Moreover, the foster mother never let the patient think independently. She discouraged the patient's striving for an education, taking her out of school at sixteen when the family could have afforded to let her go on.

Despite the repressive sex training she received, Mrs. A. had developed strong sexual appetites. In early childhood she had overheard parental intercourse, had masturbated, and had witnessed animal copulation. When she was ten or twelve, her foster brother seduced her. During the years before her marriage a dozen men tried to seduce her and most of them succeeded.

Nevertheless, sex was to her a dirty, loathsome thing that was painful for her to discuss or think about. She found sexual relations with her husband disgusting and was morbidly shy in her relations with him.

The patient had met her husband-to-be while she was working as a typist in Washington during the war. He was an Army officer and a college graduate. Her beauty enabled the patient to make a marriage that improved her social position; her husband's family were middle-class people. At the time of treatment Mrs. A. had not yet learned all the habits of middle-class life. She was still somewhat awkward about entertaining or being entertained and made glaring errors in grammar and pronunciation. She was dominated, socially subordinated, and partly rejected by her husband's family.

When they were first married, Mr. and Mrs. A. lived with his parents in a small town north of New York City and commuted to the city for work. Mrs. A. had an office job there. Later, they were able to get an apartment in New York, but they stayed with the in-laws every week end. Although she described her mother-in-law in glowing terms at the beginning of treatment, Mrs. A. later came to express considerable hostility toward her.

When she came to the psychiatrist, Mrs. A. was in great distress. She had to pay continual attention to her heart lest it stop beating. She lived under a burden of vague anxiety and had a number of specific phobias that prevented her from enjoying many of the normal pleasures of her life, such as going to the movies. She felt helpless to cope with her problems. Her constant complaints had tired out and alienated her friends. Her husband was fed up with her troubles and had threatened to divorce her. She could not get along with her foster mother and her mother-in-law had rejected her. She had no one left to talk to. She was hurt, baffled, and terrified by the thought that she might be going crazy.

Analysis in terms of conflict, repression, reinforcement

We have described Mrs. A. as of the moment when she came to treatment. The analysis of the case, however, presents the facts as they were afterward ordered and clarified by study.

Misery. Mrs. A.'s misery was obvious to her family, her therapist, and herself. She suffered from a strong, vague, unremitting fear. She was tantalized by a mysterious temptation. The phobic limitations on her life prevented her from having much ordinary fun, as by shopping or going to the movies. Her husband and mother-in-law criticized her painfully. She feared that her husband would carry out his threat and divorce her. She feared that her heart would stop. She feared to be left all alone, sick and rejected. Her friends and relatives pitied her at first, then became put out with her when her condition persisted despite well-meant advice. Her misery, though baffling, was recognized as entirely real.

Conflict. Mrs. A. suffered from two conflicts which produced her misery. The first might be described as a sex-fear conflict. Thanks to childhood circumstances she had developed strong sex appetites. At the same time strong anxieties were created in her and attached to the cues produced by sex excitement. However, she saw no connection between these remembered circumstances and the miserable life she was leading. The connective thoughts had been knocked out and the conflict was thus unconscious. The presence of the sexual appetites showed up in a kind of driven behavior in which she seemed to court seduction. Her fear was exhibited in her revulsion from sexual acts and thoughts and in her inability to take responsibility for a reasonable sexual expressiveness with her husband. The conflict was greatly intensified after her marriage because of her wish to be a dutiful wife. Guilt about the prospect of adultery was added to fear about sex motives.

Mrs. A. was involved in a second, though less severe, conflict between aggression and fear. She was a gentle person who had been very badly treated by her mother-in-law. Resentful tendencies arose in her but they were quickly inhibited by fear. She attempted to escape the anger-fear conflict by exceptionally submissive behavior, putting up meekly with slights and subordination and protesting her fondness for the mother-in-law. She was tormented by it nevertheless, especially by feelings of worthlessness and helplessness. She felt much better, late in therapy, when she was able to state her resentment and begin to put it into effect in a measured way. (After all, she had the husband and his love, and if the mother-in-law wanted to see her son and prospective grandchildren she would have to take a decent attitude toward Mrs. A.)

Stupidity. Mrs. A.'s mind was certainly of little use to her in solving her problem. She tried the usual medical help with no result. She took a trip, as advised, and got no help. Her symptoms waxed and waned in unpredictable ways. She knew that she was helpless. At the time she came for therapy she had no plans for dealing with her problem and no hope of solving it. In addition to being unable to deal with her basic problems, Mrs. A. did many things that were quite unintelligent and maladaptive. For example, in spite of the fact that she wanted very much to make a success of her marriage and was consciously trying to live a proper married life, she frequently exposed herself to danger of seduction. She went out on drinking parties with single girls. She hitchhiked rides with truck drivers. She was completely unaware of the motivation for this behavior and often unable to foresee its consequences until it was too late. While her behavior seems stupid in the light of a knowledge of the actual state of affairs, there are many ways in which Mrs. A. did not seem at all stupid—for example, when debating with the therapist to protect herself against fear-producing thoughts. She then gave hopeful evidence of what she could do with her mind when she had available all the necessary units to think with.

Repression. Mrs. A. gave abundant evidence of the laming effects of repression. At the outset she thought she had no sex feelings or appetites. She described behavior obviously motivated by fear but could not label the fear itself. The closest she came was to express the idea that she was going insane. Further, Mrs. A. thought she had an organic disease and clung desperately to this idea, inviting any kind of treatment so long as it did not force her to think about matters which would produce fear. Such mental gaps and distortions are a characteristic result of repression. They are what produce the stupidity.

Symptoms. Mrs. A.'s chief symptoms were the spreading phobia which drove her out of theaters and stores and the compulsive counting of breaths and heartbeats. These symptoms almost incapacitated her. She had lost her freedom to think and to move.

Reinforcement of symptoms. An analysis of the phobia revealed the following events. When on the streets alone, her fear of sex temptation was increased. Someone might speak to her, wink at her, make an approach to her. Such an approach would increase her sex desire and make her more vulnerable to seduction. Increased sex desire, however, touched off both anxiety and guilt, and this intensified her conflict when she was on the street. When she "escaped home," the temptation stimuli were lessened, along with a reduction of the fear which they elicited. Going home and, later, avoiding the temptation situation by anticipation were reinforced. Naturally, the basic sex-anxiety conflict was not resolved by the defensive measure of the symptom. The conflict persisted but was not so keen.

The counting of heartbeats can be analytically taken apart in a similar way. When sexy thoughts came to mind or other sex stimuli tended to occur, these stimuli elicited anxiety. It is clear that these stimuli were occurring frequently because Mrs. A. was responding with anxiety much of the time. Since counting is a highly preoccupying kind of response, no other thoughts could enter her mind during this time. While counting, the sexy thoughts which excited fear dropped out. Mrs. A. "felt better" immediately when she started counting, and the counting habit was reinforced by the drop in anxiety. Occasionally, Mrs. A. would forget to count and then her intense anxiety would recur. In this case, as in that of the phobia, the counting symptom does not resolve the basic conflict—it only avoids exacerbating it.

Chapter 28

Experiences in a concentration camp*

Viktor E. Frankl

Viktor Frankl is the originator of a new method of treatment called logotherapy. It is his contention that much present-day anxiety is caused, not by inappropriate emotional conditioning, but by failure to find a meaning and a purpose in one's existence. When such a meaning is present, an individual becomes able to undergo experiences that might previously have been impossible to bear.

It had been a bad day. On parade, an announcement had been made about the many actions that would, from then on, be regarded as sabotage and therefore punishable by immediate death by hanging. Among these were crimes such as cutting small strips from our old blankets (in order to improvise ankle supports) and very minor "thefts." A few days previously a semistarved prisoner had broken into the potato store to steal a few pounds of potatoes. The theft had been discovered and some prisoners had recognized the "burglar." When the camp authorities heard about it they ordered that the guilty man be given up to them or the whole camp would starve for a day. Naturally the 2,500 men preferred to fast.

On the evening of this day of fasting we lay in our earthen huts—in a very low mood. Very little was said and every word sounded irritable. Then, to make matters even worse, the light went out. Tempers reached their lowest ebb. But our senior block warden was a wise man. He improvised a little talk about all that was on our minds at that moment. He talked about the many comrades who had died in the last few days, either of sickness or of suicide. But he also mentioned what may have been the real reason for their deaths: giving up hope. He maintained that there should be some way of preventing possible future victims from reaching this extreme state. And it was to me that the warden pointed to give this advice.

God knows, I was not in the mood to give psychological explanations or to preach any sermons—to offer my comrades a kind of medical care of their souls. I was cold and hungry, irritable and tired, but I had to make the effort and use this unique opportunity. Encouragement was now more necessary than ever.

So I began by mentioning the most trivial of comforts first. I said that even in this Europe in the sixth winter of the Second World War, our situation was not the most terrible we could think of. I said that each of us had to ask himself what irreplaceable losses he had suffered up to then. I speculated that for most of them these losses had really been few. Whoever was still alive had reason for hope. Health, family, happiness, professional abilities, fortune, position in society—all these were things that could be achieved again or restored. After all, we still had our bones intact. Whatever we had gone through could still be an asset to us in the future. And I quoted from Nietzsche: *"Was mich nicht umbringt, macht mich stärker."* (That which does not kill me, makes me stronger.)

Then I spoke about the future. I said that to the impartial the future must seem hopeless. I agreed that each of us could guess for himself how small were his chances of survival. I told them that although there was still no typhus epidemic in the camp, I estimated my own chances at about one in twenty. But I also told them that, in spite of this, I had no intention of losing hope and giving up. For no man knew what the future would bring, much less the next hour. Even if we could not expect any sensational military events in the next few days, who knew better than we, with our experience of camps, how great chances sometimes opened up, quite suddenly, at least for the individual. For instance, one might be attached unexpectedly to a special group with exceptionally good working conditions—for this was the kind of thing which constituted the "luck" of the prisoner.

But I did not only talk of the future and the veil which was drawn over it. I also mentioned the past; all its joys, and how its light shone even in the present darkness. Again I quoted a poet—to avoid sounding like a preacher myself—who had written, *"Was Du erlebt, kann keine Macht der Welt Dir rauben."* (What you have experienced, no power on earth can take from you.) Not only our experiences, but all we have done, whatever great thoughts we may have had, and all we have suffered, all this is not lost, though it is past; we have brought it into being. Having been is also a kind of being, and perhaps the surest kind.

Then I spoke of the many opportunities of giving life a meaning. I told my comrades (who lay motionless, although occasionally a sigh could be heard) that human life, under any circumstances, never ceases to have a meaning, and that this infinite meaning of life includes suffering and dying, privation and death. I asked the poor creatures who listened to me attentively in the darkness of the hut to face up to the seriousness of our position. They must not lose hope but should keep their courage in the certainty that the hopelessness of our struggle did not detract from its dignity and its meaning. I said that someone looks down on each of us in difficult hours—a friend, a wife, somebody alive or dead, or a God—and he would not expect us to disappoint him. He would hope to find us suffering proudly—not miserably—knowing how to die.

And finally I spoke of our sacrifice, which had meaning in every case. It was in the nature of this sacrifice that it should appear to be pointless in the normal world, the world of material success. But in reality our sacrifice did have a meaning. Those of us who had any religious faith, I said frankly, could understand without difficulty. I told them of a comrade who on his arrival in camp had tried to make a pact with Heaven that his suffering and death should save the human being he loved from a painful end. For this man, suffering and death were meaningful; his was a sacrifice of the deepest significance. He did not want to die for nothing. None of us wanted that.

The purpose of my words was to find a full meaning in our life, then and there, in that hut and in that practically hopeless situation. I saw that my efforts had been successful. When the electric bulb flared up again, I saw the miserable figures of my friends limping toward me to thank me with tears in their eyes. But I have to confess here that only too rarely had I the inner strength to make contact with my companions in suffering and that I must have missed many opportunities for doing so.

Chapter 29

Two games people play*

Eric Berne

Dr. Berne has succeeded in identifying a number of social maneuvers that people employ in everyday life to gratify hidden motives of which they themselves may be unaware. In the same way one would go about analyzing a game of chess or a hand of poker, Dr. Berne shows how these "games" gratify the Child, the Adult, and the Parent within the personality of each of us.

NOW I'VE GOT YOU . . .

Thesis. This can be seen in classic form in poker games. White gets an unbeatable hand, such as four aces. At this point, if he is a NIGYSOB player, he is more interested in the fact that Black is completely at his mercy than he is in good poker or making money.

White needed some plumbing fixtures installed, and he reviewed the costs very carefully with the plumber before giving him a go-ahead. The price was set, and it was agreed that there would be no extras. When the plumber submitted his bill, he included a few dollars extra for an unexpected valve that had to be installed—about four dollars on a four-hundred-dollar job. White became infuriated, called the plumber on the phone and demanded an explanation. The plumber would not back down. White wrote him a long letter criticizing his integrity and ethics and refused to pay the bill until the extra charge was withdrawn. The plumber finally gave in.

It soon became obvious that both White and the plumber were playing games. In the course of their negotiations, they had recognized each other's potentials. The plumber made his provocative move when he submitted his bill. Since White had the plumber's word, the plumber was clearly in the wrong. White now felt justified in venting almost unlimited rage against him. Instead of merely negotiating in a dignified way that befit the Adult standards he set for himself, perhaps with a little innocent annoyance, White took the opportunity to make extensive criticisms of the plumber's whole way of living. On the surface their argument was Adult to Adult, a legitimate business dis-

*From *Games People Play: The Psychology of Human Relationships*. Reprinted by permission of Grove Press, Inc., New York, and of André Deutsch Limited Publishers, London, England. Copyright © 1964 by Eric Berne.

pute over a stated sum of money. At the psychological level it was Parent to Adult: White was exploiting his trivial but socially defensible objection (position) to vent the pent-up furies of many years on his cozening opponent, just as his mother might have done in a similar situation. He quickly recognized his underlying attitude (NIGYSOB) and realized how secretly delighted he had been at the plumber's provocation. He then recalled that ever since early childhood he had looked for similar injustices, received them with delight and exploited them with the same vigor. In many of the cases he recounted, he had forgotten the actual provocation, but remembered in great detail the course of the ensuing battle. The plumber, apparently, was playing some variation of "Why Does This Always Happen to Me?" (WAHM)....

WHY DON'T YOU—YES BUT

Thesis. "Why Don't You—Yes But" occupies a special place in game analysis, because it was the original stimulus for the concept of games. It was the first game to be dissected out of its social context, and since it is the oldest subject of game analysis, it is one of the best understood. It is also the game most commonly played at parties and groups of all kinds, including psychotherapy groups. The following example will serve to illustrate its main characteristics:

> White: "My husband always insists on doing our own repairs, and he never builds anything right."
> Black: "Why doesn't he take a course in carpentry?"
> White: "Yes, but he doesn't have the time."
> Blue: "Why don't you buy him some good tools?"
> White: "Yes, but he doesn't know how to use them."
> Red: "Why don't you have your building done by a carpenter?"
> White: "Yes, but that would cost too much."
> Brown: "Why don't you just accept what he does the way he does it?"
> White: "Yes, but the whole thing might fall down."

Such an exchange is typically followed by a silence. It is eventually broken by Green, who may say something like, "That's men for you, always trying to show how efficient they are."

YDYB can be played by any number. The agent presents a problem. The others start to present solutions, each beginning with "Why don't you . . .?" To each of these White objects with a "Yes, but. . . ."A good player can stand off the others indefinitely until they all give up, whereupon White wins. In many situations she might have to handle a dozen or more solutions to engineer the crestfallen silence which signifies her victory, and which leaves the field open for the next game in the above paradigm, Green switching into "PTA," Delinquent Husband Type.

Since the solutions are, with rare exceptions, rejected, it is apparent that this game must serve some ulterior purpose. YDYB is not played for its ostensible purpose (an Adult quest for information or solutions), but to reassure and gratify the Child. A bare transcript may sound Adult, but in the living tissue it can be observed that White presents herself as a Child inadequate to meet the situation; whereupon the others become transformed into sage Parents anxious to dispense their wisdom for her benefit.

Chapter 30

Are there such things as mental diseases?*

John B. Watson

The following excerpt from the book "Behaviorism," which first appeared in 1912, expresses rather strikingly the behavioristic view of
mental illness and the means by which it should be treated. Subsequent
refinements in conditioning technique have provided a number of treatment methods designed to implement this particular orientation, and the
number of adherents to this point of view appears to be continuously
growing.

To show the needlessness of introducing the "conception of mind" in so-
called mental diseases, I offer you a fanciful picture of a psychopathological
dog (I use the dog because I am not a physician and have no right to use a
human illustration—I hope the veterinarians will pardon me!). Without taking
any one into my counsel suppose I once trained a dog so that he would walk
away from nicely-ground, fresh hamburg steak and would eat only decayed
fish (true examples of this are now at hand). I trained him (by the use of
electric shock) to avoid smelling the female dog in the usual canine way—he
would circle around her but would come no closer than ten feet (J. J. B.
Morgan has done something very close to this on the rat). Again, by letting
him play only with male puppies and dogs and punishing him when he tried
to mount a female, I made a homosexual of him (F. A. Moss has done something closely akin to this in rats). Instead of licking my hands and becoming
lively and playful when I go to him in the morning, he hides or cowers, whines
and shows his teeth. Instead of going after rats and other small animals in the
way of hunting, he runs away from them and shows the most pronounced
fears. He sleeps in the ash can—he fouls his own bed, he urinates every half
hour and anywhere. Instead of smelling every tree trunk, he growls and fights
and paws the earth but will not come within two feet of the tree. He sleeps
only two hours per day and sleeps these two hours leaning up against a wall
rather than lying down with head and rump touching. He is thin and emaci-
ated because he will eat no fats. He salivates constantly (because I have con-

*From *Behaviorism,* New York, 1924, The Peoples Institute Publishing Co., pp. 299-300.

ditioned him to salivate to hundreds of objects). This interferes with his digestion. Then I take him to the dog psychopathologist. His physiological reflexes are normal. No organic lesions are to be found anywhere. The dog, so the psychopathologist claims, is mentally sick, actually insane; his mental condition has led to the various organic difficulties such as lack of digestion; it has "caused" his poor physical condition. Everything that a dog should do—as compared with what dogs of his type usually do—he does not do. And everything that seems foreign for a dog to do he does. The psychopathologist says I must commit the dog to an institution for the care of insane dogs; that if he is not restrained he will jump from a ten-story building, or walk into a fire without hesitation.

I tell the dog psychopathologist that he doesn't know anything about my dog; that from the standpoint of the environment in which the dog has been brought up (the way I have trained him) he is the most normal dog in the world; that the reason he calls the dog "insane" or mentally sick is because of his own absurd system of classification.

I then take the psychopathologist into my confidence. He becomes extremely angry. "Since you've brought this on, go cure him." I attempt then to correct my dog's behavior difficulties, at least up to the point where he can begin to associate with the nice dogs in the neighborhood. If he is very old or if things have gone too far, I just keep him confined; but if he is fairly young and he learns easily, I undertake to retrain him. I use behavioristic methods. I uncondition him and then condition him. Soon I get him to eating fresh meat by getting him hungry, closing up his nose and feeding him in the dark. This gives me a good start. I have something basic to use in my further work. I keep him hungry and feed him only when I open his cage in the morning; the whip is thrown away; soon he jumps for joy when he hears my step. In a few months' time I not only have cleared out the old but also have built in the new. The next time there is a dog show I proudly exhibit him, and his general behavior is such an asset to his sleek, perfect body that he walks off with the blue ribbon.

All this is an exaggeration—almost sacrilege! Surely there is no connection between this and the poor sick souls we see in the psychopathic wards in every hospital! Yes, I admit the exaggeration, but I am after elementals here. I am pleading for simplicity and ruggedness in the building stones of our science of behavior. I am trying to show by this homely illustration *that you can by conditioning not only build up the behavior complications, patterns and conflicts in diseased personalities, but also by the same process lay the foundations for the onset of actual organic changes which result finally in infections and lesions* —all without introducing the concepts of the mind-body relation ("influence of mind over the body") or even without leaving the realm of natural science. In other words, as behaviorists, even in "mental diseases" we deal with the same material and the same laws that the neurologists and physiologists deal with.

Chapter 31

The psychiatric nurse as a behavioral engineer*†

Teodoro Ayllon and Jack Michael

The behavior which leads to a person's admission to a mental hospital often involves danger to himself or others, withdrawal from normal social functions, or a dramatic change from his usual mode of behaving. The professional staff of the psychiatric hospital directs its major efforts toward the discovery of the flaw in the patient's mental apparatus which presumably underlies his disturbing and dangerous behavior. Following the medical paradigm, it is presumed that once the basic disfunction has been properly identified the appropriate treatment will be undertaken and the various manifestations of the disfunction will disappear.

While diagnosis is being made and during subsequent treatment, the patient is under the daily care of the psychiatric nurses[1] in the ward. There, he often exhibits annoying and disrupting behavior which is usually regarded as a further manifestation of his basic difficulty. This behavior is sometimes identical with that which led to his admission; but at other times it seems to originate and develop within the hospital setting. Although it is still regarded as a reflection of his basic problem, this disruptive behavior may become so persistent that it engages the full energies of the nurses, and postpones, sometimes permanently, any effort on their part to deal with the so-called basic problem.

Disrupting behaviors usually consist in the patient's failure to engage in activities which are considered normal and necessary; or his persistent engagement in activities that are harmful to himself or other patients, or disrupting in other ways. For example, failures to eat, dress, bathe, interact socially with other patients, and walk without being led are invariably disruptive. Hoarding various objects, hitting, pinching, spitting on other patients, constant attention-

---

*From *Journal of the Experimental Analysis of Behavior* 2:323-334, 1959. Copyright 1959 by Society for the Experimental Analysis of Behavior, Inc.
†Additional experiments and related research are found in *The Token Economy: a Motivational System for Therapy and Rehabilitation,* by T. Ayllon and N. Azrin, published by Appleton-Century-Crofts, 1968, New York.
[1]As used in this discussion, "psychiatric nurse" is a generic term including all those who actually work on the ward (aides, psychiatric nurses, and registered nurses).

seeking actions with respect to the nurses, upsetting chairs in the day-room, scraping paint from the walls, breaking windows, stuffing paper in the mouth and ears, walking on haunches or while in a squatting position are disruptive when they occur frequently and persistently.

At present, no systematic approach to such problems is available to the nurses. A psychodynamic interpretation is often given by psychiatrists, and psychologists; and, for that matter, the nurses sometimes construct "depth" interpretations themselves. These interpretations seldom suggest any specific remedial actions to the nurses, who then have no other recourse than to act on the basis of common sense, or to take advantage of the physical therapy in vogue. From the point of view of modern behavior theory, such strong behaviors, or behavioral deficits, may be considered the result of events occurring in the patient's immediate or historical environment rather than the manifestations of his mental disorder. The present research represents an attempt to discover and manipulate some of these environmental variables for the purpose of modifying the problem behavior.

RESEARCH SETTING

The research was carried out at the Saskatchewan Hospital, Weyburn, Saskatchewan, Canada. It is a psychiatric hospital with approximately 1500 patients. Its most relevant feaures in terms of the present experiment are:

1. The nurses are trained as psychiatric nurses in a 3-year program.

2. They are responsible for the patients in their wards and enjoy a high degree of autonomy with respect to the treatment of a patient. The psychiatrists in the hospital function as advisers to the nursing staff. This means that psychiatrists do not give orders, but simply offer advice upon request from the psychiatric nurses.

3. The nurses administer incoming and outgoing mail for the patients, visitor traffic, ground passes, paroles, and even discharge, although the last is often carried out after consultation with a psychiatrist. The nurses also conduct group therapy under the supervision of the psychiatric staff.

The official position of the senior author, hereafter referred to as E, was that of a clinical psychologist, who designed and supervised operant-conditioning "therapy" as applied by the nurses. Once his advice had been accepted, the nurses were responsible for carrying out the procedures specified by E. It was the privilege of the nurses to discontinue any treatment when they believed it was no longer necessary, when they were unable to implement it because of lack of staff, or when other ward difficulties made the treatment impossible. Whenever termination became necessary, E was given appropriate notice.

SUBJECTS

The subjects used in this investigation were all patients in the hospital. Of the total 19 patients, 14 had been classified as schizophrenic and 5 as mentally defective. Except for one female patient who was resident for only 7 months, all patients had been hospitalized for several years. Each subject presented a persistent behavior problem for which he had been referred to E by the nursing staff. None of the Ss was presently receiving psychotherapy, electroconvulsive therapy, or any kind of individual treatment.

The behaviors which were studied do not represent the most serious problems encountered in a typical psychiatric hospital. They were selected mainly because their persistence allowed them to survive several attempts at altering them.

PROCEDURE

Prior to a systemic observational study of the patient's behavior the nurses were asked about the kind and frequency of naturally occurring reinforcement obtained by the patient, the duration and frequency of the problem behavior, and the possibility of controlling the reinforcement. Next, a period of systematic observation of each patient was undertaken prior to treatment. This was done to obtain objective information on the frequency of the behavior that was a problem to the nurses, and to determine what other behaviors were emitted by the patient.

Depending on the type of behavior, two methods were used for recording it. If the behavior involved interaction with a nurse, it was recorded every time it occurred. Entering the nurses' office, and eating regular meals are examples of such behavior.

Behavior which did not naturally involve contact with the nurse was recorded by a time-sampling technique. The nurse who was in charge of the program was supplied with a mimeographed record form. She sought out the patient at regular intervals; and without interaction with him, she recorded the behavior taking place at that time. She did not actually describe the behavior occurring, but rather classified it in terms of a pre-established trichotomy: (a) the undesirable behavior; (b) incompatible behavior which could ultimately displace the undesirable behavior; and (c) incompatible behavior which was not considered shapeable, such as sleeping, eating, and dressing. (Although these latter acts are certainly susceptible to the influence of reinforcement, they were regarded as neutral behaviors in the present research.) The period of observation varied from 1 to 3 minutes. After making an observation, the nurse resumed her regular ward activities until the next interval was reached, whereupon she again sought out the patient. Except for one patient, who was observed every 15 minutes, such observations were made every 30 minutes.

The relevant aspect of the data obtained by the time-check recording is the proportion of the total number of observations (excluding observations of neutral behavior) during which the patient was engaging in the behavior being altered. This will be called the relative frequency of the behavior. As an example, on the first day of the program of extinction for psychotic talk in the case of Helen (see below), 17 nonneutral behaviors were recorded. Of these, nine were classed as psychotic talk and eight as sensible talk; the relative frequency of psychotic talk was 0.53.

Although it would have been desirable, a long pretreatment period of observation was precluded by the newness of this approach and the necessity of obtaining the voluntary cooperation of the nurses.

After the pretreatment study had been completed, E instructed the ward nurses in the specific program that was to be carried out. In all cases the instruction was given at ward meetings and usually involved the cooperation of only two shifts, the 7 a.m. to 3 p.m., and 3 p.m. to 11 p.m., since the patients were usually asleep during the 11 p.m. to 7 a.m. shift.

The pretreatment studies indicated that what maintained undesirable behavior in most of the patients was the attention or social approval of the nurses toward that behavior. Therefore, the emphasis in instructing the nursing staff was on the operation of giving or withholding social reinforcement contingent upon a desired class of behavior. What follows illustrates the tenor of E's somewhat informal instructions to the nurses. "Reinforcement is something you do for or with a patient, for example, offering candy or a cigarette. Any way you convey attention to the patient is reinforcing. Patients may be reinforced if you answer their questions, talk to them, or let them know by your reaction that you are aware of their presence. The common-sense expression 'pay no attention' is perhaps closest to what must be done to discourage the patient's behavior. When we say 'do not reinforce a behavior,' we are actually saying 'ignore the behavior and act deaf and blind whenever it occurs.' "

When reinforcement was given on a fixed-interval basis, the nurse was instructed to observe the patient for about 1 to 3 minutes at regular intervals, just as in the pretreatment observation period. If desirable behavior was occurring at the time of observation, she would reinforce it; if not, she would go on about her duties and check again after the next interval had passed. Strictly speaking, this is fixed interval with a limited-hold contingency (Ferster and Skinner, 1957). During a program of extinction the nurse checked as above; however, instead of reinforcing the patient when he exhibited the behavior being altered, she simply recorded it and continued her other work. Except for specific directions for two patients, the nurses were not given instructions on the operation of aversive control.

The programs requiring time-sample observations started after breakfast (around 9 a.m.) and ended at bedtime (around 9 p.m.), and were usually carried out by only one of the 6 to 12 nurses on each shift. Because of the daily shift changes, the monthly ward rotations, and a systematic effort to give everyone experience at this new duty, no patient's program was followed by any one nurse for any considerable length of time. Nineteen, as a minimum, different nurses were involved in carrying out each patient's program. Over 100 different nurses participated in the entire research project.

Most social ward activities took place in the dayroom, which was a large living room containing a television set, card tables, magazines, and games. It was here that reinforcement was given for social behaviors toward patients, and for nonsocial behaviors which were strengthened to compete with undesirable behaviors. The fact that the research was carried out in five wards distributed far from each other in a four-floor building made it impossible for E to observe all the nurses involved in the research at any one time. Because of the constant change in nursing personnel, most of E's time was spent in instructing new people in the routines of the programs. In addition, since E did not train the nurses extensively, he observed them, often without their knowledge, and supervised them in record keeping, administering reinforcement, extinction, etc. That the nurses performed effectively when E was absent can be at least partially determined by the ultimate results.

RESULTS

The results will be summarized in terms of the type of behavior problem and the operations used in altering the behavior. In general, the time required to change a specific behavior ranged from 6 to 11 weeks. The operations were in force for 24 hours a day, 7 days a week.

Strong behavior treated by extinction, or extinction combined with reinforcement for incompatible behavior

In the five cases treated with this program, the reinforcer was the attention of the nurses; and the withholding of this reinforcer resulted in the expected decline in frequency. The changes occurring in three of the behavior problems, scrubbing the floor, spending too much time in the bathroom, and one of the two cases of entering the nurses' offices, were not complicated by uncontrollable variables. Lucille's case is presented in detail as representative of these three. The interpretation of the changes occurring in the other two behavior problems, entering the nurses' offices, and psychotic verbal behavior, is not so clear-cut. Helen's case illustrates this point. For details concerning the cases not discussed in this paper, see Ayllon (1959).

Lucille. Lucille's frequent visits to the nurses' office interrupted and interfered with their work. She had been doing this for 2 years. During this time, she had been told that she was not expected to spend her time in the nurses' office. Frequently, she was taken by the hand or pushed back bodily into the ward. Because the patient was classified as mentally defective, the nurses had resigned themselves to tolerating her behavior. As one of the nurses put it, "It's difficult to tell her anything because she can't understand—she's too dumb."

The following instructions were given to the nurses: "During this program the patient must not be given reinforcement (attention) for entering the nurses' office. Tally every time she enters the office."

The pretreatment study indicated that she entered the office on an average of 16 times a day. . . . The average frequency was down to two entries per day by the seventh week of extinction, and the program was terminated. . . .

Helen. This patient's psychotic talk had persisted for at least 3 years. It had become so annoying during the last 4 months prior to treatment that other patients had on several occasions beaten her in an effort to keep her quiet. She was described by one of the psychiatrists as a "delusinal" patient who "feels she must push her troubles onto somebody else, and by doing this she feels she is free." Her conversation centered around her illegitimate child and the men she claimed were constantly pursuing her. It was the nurses' impression that the patient had "nothing else to talk about."

A 5-day pretreatment observation of the patient was made at 30-minute intervals to compare the relative frequencies of psychotic and sensible content in her talk. Some of the nurses reported that, previously, when the patient started her psychotic talk, they listened to her in an effort to get at the "roots of her problem." A few nurses stated that they did not listen to what she was saying but simply nodded and remarked, "Yes, I understand," or some such comment, the purpose of which was to steer the patient's conversation onto some other topic. These reports suggested that the psychotic talk was being maintained by the nurses' reaction to it. While it is recognized that a distinction between psychotic and normal talk is somewhat arbitrary, this case was included in the research because of its value as a problem involving primarily verbal behavior.

The following instructions were given to the nurses: "During this program the patient must not be given reinforcement (attention) for her psychotic talk (about her illegitimate child and the men chasing her). Check the patient every 30 minutes, and (a) tally for psychotic talk; and (b) reinforce (and tally) sensible talk. If another patient fights with her, avoid making an issue of it. Simply stop the other patient from hurting her, but do so with a matter-of-fact attitude."

The 5-day observation period resulted in a relative frequency of psychotic talk of 0.91. During treatment, the relative frequency dropped to less than 0.25; but, later on, it rose to a value exceeded only by the pretreatment level. The sudden increase in the patient's psychotic talk in the ninth week probably occurred because the patient had been talking to a social worker, who, unknown to the nurses, had been reinforcing her psychotic talk. The reinforcement obtained from the social worker appeared to generalize to her interaction with other patients and nurses. The patient herself told one of the nurses, "Well you're not listening to me. I'll have to go and see Miss _____ (the social worker) again, 'cause she told me that if she would listen to my past she could help me."

In addition to the reinforcement attributable to the social worker, two other instances of bootleg reinforcement came to light. One instance occurred when a hospital employee came to visit the ward, and, another, when volunteer ladies came to entertain the patients. These occasions were impossible to control, and indicate some of the difficulties of long-term control over verbal behavior.

It is of interest to note that since the reinforcement program began, the patient has not been attacked by the other patients and is only rarely abused verbally. These improvements were commented upon by the nurses, who were nevertheless somewhat disappointed. On the basis of the improvement shown in verbal behavior, the nurses had expected a dramatic over-all change which did not occur.

Strong behavior treated by strengthening incompatible behavior

This case represented an attempt to control violent behavior by strengthening an incompatible class of responses, and to recondition normal social approaches while the violence was under control. The first phase was quite successful; but errors in strategy plagued the last half of the program, and it was terminated by the nurses because the patient became more violent.

The immediate reason for referral was that the patient, Dotty, had become increasingly violent over the last 5 years, and recently attacked several patients and hospital personnel without any apparent reason. Since admission and up to the present, she had received many electroconvulsive-therapy treatments aimed at reducing this violence, with little or no success. In 1947, a physician recommended her as a good case for psychosurgery. In December of the same year, she attempted to strangle her mother who was visiting her at the time. In July 1948, the patient had a leucotomy. The situation had recently become so serious that at the least suspicious move on her part the nurses would put her in the seclusion room. She spent from 3 to 12 hours daily in that room.

A 5-day pretreatment study, at 15-minute intervals, indicated that one of the nonviolent behaviors exhibited fairly often was "being on the floor" in the dayroom. The response included lying, squatting, kneeling, and sitting on the floor. Strengthening this class of responses would control the violence and, at the same time, permit the emotional behavior of other patients and nurses toward her to extinguish. To strengthen the patient's own social behavior, her approaches to the nurses were to be reinforced. The response "approach to nurse" was defined as spontaneous requests, questions or comments made by the patient to the nurse. Ultimately, the plan was to discontinue reinforcing being on the floor once the patient-nurse social interaction appeared somewhat normal. Presumably, this would have further increased the probability of approach to the nurses.

For the duration of the program, continuous social reinforcement was to be available for her approach to the nurses. Social reinforcement was to be available for the first 4 weeks only, on a fixed interval of 15 minutes, contingent on the response being on the floor. For the last 4 weeks, social reinforcement was to be withheld for being on the floor.

The following instructions were given to the nurses for the first 4 weeks of the program: "Reinforce (and tally) her approaches to you every time they occur. Check the patient every 15 minutes, and reinforce (and tally) the behavior being on the floor."

From the fifth week on the instructions were modified as follows: "Continue reinforcing (and tallying) her approaches to you every time they occur. Check the patient every 15 minutes, and tally but do not reinforce the behavior being on the floor."

During the period of reinforcement the relative frequency of the response being on the floor increased from the pretreatment level of less than 0.10 to a value of 0.21. During the succeeding 4 weeks of extinction, the frequency of being on the floor returned to the pretreatment level.

It was clear that being on the floor was incompatible with the fighting behavior and that the latter could be controlled by reinforcing the former. During the period of reinforcement for being on the floor, she attacked a patient once; but during the period of extinction, she made eight attacks on others. Her approaches to nurses increased over-all during the 4 weeks of reinforcement, but they decreased during the last 4 weeks, even though they were still being reinforced. This decrease paralleled the decrease in being on the floor. While being on the floor was undergoing extinction, attacks on the patients and nurses increased in frequency, and the nurses decided to return to the practice of restraining the patient. The program was terminated at this point.

The patient's failure to make the transition from being on the floor to approaching the nurses suggests that the latter response was poorly chosen. It was relatively incompatible with being on the floor. This meant that a previously reinforced response would have to be extinguished before the transition was possible, and this, too, was poor strategy with a violent patient.

Weak behavior strengthened by escape and avoidance conditioning

Two female patients generally refused to eat unless aided by the nurses. One, Janet, had to be forcefully taken to the dining room, where she would permit the nurses to spoonfeed her. The other patient, Mary, was spoonfed in a room adjacent to the dining room. Both patients had little social contact with others and were reported to be relatively indifferent to attention by the nurses. Both were also reported to care only for the neat and clean appearance of their clothing. Mary had been at the hospital for 7 months, and Janet had been there for 28 years. These two patients were in different wards and apparently did not know each other.

The program involved a combination of escape and avoidance conditioning, with food spilling as the aversive stimulus. All spoonfeeding was to be accompanied by some food spilling which the patient could escape by feeding herself after the first spilling, or avoid by feeding herself the entire meal. Social reinforcement was to be given contingent on feeding herself.

It was hoped that once self-feeding began to occur with some regularity, it would come under the control of environmental variables which maintain this behavior in most people, such as convenience, social stimulation at meal time, etc. In both cases, the program ultimately resulted in complete self-feeding, which now has been maintained for over 10 months. Janet's behavior change was complicated by a history of religious fasting, and her change took a little longer. Mary's case will be given here in detail.

The following instructions were given to the nurses: "continue spoonfeeding the patient; but from now on, do it in such a careless way that the patient will have a few drops of food fall on her dress. Be sure not to overdo the food dropping, since what we want to convey to the patient is that it is difficult to spoonfeed a grown-up person, and not that we are mean to her. What we expect is that the patient will find it difficult to depend on your skill to feed her. You will still be feeding her, but you will simply be less efficient in doing a good job of it. As the patient likes having her clothes clean, she will have to choose between feeding herself and keeping her clothes clean, or being fed by others and risking getting her clothes soiled. Whenever she eats on her own, be sure to stay with her for a while (3 minutes is enough), talking to her, or simply being seated with her. We do this to reinforce her eating on her own. In the experience of the patient, people become nicer when she eats on her own."

During the 8-day pretreatment study, the patient ate 5 meals on her own, was spoonfed 12, and refused to eat 7. Her weight at this time was 99 pounds. Her typical reaction to the schedule was as follows: the nurse would start spoonfeeding her; but after one or two "good" spoonfuls, the nurse would carelessly drop some food on her dress. This was continued until either the patient requested the spoon, or the nurse continued spoonfeeding her the entire meal. The behaviors the patient adopted included (a) reaching for the spoon after a few drops had fallen on her dress; (b) eating completely on her own; (c) closing her mouth so that spoonfeeding was terminated; or (d) being spoonfed the entire meal. Upon starting the schedule, the most frequent of all these alternatives was the first; but after a while, the patient ate on her own immediately. On the 12th day, the patient ate all three meals on her own for the first time. Four meals were refused out of the last 24; one meal was missed because she stated she didn't like "liver" and the other three because she said she was not hungry. Her weight when she left the hospital was 120 pounds, a gain of 21 pounds over her pretreatment weight.

Mary's relapse in the fifth week, after she had been eating well for 2 weeks, was quite unexpected. No reasonable explanation is suggested by a study of her daily records; but, after she had been spoonfed several meals in a row, the rumor developed that someone had informed the patient that the food spilling was not accidental. In any event, the failure to feed herself lasted only about 5 days.

Since the patient's hospital admission had been based on her refusal to eat, accompanied by statements that the food was poisoned, the success of the program led to her discharge. It is to be noted that although nothing was done to deal directly with her claims that the food was poisoned, these statements dropped out of her repertoire as she began to eat on her own.

Strong behavior weakened through a combination of extinction for social attention and stimulus satiation

For 5 years, several mentally defective patients in the same ward, Harry, Joe, Tom, and Mac, had collected papers, rubbish, and magazines and carried these around with them inside their clothing next to their body. The most serious offender was Harry, whose hoarding resulted in skin rashes. He carried so much trash and so persistently that for the last 5 years the nurses routinely "dejunked" him several times during the day and before he went to bed.

An analysis of the situation indicated that the patient's hoarding behavior was probably maintained by the attention he derived because of it and by the actual scarcity of printed matter. There were few papers or magazines in the ward. Some were brought in occasionally; but since they were often torn up and quickly disappeared, the nurses did not bring them in very often.

It was expected that flooding the ward with magazines would decrease the hoarding behavior after the paradigm of satiation. Similarly, the availability of many magazines was expected to result in their being the major object of hoarding. The latter would facilitate an easier measurement of this behavior.

In addition, social reinforcement was to be withheld for hoarding magazines and rubbish. The results for all patients were essentially similar: a gradual decrease in hoarding. After 9 weeks of satiation and extinction, the program was terminated, since hoarding was no longer a problem. This improvement has been maintained for the last 6 months.

The following instructions were given to the nurses: "During this program the patients Harry, Mac, Joe, and Tom must not be given reinforcement (attention) for hoarding. There will be a full supply of magazines in the dayroom. Every night, after all patients have gone to bed, replenish the magazine supply in the dayroom. Every night while the patients are in bed, check their clothes to record the amount of hoarding. Do not, however, take their hoarding from them."

The original plan was to count the number of magazines in the patients' clothing after they had gone to bed. The recording for Harry had to be changed, however; after 4 days of the program, he no longer carried the rubbish or magazines in his clothing. Instead, he kept a stack of magazines on his lap while he was sitting in the dayroom. The number of magazines in this stack was counted when he left the dayroom for supper. . . . (Mac was out of the ward for 3 weeks because of illness.)

Prior to the program, one of the nurses questioned the possibility and even advisability of changing Harry's behavior. Her argument was that "behavior has its roots in the personality of the individual. The fact that he hoards so much indicates that Harry has a strong need for security. I don't see how we are going to change this need, and I also wonder if it is a good thing to do that." This was a point of view commonly encountered, especially regarding relatively nonverbal patients.

It would seem in this case that Harry transferred his security needs from hoarding rubbish and magazines to sitting in the dayroom and looking at magazines, especially during T.V. commercials. The transfer occurred with no apparent signs of discomfort on his part.

Other cases

Combinations of extinction, reinforcement, and avoidance programs were set up for three patients; in two of these the problem behavior was eliminated in only a few weeks. The program of the third patient was followed for 20 days and then terminated since he had shown no changes by that time. An interpretation of the outcome of each of these programs is rendered questionable by the number of controlling variables involved and the nature of the changes.

The pretreatment study of four additional patients showed that the problem behavior of three of them did not occur often enough to justify carrying through a program; and in the fourth case, no easily controllable variables were available and, again, no program was undertaken.

DISCUSSION

On the basis of this work, further research along the same lines is now under way (see Ayllon, 1963). The present results are presented in this preliminary form in the hopes that they will provide encouragement to those who are in a position to conduct similar research. Therefore, it will be useful to mention a few other aspects of this work.

A major problem concerns the use of nurses as experimental assistants as well as substitutes for the recording and programming apparatus of the laboratory. There is no question as to the greater reliability of the ordinary laboratory component. In large part, however, the nurses' failures in carrying out *E*'s instructions were unsystematic with respect to the results obtained, and although undesirable, they do not by any means render this kind of work uninterpretable. Systematic errors in observation can be reduced to some extent by dealing with response classes that are relatively easily identified. But, of course, this problem will become more serious as efforts are made to alter more subtle aspects of behavior. Perhaps the only solution is to be dissatisfied with one's techniques and principles until the behavioral changes are so obvious as to render statistical analysis superfluous.

Another question concerns the acceptability of this approach to the hospital staff. The nurses and psychiatrists who were familiar with the "reinforcement programs," as they were called, were given questionnaires and interviews to determine their attitudes toward this work. The results indicate a mildly favorable reception in general, with some enthusiastic support from both nurses and psychiatrists.

Regarding time actually spent in carrying out the programs, it might seem unreasonable to expect the already overworked nurse to devote 2 or 3 minutes every half-hour to observation and recording. However, this is only about 40 minutes of an 8-hour shift; and, besides, much of her work stems from patients' behavior problems, the elimination of which would make the 40 minutes an excellent investment of time.

Two sources of possible misunderstanding between E and nurses should be pointed out. First, when nurses were asked about the sort of problems they had in the ward, if no dramatic behaviors, such as attempts at suicide, or violent acts, had been recently reported, they often denied having any problems. Problems also went unrecognized because they were considered unsolvable. For example, since most nurses attributed the behavior of a patient to his diagnosis or age, little or no effort was made to discover and manipulate possibly relevant environmental variables.

Second, even after a behavior had been modified, it was not uncommon to hear nurses remark, "We've changed her behavior. So what? She's still psychotic." It seemed that once a persistent problem behavior was eliminated, its previous importance was forgotten and other undesirable aspects of the patient's repertoire were assumed to be the most important ones. In general, their specific expectations were unclear or unverbalized, and they tended to be somewhat dissatisfied with any change less than total "cure."

Finally, an objection often raised against this approach is that the behavior changes may be only temporary. However, permanent elimination of ward behavior problems requires a permanent elimination of the environmental variables that shape them up and maintain them. The clinical belief that a favorable behavioral change, if properly accomplished, will be permanent probably rests on a faulty evaluation of the role of environmental variables in controlling behavior. Certainly, it is not based on any actual accomplishments in the field of mental health.

Chapter 32

An incident of mass hysteria*

Edgar A. Schuler and Vernon J. Parenton

Perhaps the most important thing one can learn in the study of psychology is that there is no such thing as human behavior without reasons behind it. These "reasons" are in reality basic laws of behavior that affect the conduct of everyone, no matter how bizarre that conduct may at first appear to the casual observer. The following article presents an account of a "mental epidemic" at a girls' high school in Louisiana and an analysis of these events in psychological terms. What similarities and differences in orientation do you note between this discussion and the preceding one?

The chronological sequence of the major occurrences which took place in Bellevue leading up to and including the hysterical epidemic, so far as we have been able to reconstruct it, was as follows:

Saturday, Jan. 28. Helen developed an involuntary twitching in the large muscles of her right leg while she was watching the dancing going on at the annual Alumni Homecoming Dance.

Tuesday, Feb. 16. Second annual Bellevue High School Carnival Ball.

Tuesday, Feb. 21. (Mardi Gras). That night a public dance was held at Ferryville, about three miles from Bellevue. This dance was attended by at least two of the girls who subsequently developed the hysterical symptoms, Millie and Frances. Millie was concluding a very active week and at the home of the one family which she visited in Bellevue. Soon after returning to her friends' home, about one o'clock Wednesday morning, she suddenly developed an involuntary convulsive jerking in the diaphragm, chest, and neck.

Wednesday, Feb. 22. Millie's disturbance continued during the day, but she attended all her classes. At noon she visited a local doctor, and upon returning home that afternoon she was examined by her family's physician who prescribed rest at home for a few days.

Thursday, Feb. 23. The morning was rainy, and the pupils gathered in the assembly hall before the beginning of classes. At this time Helen was observed

*Excerpt from A Recent Epidemic of Hysteria in a Louisiana High School, *Journal of Social Psychology* 17:221-235, 1943.

by many of the high school pupils experiencing one of her attacks which, by this time, had become a common occurrence.

Apparently nothing unusual took place during the first class period. But early in the second hour (9:30-10:30), in a French class, Frances began her involuntary spasmodic movements, which continued for some time without interruption, soon becoming noticeable to the entire class. She was then taken to the infirmary where some of the older students attempted to care for her. In the meantime, her friend, Geraldine P., aged 16, who sat at the adjacent desk, had been getting more and more nervous. In her own words: "First I trembled a little. Then everybody kept saying, 'Look at Geraldine.' And then I started jumping. Then they carried me upstairs to the infirmary, and I started crying. They gave me ammonia, but that didn't help. Plenty girls tried to hold me down, but they couldn't." One can well imagine the spreading of the disturbance entailed by the foregoing procedure.

Sometime in the course of the events described in the preceding paragraph, and possibly even precipitating the epidemic itself, another unusual development was taking place. A greatly agitated and none too well-informed mother from Ferryville had driven up in the family truck and loudly demanded her children.[1] Over the public address system, which reached every room and the playground, and was clearly audible for blocks around, the principal requested the specified children to report to his office at once. Shortly these children returned to their respective rooms to get their belongings, whereupon they left precipitantly. Soon (for Ferryville is only three miles distant) more cars and trucks began to stream in, and more and more children were called from their classes. With these further unexplained departures, coupled with the sounds of nervous crying, and hurried running to and fro in the halls, the curiosity and anxiety of the school children began to know no bounds. The tension became so pronounced that the principal, who had vainly attempted to reassure the panicky students as well as the nervous and fearful parents, found it necessary to call a special assembly in the hope of restoring order—but to no avail. In the meantime, as news and rumors of the "strange goings-on" at the Bellevue High School were spread around Ferryville by the returning parents and children, the noise and confusion of arriving and departing cars increased.

With the break-up of assembly, and the beginning of recess, the children scurried around and pressed forward in an attempt to see and hear what they could of the hysterical subjects. Some were to be seen in the principal's office; others were being administered ammonia-water by a practical nurse in the infirmary; still others, who had not developed the motor disturbances, but who contributed even more largely to the general confusion because of their uncontrolled fearful crying, had been taken to the nearby teacherage. As one of the witnesses said, "You've seen a stampede? That's how it was. The children were running up and down and all around trying to get a whiff here and a whiff there."

---

[1] Her explanation to the writers for this action was that she had overheard some people talking about recent developments at the school, and when she heard that the school was "having fits" she decided it was high time that she do something to rescue her own children and those of what neighbors and friends she was able—hence the truck.

The disorganization by this time was too much to be handled by ordinary measures, so the school bus drivers were assembled, and school was dismissed by authority of the Parish Health Officer. The children who still remained, practically all from Ferryville having already been called for by their parents, were then taken home.

In one of the school buses, on the way home, the last reported case of hysteria appeared in one of the girls, induced, apparently, by the chance remark of the bus driver. The children had been talking and joking about the morning's developments, and the driver reputedly said, "If you want to talk about the jerks, why don't you practice them?" And forthwith, Mildred Wilson, aged 17, began to jerk and twitch in the same manner as all the other cases of the morning.

In the meantime the director of the Parish Health Unit had been notified, and that afternoon he, together with other physicians, including two representatives of the State Board of Health (one of whom was also a psychiatrist and neurologist) investigated several of the cases. The possibility that the epidemic might have a bacteriological basis was explored and eliminated. Accordingly, little more was done concerning the matter by the physicians.[2] Sedatives were prescribed together with rest and absention from school for one or two weeks. School re-opened the following Monday with not only the afflicted girls, but about half of the other pupils, absent. The entire school was assembled and addressed in a firm and assuring manner by the director of the Parish Health Unit. In his remarks he emphasized the groundlessness of the current fears, and tried to instill confidence by declaring that nothing contagious was involved. Said the doctor: "You can't catch a broken arm." Nevertheless, the attendance crept up so slowly that it was a full week before it had returned to normal.

The writers' attempt to discover whether there had been any subsequent manifestation of hysteria by any of the afflicted girls yielded negative findings, with two exceptions. Frances reported that several times since the epidemic, especially when she was away from home, and had "the blues," she had started by crying, not quietly to herself, but "out loud," and ended with an attack. The attention gaining aspect of this too-loud crying should not be overlooked, together with the implication of recurrent hysteria. But this is an individual matter, and represents nothing in the nature of another epidemic. Second, Helen has also reported the leg twitchings have appeared on rare occasions, but only when she was very much fatigued.

INTERPRETATION

As a basis for attempting to interpret our findings, three distinct phases in the course of the epidemic may be pointed out: first, the period during which

[2]It should be stated that a typhoid fever epidemic, which was raging at this time not far distant, prevented more extensive medical investigation. See H. N. Old and S. L. Gill, M.D., "A typhoid fever epidemic caused by carrier 'bootlegging' oysters," *Amer. J. Public Health,* Vol. 30 (June, 1940) pp. 633-640. Furthermore, it was thought by the investigating physicians that the less attention was called to the hysterical symptoms, the sooner they would be likely to pass away.

only one person displayed the hysterical symptoms of involuntary nervous twitching; second, the period in which a number of persons, apparently unconsciously influenced by the repeated suggestion of the initial case, but possibly rendered more suggestible by the strain and fatigue induced by the events of the preceding days and nights, developed similar behavior patterns; and finally, the period in which some of the more easily excitable and less fully informed adults in a neighboring community, fearing that the malady was contagious and seriously dangerous, acted on the worthy impulse to save their children from a fate not clearly understood, and therefore all the more fearful.

Without techniques which the investigators did not have at their disposal it would hardly be possible to attempt a full explanation of the initial case. Nevertheless, it seems to display the characteristic pattern of hysteria as an escape mechanism, in this case an unconscious attempt to avoid a situation in which the subject, Helen, was being called upon, and eventually compelled, to participate in an activity for which she had no desire, in which she was not only not skilled (as contrasted with other activities in which she was outstanding), but in which she was entirely inexperienced. The jerking of her leg muscles obviously made it impossible for her to dance, and so the painful conflict situation was resolved with no discredit to the subject. Furthermore, the attack brought her the attention and sympathy which very probably she was unconsciously craving, since the affections of her boy friend, Maurice, were being alienated by Gretchen, the vivacious freshman newcomer.

Since the initial case occurred in a person who had high prestige within the social universe of the community and the High School, there was obviously no ostracism or penalty to be attached to an unconscious imitation of her behavior. If anything, in fact, it apparently served as a satisfactory device for gaining attention in the next two cases. This type of development, however, was definitely discouraged by the school authorities, and it is unlikely that it was of significance in any but a thoroughly unconscious or unintentional manner.

It will be recalled that the closest associates of the first subject, that is, those who were apparently already in the inner circle, without exception failed to develop any of the hysterical symptoms. They paid no attention to Helen's difficulty other than to sympathize with her; they regarded it as a purely nervous condition, involving nothing contagious or dangerous to themselves. On the other hand, there was apparently no unconscious desire to identify themselves further with her by a display of her distinctive behavior patterns, for her closest friends were precisely the genuine leaders of the school—their desires for prestige were already adequately satisfied.

The appearance of the third case, which was followed by the four or more others whose motor and emotional disturbances constituted the epidemic itself, has been accounted for by the members of the community in a number of ways. *(a)* Since Helen was known to over-indulge in her eating of candy bars, it was thought there may have been "something wrong with the candy." *(b)* The drinking water of the community had at the time a notoriously bad taste. Accordingly, the public water supply was investigated, but was found to be perfectly safe. *(c)* Since the hysteria developed shortly after the termination of an epidemic of measles, it was thought there was a causal connection between the two epidemics. However, none of the hysterical subjects had had the measles. *(d)* For the first time in the history of the Bellevue High School, a formal program of physical education had been instituted the preceding fall. The regulation gymnasium suits worn by the girls, contrary to the desires of the more conservative parents, consisted of short-sleeved sweaters and very much abbreviated shorts. Although the objections to these costumes for the girls may have been based as much on the grounds of morals as of health, at any rate the physical exposure of the girls in outdoor gymnasium classes was thought to have been a factor in the hysterical epidemic. *(e)* In the course of the winter the dance known as the "jitterbug" had become very much the vogue among the high school students. The importance in Bellevue of social dancing has already been indicated. The abrupt termination of this dance, with the beginning of Lent, therefore, was thought to have been responsible for the appearance of the muscular jerking. *(f)* Finally, it must be emphasized that many of the adults in the communities of the area regarded the entire episode as little more than a hoax on the part of some prankish youngsters who would willingly put on quite a show if they could thereby get out of a little school work.

The parents who participated in the unreasoning rush upon the school possibly feared for their children's safety because of the typhoid fever epidemic which was then going on in a nearby area, but from which children were coming regularly to the Bellevue High School. Although the student body involved in the epidemic of hysteria was in no way endangered by the cases of typhoid, it may well be that the fears aroused thereby served to intensify any uneasiness caused by rumors regarding the first cases of hysteria at the Bellevue High School.

In conclusion it may be stated that this case of a minor mental epidemic, brief and trivial as in itself it is, seems to be of significance in several ways:

First, it is clear that the phenomenon of the "mental epidemic" is not exclusively historical, nor is it confined necessarily to ignorant and backward populations. On the contrary, it may occur even though it be accurately diagnosed and clearly understood by the intelligent and informed members of the community.

Second, it is hoped hereby to stimulate further research in this borderline field of social psychology and abnormal psychology.

Third, the study and comparison of cases of these phenomena may throw additional light on such socio-psychological mechanisms as are operative in the closely related problems of mass suggestion, hysteria in crisis, and rumor, which occur more frequently and in less dramatic forms than in the type of case here described.

Part XII

Social psychology

Chapter 33

Attitude development as a function of reference groups: the Bennington study*

T. M. Newcomb

The following article illustrates the restraining effect of group membership on individual freedom. The second article in this section provides an example of how group membership may serve to enhance the range of individual choice. The concluding article in the series demonstrates some of the conditions under which groups themselves function either in an atmosphere of rivalry and mutual constraint or in a spirit of harmony and mutual cooperation.

In a membership group in which certain attitudes are approved (i.e., held by majorities, and conspicuously so by leaders), individuals acquire the approved attitudes to the extent that the membership group (particularly as symbolized by leaders and dominant subgroups) serves as a positive point of reference. The findings of the Bennington study seem to be better understood in terms of this thesis than any other. The distinction between membership group and reference group is a crucial one, in fact, although the original report did not make explicit use of it.

The above statement does not imply that no reference groups other than the membership group are involved in attitude formation; as we shall see, this is distinctly not the case. Neither does it imply that the use of the membership group as reference group necessarily results in adoption of the approved attitudes. It may also result in their rejection; hence the word "positive" in the initial statement. It is precisely these variations in degree and manner of relationship between reference group and membership group which must be known in order to explain individual variations in attitude formation, as reported in this study.

The essential facts about the Bennington membership group are as follows:

*From pp. 139-155 in *An Outline of Social Psychology* by Muzafer Sherif. Copyright 1948 by Harper & Row, Publishers, Inc. By permission of the publishers.

221

(1) It was small enough (about 250 women students) so that data could be obtained from every member. (2) It was in most respects self-sufficient; college facilities provided not only the necessities of living and studying, but also a cooperative store, post office and Western Union office, beauty parlor, gasoline station, and a wide range of recreational opportunities. The average student visited the four-mile-distant village once a week, and spent one week-end a month away from the college. (3) It was self-conscious and enthusiastic, in large part because it was new (the study was begun during the first year in which there was a senior class) and because of the novelty and attractiveness of the college's educational plan. (4) It was unusually active and concerned about public issues, largely because the faculty felt that its educational duties included the familiarizing of an oversheltered student body with the implications of a depression-torn America and a war-threatened world. (5) It was relatively homogeneous in respect to home background; tuition was very high, and the large majority of students came from urban, economically privileged families whose social attitudes were conservative.

Most individuals in this total membership group went through rather marked changes in attitudes toward public issues, as noted below. In most cases the total membership group served as the reference group for the changing attitudes. But some individuals changed little or not at all in attitudes during the four years of the study; attitude persistence was in some of these cases a function of the membership group as reference group and in some cases it was not. Among those who did change, moreover, the total membership group sometimes served as reference group but sometimes it did not. An over simple theory of "assimilation into the community" thus leaves out of account some of those whose attitudes did and some of those whose attitudes did not change; they remain unexplained exceptions. A theory which traces the impact of other reference groups as well as the effect of the membership group seems to account for all cases without exception.

The general trend of attitude change for the total group is from freshman conservatism to senior non-conservatism (as the term was commonly applied to the issues toward which attitudes were measured). During the 1936 presidential election, for example, 62 per cent of the freshmen and only 14 per cent of the juniors and seniors "voted" for the Republican candidate, 29 per cent of freshmen and 54 per cent of juniors and seniors for Roosevelt, and 9 per cent of freshmen as compared with 30 per cent of juniors and seniors for the Socialist or Communist candidates. Attitudes toward nine specific issues were measured during the four years of the study, and seniors were less conservative in all of them than freshmen; six of the nine differences are statistically reliable. These differences are best shown by a Likert-type scale labeled Political and Economic Progressivism (PEP) which dealt with such issues as unemployment, public relief, and the rights of organized labor, which were made prominent by the New Deal. Its odd-even reliability was about .9, and it was given once or more during each of the four years of the study to virtually all students. The critical ratios of the differences between freshmen and juniors-seniors in four successive years ranged between 3.9 and 6.5; the difference between the average freshman and senior scores of 44 individuals (the entire class that graduated in 1939) gives a critical ratio of 4.3.

As might be anticipated in such a community, *individual prestige was associated with non-conservatism*. Frequency of choice as one of five students "most worthy to represent the College" at an intercollegiate gathering was used as a measure of prestige. Nominations were submitted in sealed envelopes by 99 per cent of all students in two successive years, with almost identical results. The non-conservatism of those with high prestige is not merely the result of the fact that juniors and seniors are characterized by both high prestige and non-conservatism; in each class those who have most prestige are least conservative. For example, 10 freshmen receiving 2 to 4 choices had an average PEP score of 64.6 as compared with 72.8 for freshmen not chosen at all (high scores are conservative); eight sophomores chosen 12 or more times had an average score of 63.6 as compared with 71.3 for those not chosen; the mean PEP score of five juniors and seniors chosen 40 or more times was 50.4 and of the 15 chosen 12 to 39 times 57.6, as compared with 69.0 for those not chosen. In each class, those intermediate in prestige are also intermediate in average PEP score.

Such were the attitudinal characteristics of the total membership group, expressed in terms of average scores. Some individuals, however, showed these characteristics in heightened form and others failed to show them at all. An examination of the various reference groups in relation to which attitude change did or did not occur, and of the ways in which they were brought to bear, will account for a large part of such attitude variance.

Information concerning reference groups was obtained both directly, from the subjects themselves, and indirectly, from other students and from teachers. Chief among the indirect procedures was the obtaining of indexes of "community citizenship" by a guess-who technique. Each of 24 students, carefully selected to represent every cross-section and grouping of importance within the community, named three individuals from each of three classes who were reputedly most extreme in each of 28 characteristics related to community citizenship. The relationship between reputation for community identification and non-conservatism is a close one, in spite of the fact that no reference was made to the latter characteristic when the judges made their ratings. A reputation index was computed, based upon the frequency with which individuals were named in five items dealing with identification with the community, minus the number of times they were named in five other items dealing with negative community attitude. Examples of the former items are: "absorbed in college community affairs," and "influenced by community expectations regarding codes, standards, etc."; examples of the latter are: "indifferent to activities of student committees," and "resistant to community expectations regarding codes, standards, etc." The mean senior PEP score of 15 individuals whose index was +15 or more was 54.4; of 63 whose index was +4 to –4, 65.3; and of ten whose index was –15 or less, 68.2.

To have the reputation of identifying oneself with the community is not the same thing, however, as to identify the community as a reference group for a specific purpose—e.g., in this case, as a point of reference for attitudes toward public issues. In short, the reputation index is informative as to degree and direction of tendency to use the total membership group as a *general* reference group, but not necessarily as a group to which social attitudes are referred. For this purpose information was obtained directly from students.

Informal investigation had shown that whereas most students were aware of the marked freshman-to-senior trend away from conservatism, a few (particularly among the conservatives) had little or no awareness of it. Obviously, those not aware of the dominant community trend could not be using the community as a reference group for an attitude. (It does not follow, of course, that all those who are aware of it are necessarily using the community as reference group.) A simple measure of awareness was therefore devised. Subjects were asked to respond in two ways to a number of attitude statements taken from the PEP scale: first, to indicate agreement or disagreement (for example, with the statement: "The budget should be balanced before the government spends any money on social security"); and second, to estimate what percentage of freshmen, juniors and seniors, and faculty would agree with the statement. From these responses was computed an index of divergence (of own attitude) from the estimated majority of juniors and seniors. Thus a positive index on the part of a senior indicates the degree to which her own responses are more conservative than those of her classmates, and a negative index the degree to which they are less conservative. Those seniors whose divergence index more or less faithfully reflects the true difference between own and class attitude may (or may not) be using the class as an attitude reference group; those whose divergence indexes represent an exaggerated or minimized version of the true relationship between own and class attitude are clearly not using the class as an attitude reference group, or if so, only in a fictitious sense. (For present purposes the junior-senior group may be taken as representative of the entire student body, since it is the group which "sets the tone" of the total membership group.)

These data were supplemented by direct information obtained in interviews with seniors in three consecutive classes, just prior to graduation. Questions were asked about the resemblance between own attitudes and those of class majorities and leaders, about parents' attitudes and own resemblance to them, about any alleged "social pressure to become liberal," about probable reaction if the dominant college influence had been conservative instead of liberal, etc. Abundant information was also available from the college Personnel Office and from the college psychiatrist. It was not possible to combine all of these sources of information into intensive studies of each individual, but complete data were assembled for (roughly) the most conservative and least conservative sixths of three consecutive graduating classes. The 24 non-conservative and 19 conservative seniors thus selected for intensive study were classified according to their indexes of conservative divergence and of community reputation. Thus eight sets of seniors were identified, all individuals within each set having in common similar attitude scores, similar reputations for community identification, and similar degrees of awareness (based upon divergence index) of own attitude position relative to classmates. The following descriptions of these eight sets of seniors will show that there was a characteristic pattern of relationship between membership group and reference group within each of the sets.

1. *Conservatives, reputedly negativistic, aware of their own relative conservatism.* Four of the five are considered stubborn or resistant by teachers (all five, by student judges). Three have prestige scores of 0, scores of the other

two being about average for their class. Four of the five are considered by teachers or psychiatrist, or by both, to be overdependent upon one or both parents. All of the four who were interviewed described *their major hopes,* on entering college, *in terms of social rather than academic prestige;* all four felt that they had been defeated in this aim. The following verbatim quotations are illustrative:

E2: "Probably the feeling that (my instructors) didn't accept me led me to reject their opinions." (She estimates classmates as being only moderately less conservative than herself, but faculty as much less so.)

G32: "I wouldn't care to be intimate with those so-called liberal student leaders." *(She claims to be satisfied with a small group of friends.* She is chosen as friend, in a sociometric questionnaire responded to by all students, only twice, and reciprocates both choices; both are conservative students.)

F22: "I wanted to disagree with all the noisy liberals, but I was afraid and I couldn't. *So I built up a wall inside me against what they said. I found I couldn't compete, so I decided to stick to my father's ideas. For at least two years I've been insulated against all college influences.*" (She is chosen but once as a friend, and does not reciprocate that choice.)

Q10: (who rather early concluded that she had no chance of social success in college) "It hurt me at first, but now I don't give a damn. *The things I really care about are mostly outside the college.* I think radicalism symbolizes the college for me more than anything else." (Needless to say, she has no use for radicals.)

For these four individuals (and probably for the fifth also) the community serves as reference group in a *negative* sense, and the home-and-family group in a positive sense. Thus their conservatism is dually reinforced.

2. *Conservatives, reputedly negativistic, unaware of their own relative conservatism.* All five are described by teachers, as well as by Guess-Who judges, to be stubborn or resistant. Four have prestige scores of 0, and the fifth a less than average score. Each reciprocated just one friendship choice. Four are considered insecure in social relationships, and all five are regarded as extremely dependent upon parents. In interviews four describe with considerable intensity, and the fifth with more moderation, pre-college experiences of rebuff, ostracism, or isolation, and all describe their hopes, on entering college, in terms of making friends or avoiding rebuff rather than in terms of seeking prestige. All five felt that their (rather modest) aims had met with good success. Each of the five denies building up any resistance to the acceptance of liberal opinions (but two add that they would have resented any such pressure, if felt). Three believe that only small, special groups in the college have such opinions, while the other two describe themselves as just going their own way, *paying no attention to anything but their own little circles and their college work.* Typical quotations follow:

Q47: "I'm a perfect middle-of-the-roader, neither enthusiast nor critic. I'd accept anything if they just let me alone . . . I've made all the friends I want." (Only one of her friendship choices is reciprocated.)

Q19: "*In high school I was always thought of as my parents' daughter.* I never felt really accepted for myself . . . I wanted to make my own way here, socially, but independence from my family has never asserted itself in other ways." (According to Guess-Who ratings, she is highly resistant to faculty authority.)

L12: "What I most wanted was to get over being a scared bunny . . . I always resent doing the respectable thing just because it's the thing to do, but I didn't realize I was so different, politically, from my classmates. At least I agree with the few people I ever talk to about such matters." (Sociometric responses place her in a small, conservative group.)

Q81: "I hated practically all my school life before coming here. I had the perfect inferiority complex, and I pulled out of school social life—out of fear. I didn't intend to repeat that mistake here. . . . I've just begun to be successful in winning friendships, and I've been blissfully happy here." (She is described by teachers as "pathologically belligerent"; she receives more than the average number of friendship choices, but reciprocates only one of them.)

For these five individuals, who are negativistic in the sense of being near-isolates rather than rebels, the community does not serve as reference group for public attitudes. To some extent, their small friendship groups serve in this capacity, but in the main they still refer such areas of their lives to the home-and-family group. They are too absorbed in their own pursuits to use the total membership group as a reference group for most other purposes, too.

3. *Conservatives, not reputedly negativistic, aware of their own relative conservatism.* Three of the five are described by teachers as "cooperative" and "eager," and none as stubborn or resistant. Four are above average in prestige. Four are considered by teachers or by Guess-Who raters, or both, to retain very close parental ties. All four who were interviewed had more or less definite ambitions for leadership on coming to college, and all felt that they had been relatively successful—though, in the words of one of them, none ever attained the "really top-notch positions." All four are aware of conflict between parents and college community in respect to public attitudes, and all quite consciously decided to "string along" with parents, feeling self-confident of holding their own in college in spite of being atypical in this respect. Sample quotations follow:

Q73: *"I'm all my mother has in the world. It's considered intellectually superior here to be liberal or radical. This puts me on the defensive,* as I refuse to consider my mother beneath me intellectually, as so many other students do. Apart from this, I have loved every aspect of college life." (A popular girl, many of whose friends are among the non-conservative college leaders.)

Q78: *"I've come to realize how much my mother's happiness depends on me, and the best way I can help her is to do things with her at home as often as I can.* This has resulted in my not getting the feel of the college in certain ways, and I know my general conservatism is one of those ways. But it has not been important enough to me to make me feel particularly left out. If you're genuine and inoffensive about your opinions, no one really minds here if you remain conservative." (Another popular girl, whose friends were found among many groups.)

F32: *"Family against faculty has been my struggle here.* As soon as I felt really secure here I decided not to let the college atmosphere affect me too much. Every time I've tried to rebel against my family I've found out how terribly wrong I am, and so I've naturally kept to my parents' attitudes." (While not particularly popular, she shows no bitterness and considerable satisfaction over her college experience.)

Q35: "I've been aware of a protective shell against radical ideas. When I found several of my best friends getting that way, I either had to go along or just shut out that area entirely. I couldn't respect myself if I had changed my opinions just for that reason, and so I almost deliberately lost interest—really, *it was out of fear of losing my friends.*" (A very popular girl, with no trace of bitterness, who is not considered too dependent upon parents.)

For these five the total membership group does not serve as reference group in respect to public attitudes, but does so serve for most other purposes. At some stage in their college careers the conflict between college community and home and family as reference group for public attitudes was resolved in favor of the latter.

4. *Conservatives, not reputedly negativistic, not aware of their own relative conservatism.* All four are consistently described by teachers as conscientious and cooperative; three are considered overdocile and uncritical of authority. All are characterized by feelings of inferiority. All are low in prestige, two receiving scores of 0; all are low in friendship choices, but reciprocate most of these few choices. Two are described as in conflict about parental authority, and two as dependent and contented. All four recall considerable anxiety as to whether they would fit into the college community; all feel that they have succeeded better than they had expected. Sample statements from interviews follow:

D22: "I'd like to think like the college leaders, but I'm not bold enough and I don't know enough. So the college trend means little to me; I didn't even realize how much more conservative I am than the others. *I guess my family influence has been strong enough to counterbalance the college influence.*" (This girl was given to severe emotional upsets, and according to personnel records, felt "alone and helpless except when with her parents.")

M12: "It isn't that I've been resisting any pressure to become liberal. The influences here didn't matter enough to resist, I guess. *All that's really important that has happened to me occurred outside of college,* and so I never became very susceptible to college influences." *(Following her engagement to be married, in her second year, she had "practically retired" from community life.)*

Q68: "If I'd had more time here I'd probably have caught on to the liberal drift here. But I've been horribly busy making money and trying to keep my college work up. *Politics and that sort of thing I've always associated with home instead of with the college.*" (A "town girl" of working-class parentage.)

Q70: "Most juniors and seniors, if they really *get excited about their work, forget about such community enthusiasms as sending telegrams to Congressmen.* It was so important to me to be accepted, I mean intellectually, *that I naturally came to identify myself in every way with the group which gave me this sort of intellectual satisfaction.*" (One of a small group of science majors, nearly all conservative, who professed no interests other than science and who were highly self-sufficient socially.)

For none of the four was the total membership group a reference group for public attitudes. Unlike the non-negativistic conservatives who are aware of their relative conservatism, they refer to the total membership group for few if any other purposes. Like the negativistic conservatives who are unaware of their relative conservatism, their reference groups for public attitudes are almost exclusively those related to home and family.

5. *Non-conservatives, reputedly community-identified, aware of their relative non-conservatism.* Each of the seven is considered highly independent by teachers, particularly in intellectual activities; all but one are referred to as meticulous, perfectionist, or overconscientious. Four are very high in prestige, two high, and one average; all are "good group members," and all but one a "leader." None is considered overdependent upon parents. All have come to an understanding with parents concerning their "liberal" views; five had "agreed to differ," and the other two describe one or both parents as "very liberal." All take their public attitudes seriously, in most cases expressing the feeling that they have bled and died to achieve them. Interview excerpts follow:

B72: *"I bend in the direction of community expectation*—almost more than I want to. I constantly have to check myself to be sure it's real self-conviction and not just social respect." (An outstanding and deeply respected leader.)

M42: "My family has always been liberal, but the influences here made me go further, and for a while I was pretty far left. Now I'm pretty much in agreement with my family again, but it's my own and it means a lot. It wouldn't be easy for me to have friends who are very conservative." (Her friendship choices are exclusively given to non-conservatives.)

E72: "I had been allowed so much independence by my parents that I needed desperately to identify myself with an institution with which I could conform conscientiously. Bennington was perfect. I drank up everything the college had to offer, including social attitudes, though not uncritically. I've become active in radical groups and constructively critical of them." (Both during and after college she worked with CIO unions.)

H32: "I accepted liberal attitudes here because *I had always secretly felt that my family was narrow and intolerant, and because such attitudes had prestige value.* It was all part of my generally expanding personality—*I had never really been part of anything before.* I don't accept things without examining things, however, and I was sure I meant it before I changed." (One of those who has "agreed to differ" with parents.)

Q43: "It didn't take me long to see that liberal attitudes had prestige value. But all the time I felt inwardly superior to persons who want public acclaim. Once I had arrived at a feeling of personal security, I could see that it wasn't important—it wasn't enough. *So many people have no security at all. I became liberal at first because of its prestige value.* I remain so because the problems around which my liberalism centers are important. What I want now is to be effective in solving the problems." (Another conspicuous leader, active in and out of college in liberal movements.)

The total membership clearly serves as reference group for these individuals' changing attitudes, but by no means as the only one. For those whose parents are conservative, parents represent a negative reference group, from whom emancipation was gained via liberal attitudes. And for several of them the college community served as a bridge to outside liberal groups as points of reference.

6. *Non-conservatives, reputedly community-identified, not aware of their own relative non-conservatism.* The word "enthusiastic" appears constantly in the records of each of these six. All are considered eager, ambitious, hard-working, and anxious to please. Four are very high in prestige, the other two about average. None is considered overdependent upon parents, and only two

are known to have suffered any particular conflict in achieving emancipation. Each one came to college with ambitions for leadership, and each professes extreme satisfaction with her college experience. Sample quotations follow:

Qx: "Every influence I felt tended to push me in the liberal direction: my under-dog complex, *my need to be independent of my parents, and my anxiousness to be a leader here.*"

Q61: "I met a whole body of new information here; I took a deep breath and plunged. When I talked about it at home my family began to treat me as if I had an adult mind. *Then too, my new opinions gave me the reputation here of being open-minded and capable of change.* I think I could have got really radical but I found it wasn't the way to get prestige here." (She judges most of her classmates to be as non-conservative as herself.)

Q72: "I take everything hard, and so of course I reacted hard to all the attitudes I found here. I'm 100% enthusiastic about Bennington, and that includes liberalism (but not radicalism, though I used to think so). Now I know that you can't be an *extremist if you're really devoted to an institution,* whether it's a labor union or a college." (A conspicuous leader who, like most of the others in this set of six, *judges classmates to be only slightly more conservative than herself.*)

Q63: "*I came to college to get away from my family,* who never had any respect for my mind. Becoming radical meant thinking for myself and, figuratively, thumb-ing my nose at my family. *It also meant intellectual identification with the faculty and students that I most wanted to be like.*" (She has always felt op-pressed by parental respectability and sibling achievements.)

Q57: "It's very simple. *I was so anxious to be accepted that I accepted the political complexion of the community here.* I just couldn't stand out against the crowd unless I had many friends and strong support." (Not a leader, but many close friends among leaders and non-conservatives.)

For these six, like the preceding seven, the membership group serves as refer-ence group for public affairs. They differ from the preceding seven chiefly in that they are less sure of themselves and are careful "not to go too far." Hence they tend to repudiate "radicalism," and to judge classmates as only slightly less conservative than themselves.

7. *Non-conservatives, not reputedly community-identified, aware of own relative non-conservatism.* Each of the six is described as highly independent and critical-minded. Four are consistently reported as intellectually outstand-ing, and the other two occasionally so. All describe their ambitions on coming to college in intellectual rather than in social terms. Four of the five who were interviewed stated that in a conservative college they would be "even more radical than here." Two are slightly above average in prestige, two below average, and two have zero scores. Three have gone through rather severe bat-tles in the process of casting off what they regard as parental shackles; none is considered overdependent upon parents. Sample interview excerpts follow:

Q7: "*All my life I've resented the protection of governesses and parents.* What I most wanted here was the intellectual approval of teachers and the more ad-vanced students. Then I found you can't be reactionary and be intellectually respectable." (Her traits of independence became more marked as she achieved academic distinction.)

Q21: "I simply got filled with new ideas here, and the only possible formulation of all of them was to adopt a radical approach. *I can't see my own position in the world in any other terms. The easy superficiality with which so many prestige-hounds here get 'liberal' only forced me to think it out more intensely.*" (A highly gifted girl, considered rather aloof.)

C32: "*I started rebelling against my pretty stuffy family before I came to college.* I felt apart from freshmen here, because I was older. Then I caught on to faculty attempts to undermine prejudice. I took sides with the faculty immediately, against the immature freshmen. I crusaded about it. *It provided just what I needed by way of family rebellion,* and bolstered up my self-confidence, too." (A very bright girl, regarded as sharp tongued and a bit haughty.)

J24: "*I'm easily influenced by people whom I respect,* and the people who rescued me when I was down and out, intellectually, gave me a radical intellectual approach; they included both teachers and advanced students. *I'm not rebelling against anything.* I'm just doing what I had to do to stand on my own feet intellectually." (Her academic work was poor as a freshman, but gradually became outstanding.)

For these six students it is not the total membership group, but dominant sub-groups (faculty, advanced students) which at first served as positive reference groups, and for many of them the home group served as a negative point of reference. Later, they developed extra-college reference groups (left-wing writers, etc.). In a secondary sense, however, the total membership group served as a negative point of reference—i.e., they regarded their non-conservatism as a mark of personal superiority.

8. *Non-conservatives not reputedly community-identified, not aware of own relative non-conservatism.* Each of the five is considered hard-working, eager and enthusiastic but (especially during the first year or two) unsure of herself and too dependent upon instructors. They are "good citizens," but in a distinctly retiring way. Two are above average in prestige, and the other three much below average. None of the five is considered overdependent upon parents; two are known to have experienced a good deal of conflict in emancipating themselves. All regard themselves as "pretty average persons," with strong desire to conform; they describe their ambitions in terms of social acceptance instead of social or intellectual prestige. Sample excerpts follow:

E22: "*Social security is the focus of it all with me.* I became steadily less conservative as long as I was *needing to gain in personal security, both with students and with faculty.* I developed some resentment against a few extreme radicals who don't really represent the college viewpoint, and that's why I changed my attitudes so far and no further." (A girl with a small personal following, otherwise not especially popular.)

D52: "*Of course there's social pressure here to give up your conservatism.* I'm glad of it, because for me this became the *vehicle for achieving independence from my family.* So changing my attitudes has gone hand in hand with two *very important things: establishing my own independence and at the same time becoming a part of the college organism.*" (She attributes the fact that her social attitudes changed, while those of her younger sister, also at the college, did not, to the fact that she had greater need both of family independence and of group support.)

Q6: "I was ripe for developing liberal or even radical opinions because so many of my friends at home were doing the same thing. So it was really wonderful that I could agree with all the people I respected here and the same time move in the direction that my home friends were going." (A girl characterized by considerable personal instability at first, but showing marked improvement.)

Qy: "I think my change of opinions has given me *intellectual and social self-respect at the same time.* I used to be too timid for words, and I never had an idea of my own. As I gradually became more successful in my work and made more friends, I came to feel that it didn't matter so much whether I agreed with my parents. It's all part of the feeling that I really belong here." (Much other evidence confirms this; she was lonely and pathetic at first, but really belonged later.)

These five provide the example *par excellence* of individuals who came to identify themselves with "the community" and whose attitudes changed *pari passu* with the growing sense of identity. Home-and-family groups served as supplementary points of reference, either positive or negative. To varying degrees, subgroups within the community served as focal points of reference. But, because of *their need to be accepted, it was primarily the membership group as such which served as reference group for these five.*

SUMMARY

In this community, as presumably in most others, all individuals belong to the total membership group, but such membership is not necessarily a point of reference for every form of social adaptation, e.g., for acquiring attitudes toward public issues. *Such attitudes, however, are not acquired in a social vacuum. Their acquisition is a function of relating oneself to some group or groups, positively or negatively.* In many cases (perhaps in all) the referring of social attitudes to one group negatively leads to referring them to another group positively, or vice versa, so that the attitudes are dually reinforced.

An individual is, of course, "typical" in respect to attitudes if the total membership group serves as a positive point of reference for that purpose, but "typicality" may also result from the use of other reference groups. It does not follow from the fact that an individual is "atypical" that the membership group does not serve for reference purposes; it may serve as negative reference group. Even if the membership group does not serve as reference group at all (as in the case of conservatives in this community who are unaware of the general freshman-to-senior trend), it cannot be concluded that attitude development is not a function of belonging to the total membership group. The unawareness of such individuals is itself a resultant adaptation of particular individuals to a particular membership group. The fact that such individuals continue to refer attitudes toward public issues primarily to home-and-family groups is, in part at least, a result of the kind of community in which they have membership.

In short, the Bennington findings seem to support the thesis that, in a community characterized by certain approved attitudes, the individual's attitude development is a function of the way in which he relates himself both to the total membership group and to reference group or groups.

Chapter 34

Liberating effects of group pressure*

Stanley Milgram

It is said that Adolf Hitler once worked himself into such a frenzy during a speech that he could think of nothing more to say. Finally, he
simply bellowed "Gehorsamkeit!" or "Obedience!", to which the audience automatically responded with "Heil Hitler!" The following investigation of the strength of obedience as a generalized reinforcer would
suggest that the Nazis had no monopoly on its potential antisocial use,
but its influence is considerably weakened when group pressure is in-
voked to oppose rather than to support it.

In laboratory research, the effect of group pressure has most often been
studied in its negative aspect; the conspiratorial group is shown to limit, con-
strain, and distort the individual's responses (Asch, 1951; Blake & Brehm,
1954; Milgram, 1964). Edifying effects of the group, although acknowledged,
have rarely been demonstrated with the clarity and force of its destructive potential. Particularly in those areas in which a morally relevant choice is at issue, experimentalists typically examine pressures that diminish the scope of individual action. They have neglected effects that enhance the individual's sense
of worth, enlarge the possibilities for action, and help the subject resolve conflicting feelings in a direction congruent with his ideals and values. Although in
everyday life occasions arise when conformity to group pressures is constructive,
in the laboratory "thinking and investigation have concentrated almost obses-
sively on conformity in its most sterile forms [Asch, 1959]."

There are technical difficulties to demonstrating the value enhancing potential of group pressure. They concern the nature of the base line from which
the group effect is to be measured. The problem is that the experimental subject ordinarily acts in a manner that is socially appropriate. If he has come to
the laboratory to participate in a study on the perception of lines, he will generally report what he sees in an honest manner. If one wishes to show the
effects of group influence by producing a change in his performance, the only

*From *Journal of Personality and Social Psychology* 1(2):127-134, 1965. By permission
of the author and American Psychological Association.

direction open to change is that of creating some deficiency in his performance, which can then be attributed to group influences.

If men tend to act constructively under usual circumstances the obvious direction of an induced and measurable change is toward inappropriate behavior. It is this technical need rather than the inherently destructive character of group forces that has dictated the lines of a good deal of laboratory research. The experimental problem for any study of *constructive* conformity is to create a situation in which undesirable behavior occurs with regularity and then to see whether group pressure can be applied effectively in the direction of a valued behavior outcome.[1]

EXPERIMENT I: BASE-LINE CONDITION

A technique for the study of destructive obedience (Milgram, 1963) generates the required base line. In this situation a subject is ordered to give increasingly more severe punishment to a person. Despite the apparent discomfort, cries, and vehement protests of the victim, the experimenter instructs the subject to continue stepping up the shock level.

Technique

Two persons arrive at a campus laboratory to take part in a study of memory and learning. (One of them is a confederate of the experimenter.) Each subject is paid $4.50 upon arrival, and is told that payment is not affected in any way by performance. The experimenter provides an introductory talk on memory and learning processes and then informs the subjects that in the experiment one of them will serve as teacher and the other as learner. A rigged drawing is held so that the naive subject is always assigned the role of teacher and the accomplice becomes the learner. The learner is taken to an adjacent room and is strapped into an electric chair.

The naive subject is told that it is his task to teach the learner a list of paired associates, to test him on the list, and to administer punishment whenever the learner errs in the test. Punishment takes the form of electric shock, delivered to the learner by means of a shock generator controlled by the naive subject. The teacher is instructed to increase the intensity of the electric shock one step on the generator on each error. The generator contains 30 voltage levels ranging from 15 to 450 volts, and verbal designations ranging from Slight Shock to Danger: Severe Shock. The learner, according to plan, provides many wrong answers, so that before long the naive subject must give him the strongest shock on the generator. Increases in shock level are met by increasingly insistent demands from the learner that the experiment be stopped because of growing discomfort to him. However, the experimenter instructs the teachers to continue with the procedure in disregard of the learner's protests.

A quantitative value is assigned to the subject's performance based on the maximum intensity shock he administered before breaking off. Thus any subject's score may range from 0 (for a subject unwilling to administer the first shock level) to 30 (for a subject who proceeds to the highest voltage level on the board).

---

[1]Another solution would be to wait until people who perform in a naturally destructive way come to the laboratory and to use them as subjects. One might deliberately seek out a group of recidivist delinquents who would ordinarily behave in a disvalued manner, and then study group effects on their performance. This would, of course, limit the study to an atypical population.

Subjects

The subjects used in the several experimental conditions were male adults residing in the greater New Haven area, aged 20-50 years, and engaged in a wide variety of occupations. Each experimental condition described here employed 40 fresh subjects and was carefully balanced for age and occupational types (see Milgram, 1963, Table 1, for details).

Results and discussion

In this situation a subject is instructed to perform acts that are in some sense incompatible with his normal standards of behavior. In the face of the vehement protests of an innocent individual, many subjects refuse to carry out the experimenter's orders to continue with the shock procedure. They reject the role assignment of *experimental subject,* assert themselves as persons, and are unwilling to perform actions that violate personal standards of conduct. The distribution of break-off points for this condition is shown in Table 11, Column 1. Fourteen of the 40 subjects withdraw from the experiment at some point before the completion of the command series.

The majority of subjects, however, comply fully with the experimenter's commands, despite the acute discomfort they often experience in connection with shocking the victim. Typically these obedient subjects report that they do not wish to hurt the victim, but they feel obligated to follow the orders of the experimenter. On questioning they often state that it would have been "better" not to have shocked the victim at the highest voltage levels. Consider, for example, the remarks of the following obedient subject. He has completed the experiment and is now questioned by an interviewer (who is not the experimenter).

I'd like to ask you a few questions. How do you feel? I feel all right, but I don't like what happened to that fellow in there [the victim]. He's been hollering and we had to keep giving him shocks. I didn't like that one bit. I mean he wanted to get out but he [the experimenter] just kept going, he kept throwing 450 volts. I didn't like that.

Who was actually pushing the switch? I was, but he kept insisting. I told him "No," but he said you got to keep going. I told him it's time we stopped when we get up to 195 or 210 volts.

Why didn't you just stop? He wouldn't let me. I wanted to stop. I kept insisting to stop, but he said "No." . . . I figured the voltage we were giving him was quite a bit. I wanted to stop but he [the experimenter] kept insisting not to stop. I mean the fellow in there is hollering "I don't want to do it. I want to get out of here. I want to get out of here!"

Why didn't you just disregard what the experimenter said? He says it's got to go on, the experiment.

Do you feel a little upset? Well, I mean I feel concerned about the gentlemen in there, I do sir . . . I was getting ready to walk out . . . I couldn't see the point of going on when the guy is suffering in there. I figured he was having a heart attack or something. That's the reason I wanted to stop. . . .

The subject was then dehoaxed carefully and had a friendly reconciliation with the victim.

There is additional evidence that, in shocking the victim to the end of the command series, subjects are engaging in behavior which they disvalue and see as antithetical to personal and social ideals:

Spontaneous shock levels. In an experimental control reported elsewhere

Table 11. Distribution of break-off points by condition

Shock level	Verbal designation and voltage level	Base-line condition (n = 40) (1)	Hypothetical subjects (n = 40) (2)	Disobedient groups (n = 40) (3)	Obedient groups (n = 40) (4)
	Slight shock		3[a]		
1	15	0	0	0	0
2	30	0	0	0	0
3	45	0	1	0	0
4	60	0	1	0	0
	Moderate shock				
5	75	0	7	0	1
6	90	1	1	0	0
7	105	0	1	1	1
8	120	0	3	0	0
	Strong shock				
9	135	0	2	0	0
10	150	6	9	3←	2
11	165	0	2	4	0
12	180	1	3	1	1
	Very strong shock				
13	195	0	1	4	0
14	210	0	0	12←	0
15	225	0	1	0	0
16	240	0	1	0	0
	Intense shock				
17	255	0	1	0	0
18	270	2	0	4	4
19	285	0	0	0	0
20	300	1	3	2	0
	Extreme intensity shock				
21	315	1	0	3	2
22	330	1	0	0	0
23	345	0	0	0	0
24	360	0	0	1	0
	Danger: severe shock				
25	375	1	0	0	0
26	390	0	0	1	0
27	405	0	0	0	0
28	420	0	0	0	0
	XXX				
29	435	0	0	0	0
30	450	26	0	4	29
	Mean maximum shock	24.55	9.00	16.45	25.70
	Percentage defiant subjects	35.0%	100.0%	90.0%	27.5%

[a] These 3 subjects indicated they would refuse to administer even the lowest shock.

(Milgram, 1964), subjects administer any voltage level they wish in the absence of group or authoritarian pressure. Under this condition the mean maximum shock for 40 subjects is 82.5 volts (level = 5.50); in contrast, under command of the experimenter (in the base-line condition described above) the mean maximum shock is 368.25 volts (level = 24.55). When left on their own, subjects administer far lower shock levels than when under command.

Self-image. When persons who have not performed in the experiment are provided with a description of the experimental situation, and are asked to predict their own performance, almost all subjects see themselves as defying the experimenter at some point in the command series. Moreover, they justify their hypothetical behavior in terms of positive qualities of character, employing such statements as "I'm not the kind of person who is willing to hurt others even for the cause of science."

Column 2 of Table 11 shows the anticipated break-off points of 40 adult respondents who were asked to predict their own experimental performance. Hypothetical subjects respond in terms of ideals, values, and positive self-conceptions; these values are frequently overridden by the forces engendered in the concrete laboratory situation.

Moral judgment. Twenty undergraduates were asked to render a moral judgment on the issue of obeying or disobeying the experimenter. After describing the experiment to the respondents in concrete detail, the experimenter asked:

In terms of the moral and ethical values most important to you, and taking into account the scientific goals served by the research, how *should* you perform in the experimental situation? Should you go through to the end of the experiment or should you break off at some point?

Valued break-off points ranged from 0 to 255 volts with the median at 150 volts. Subjects were also asked to explain at length the values that should guide their behavior in the laboratory situation. A sample statement is given below:

I would say that one should not even start the shocks, but rather, forcibly withdraw the moment that the outline of the experiment becomes evident. My reasons for saying this are very complex . . . The first is that the society's morals, which I have absorbed, teach that it is wrong to hurt a man. Morals are usually tied in with religion and this is especially true with Christianity. Having been raised, then, in an old fashioned, staunchly Lutheran family I have internalized the view that hurting a man is wrong, and no amount of intellectual reasoning can shake this belief.

Thus, there is a clear consensus that the only behavior consistent with social values and individual conscience is to defy the experimenter at some point before the completion of the command series. Yet there is a marked discrepancy between this value judgment and the actual performance of subjects in the laboratory. Despite their protests and obvious conflict in shocking the victim, a substantial number of subjects are unable to defy the experimenter's authority, and proceed to administer the highest shock levels commanded by him.

EXPERIMENT II: GROUPS FOR DISOBEDIENCE

We may now examine in what degree group influence can release the subject from authoritarian control, and allow him to act in a direction congruent with his values and personal standards.

The strategy is to replicate Experiment I, but with this difference: the subject is placed in the midst of two peers who defy the experimenter and refuse to punish the victim against his will. In what degree will the pressure created by their action affect the naive subject's behavior?

Technique

Forty fresh subjects were studied in this condition. The procedure is identical to Experiment I with these exceptions: Four persons appear at the laboratory to take part in an experiment on "the effects of collective teaching and punishment on memory and learning." Three subjects are confederates of the experimenter and one is a naive subject. The experimenter explains that three teachers and one learner are to be used in the study, and by means of a rigged drawing, the naive subject is assigned the position of Teacher 3. The roles of Teacher 1, Teacher 2, and learner are filled by the confederates. The learner is strapped into the electric chair and the three teachers are seated before the shock generator. Teacher 1 is told to read the list of word pairs, Teacher 2 informs the subject if he is correct or incorrect in his answers, and Teacher 3 (the naive subject) administers punishment. As in Experiment I, the subjects are instructed to raise the shock level one step each time the learner makes an error. (More detailed descriptions of the group technique can be found in Milgram, 1964.)

Behavior of confederates. The confederates comply with the experimenter through the 150-volt shock. After the 150-volt level is administered Teacher 1 informs the experimenter that he does not wish to participate further, because of the learner's complaints. (It is at the 150-volt shock level that the learner makes his first vehement protest.) The experimenter insists that the subject continue. However, Teacher 1 is not swayed by the experimenter's commands, gets up from his chair in front of the shock generator, and takes a seat in another part of the room. Since the experimenter's efforts to get the subject to return to the generator are futile, the experimenter instructs the remaining two subjects to continue with the experiment. Teacher 3 (the naive subject) is to handle the reading of word pairs, in addition to his regular job of administering electric shock to the learner.

After Shock Level 14 (210 volts) is administered, Teacher 2, expressing concern for the learner, refuses to participate further. The experimenter makes strong efforts to have him continue, but he too leaves his chair in front of the generator and seats himself at an opposite corner of the room, saying "I'm willing to answer any of your questions, but I'm not willing to shock that man against his will; I'll have no part of it."

At this point the naive subject is seated alone in front of the shock generator. He has witnessed the defiant actions of two peers. The experimenter orders the naive subject to continue with the experimental procedure by himself, indicating that it is essential that the experiment be completed.

Results and discussion

The break-off points of the naive subjects in Experiment II are shown in Table 11, Column 3. The arrows at Shock Levels 10 and 14 indicate the points at which each of the confederates defied the experimenter.

Comparing the proportion of obedient to defiant subjects in Experiments I and II, we see that the effect of the confederates' pressure was substantial. In Experiment I, 26 subjects proceeded to the end of the command series; less than one-sixth of this number obeyed fully in the group setting (obedient versus defiant subjects $\chi^2 = 25.81$, $df = 1$, $p < .001$). The mean maximum shock in Experiment II (16.45) was also significantly lower than in Experiment I (24.55, $p < .001$).[2]

---

[2]Of course the mean maximum shock in the experimental condition is tied to the precise point in the voltage series where the confederates' break-off is staged. In this experiment it is not until Level 14 that both confederates have defied the experimenter.

After Shock Level 14 the second confederate defies the experimenter. Before Level 15 is administered, 25 naive subjects have followed the defiant group, while at the corresponding point in Experiment I only 8 subjects have refused to follow the experimenter's orders. The confederates appear to exert some influence, however, even on those subjects who do not follow them immediately. Between Voltage Levels 17 and 29, 11 subjects in Experiment II break off, while only 6 subjects do so in Experiment I.

In sum, in the group setting 36 of the 40 subjects defy the experimenter while the corresponding number in the absence of group pressure is 14. The effects of peer rebellion are most impressive in undercutting the experimenter's authority. Indeed, of the score of experimental variations completed in the Yale study on obedience none was so effective in undermining the experimenter's authority as the manipulation reported here.[3]

How should we account for the powerful effect of the experimental manipulation? It is probable that in Experiment I many subjects come near to performing the defiant action but cannot quite bring themselves to the point of disobedience. The additional pressure of the group members leads to an increment in the forces oriented toward defiance; the increment is of sufficient strength so that, in combination with pressures for defiance already present, many subjects are carried over the threshold of disobedience.

The strong liberating effect of the peers brings to mind the powerful effect of a partner in Asch's (1951) study. In that experiment negative pressures originated within the group itself so that the conflicting agents (partner versus majority) were internal to the group boundary; in the present study the peers free the subject from an influence that is *external* to the group. Additionally, the partner's support in Asch's study leads to a response that is fundamentally similar in form but different in value from that of the erring majority. In the present study the peers initiate a radically different order of response, one which has no antecedent in the course of the laboratory hour, and which destroys the very framework of the experiment.

Reactions to the confederates. The reactions of naive subjects to the defiant confederates varied considerably and were in part dependent on the exact point where the subject himself defied the experimenter. A subject who quit simultaneously with the first confederate stated, "Well, I was already thinking about quitting when the guy broke off." Most defiant subjects praised the confederates with such statements as, "I thought they were men of good character, yes I do. When the victim said 'Stop,' they stopped [Shock Level 11]."[4] "I think they were very sympathetic people . . . and they were totally unaware of what was in store for them [Shock Level 14]."

A subject who defied the experimenter at Level 21 qualified his approval: "Well I think they should continue a little further, but I don't blame them for backing out when they did."

A few subjects acknowledged the importance of the confederates in leading to their own defiance: "The thought of stopping didn't enter my mind until it was put there by the other two [Shock Level 14]." "The reason I quit was that

---

[3]See Milgram (1963) for additional experiments.

[4]Numerals in brackets indicate the break-off point of the subject quoted.

I did not wish to seem callous and cruel in the eyes of the other two men who had already refused to go on with the experiment [Shock Level 14]." The majority of subjects, however, denied that the confederates' action was the critical factor in their own defiance.[5]

The fact that obedient subjects failed to follow the defiant group should not suggest that they did not feel the pressure of the confederates' action. One obedient subject stated:

I felt that I would just look like a real Simon Legree to these guys if I just went on cooly and just kept administering lashes. I thought they reacted normally, and the first thing that came to my mind was to react as they did. But I didn't, because if they reacted normally, and stopped the experiment, and I did the same, I don't know how many months and days you'd have to continue before you got done.

Thus this subject felt the burden of the group judgment, but sensed that in the light of two defections he had a special obligation to help the experimenter complete his work. Another obedient subject, when asked about the nervousness he displayed in the experiment, replied:

I think it was primarily because of their actions. Momentarily I was ready to go along with them. Then suddenly I felt that they were just being ridiculous. What was I doing following the crowd? . . . They certainly had a right to stop, but I felt they lost all control of themselves.

And a third obedient subject criticized the confederates more directly, stating:

I don't think they should have quit. They came here for an experiment, and I think they should have stuck with it.

A closer analysis of the experimental situation points to a number of specific factors that may contribute to the group's effectiveness:

1. The peers instill in the subject the *idea* of defying the experimenter. It may not have occurred to some subjects as a response possibility.

2. The lone subject has no way of knowing whether, in defying the experimenter, he is performing in a bizarre manner or whether this action is a common occurrence in the laboratory. The two examples of disobedience he sees suggest that defiance is a natural reaction to the situation.

3. The reactions of the defiant confederates define the act of shocking the victim as improper. They provide social confirmation to the naive subject's suspicion that it is wrong to punish a man against his will, even in the context of a psychological experiment.

4. The defiant confederates remain in the laboratory even after withdrawing from the experiment (they have agreed to answer postexperimental questions). Each additional shock administered by the naive subject now carries with it a measure of social disapproval from the two confederates.

5. As long as the two confederates participate in the experimental pro-

---

[5]Twenty-seven of the defiant subjects stated that they would have broken off without the benefit of the confederates' example; four subjects definitely acknowledged the confederates' rebellion as the critical factor in their own defiance. The remaining defiant subjects were undecided on this issue. In general, then, subjects underestimate the degree to which their defiant actions are dependent on group support.

cedure there is a dispersion of responsibility among the group members for shocking the victim. As the confederates withdraw, responsibility becomes focused onto the naive subject.

6. The naive subject is a witness to two instances of disobedience and observes the *consequences* of defying the experimenter to be minimal.

7. There is identification with the disobedient confederates and the possibility of falling back on them for social support when defying the experimenter.

8. Additionally, the experimenter's power may be diminished by the very fact of failing to keep the two confederates in line, following the general rule that every failure of authority to exact compliance to its commands weakens the perceived power of the authority (Homans, 1961).

Hypothesis of arbitrary direction of group effects

The results examined thus far show that group influence serves to liberate individuals effectively from submission to destructive commands. There are some who will take this to mean that the direction of group influence is arbitrary, that it can be oriented toward destructive or constructive ends with equal impact, and that group pressure need merely be inserted into a social situation on one side of a standard or the other in order to induce movement in the desired direction.

This view ought to be questioned. Does the fact that a disobedient group alters the behavior of subjects in Experiment II necessarily imply that group pressure can be applied in the other direction with similar effectiveness? A competing view would be that the direction of possible influence of a group is not arbitrary, but is highly dependent on the general structure of the situation in which influence is attempted.

To examine this issue we need to undertake a further experimental variation, one in which the group forces are thrown on the side of the experimenter, rather than directed against him. The idea is simply to have the members of the group reinforce the experimenter's commands by following them unfailingly, thus adding peer pressures to those originating in the experimenter's commands.

EXPERIMENT III: OBEDIENT GROUPS

Forty fresh subjects, matched to the subjects in Experiments I and II, for sex, age, and occupational status, were employed in this condition. The procedure was identical to that followed in Experiment II with this exception: at all times the two confederates followed the commands of the experimenter; at no point did they object to carrying out the experimental instructions. Nor did they show sympathy for or comment on the discomfort of the victim. If a subject attempted to break off they allowed the experimenter primary responsibility for keeping him in line, but contributed background support for the experimenter; they indicated their disapproval of the naive subject's attempts to leave the experiment with such remarks as: "You can't quit *now;* this experiment has got to get done." As in Experiment II the naive subject was seated between the two confederates, and in his role of Teacher 3, administered the shocks to the victim.

Results and discussion

The results, presented in Table 11, Column 4, show that the obedient group had very little effect on the overall performance of subjects. In Experiment I,

26 of the 40 subjects complied fully with the experimenter's commands; in the present condition this figure is increased but 3, yielding a total of 29 obedient subjects. This increase falls far short of statistical significance ($\chi^2 = .52$, $df = 1$, $p > .50$). Nor is the difference in mean maximum shocks statistically reliable. The failure of the manipulation to produce a significant change cannot be attributed to a ceiling artifact since an obedient shift of even 8 of the 14 defiant subjects would yield the .05 significance level by chi square.

Why the lack of change when we know that group pressure often exerts powerful effects? One interpretation is that the authoritarian pressure already present in Experiment I has preempted subjects who would have submitted to group pressures. Conceivably, the subjects who are fully obedient in Experiment I are precisely those who would be susceptible to group forces, while those who resisted authoritarian pressure were also immune to the pressure of the obedient confederates. The pressures applied in Experiment III do not show an effect because they overlap with other pressures having the same direction and present in Experiment I; all persons responsive to the initial pressure have already been moved to the obedient criterion in Experiment I. This possibility seems obvious enough in the present study. Yet every other situation in which group pressure is exerted also possesses a field structure (a particular arrangement of stimulus, motive, and social factors) that limits and controls potential influence within that field. Some structures allow group influence to be exerted in one direction but not another. Seen in this light, the hypothesis of the arbitrary direction of group effects is inadequate.

In the present study Experiment I defines the initial field: the insertion of group pressure in a direction opposite to that of the experimenter's commands (Experiment II) produces a powerful shift toward the group. Changing the direction of group movement (Experiment III) does not yield a comparable shift in the subject's performance. The group success in one case and failure in another can be traced directly to the configuration of motive and social forces operative in the starting situation (Experiment I).

Given any social situation, the strength and direction of potential group influence is predetermined by existing conditions. We need to examine the variety of field structures that typify social situations and the manner in which each controls the pattern of potential influence.

Chapter 35

The Robbers Cave experiment*

Muzafer Sherif and Carolyn W. Sherif

In the summer of 1954, the third experiment on group relations was carried out under the direction of M. Sherif. The general plan of the study followed the 1949 and 1953 experiments.

The crucial problem of the 1954 experiment was the *reduction* of intergroup friction and conflict. It was carried out in three successive stages:

 I. *The stage of in-group formation.* In order to study intergroup relations, there have to be groups with definite structures and norms of
 their own.
 II. *The stage of intergroup friction and conflict.* Before tackling the main
 problem, namely, that of changing unfavorable intergroup attitudes
 toward friendship and cooperation, it was necessary first to produce
 unmistakable manifestations of intergroup conflict.
 III. *The stage of reduction of intergroup friction.* This stage is the crucial
 one and constitutes the really new step beyond the previous experiments in this series.

The study was carried out in Robbers Cave State Park, about 150 miles
southeast of Oklahoma City. The 200-acre camp site is wooded, hilly, and
completely surrounded by the state park. The camp site and surrounding areas
afforded ample facilities for separate housing for the groups, varied activities,
and lifelike problem situations.

Subjects were 22 boys of about 11 years of age. They all came from established, middle socioeconomic class, stable, Protestant families. None came from
broken homes. None was a problem case in school, home, or neighborhood.
They were all in the upper half of their class in scholastic standing and had
above average IQ's. They were all healthy, socially well-adjusted boys.

Since the subjects came from a homogeneous socioeconomic, religious, and
ethnic background, the results cannot be explained on the basis of social background differences. Neither can they be explained on the basis of failure, excessive frustration, maladjustment suffered in their life histories, or scholastic
retardation or intellectual ineptitude. Since the subjects were not acquainted

*From pp. 301-324 in *An Outline of Social Psychology,* rev. ed., by Muzafer Sherif and
Carolyn W. Sherif. Copyright, 1948, 1956 by Harper & Row, Publishers, Inc. Reprinted
by permission of the publishers.

with one another prior to the experiment, groups were not formed around previously existing personal relationships.

The subjects were divided into two bunches prior to the experiment. These two bunches were matched in as many respects as possible (physical size, athletic ability, swimming, cooking, musical proficiency, and so on). The two bunches of boys were taken to the experimental site in separate buses and at different times. Until the last days of Stage I (group formation), the two groups carried on in-group activities unaware of each other's presence and activities in the camp.

The nature of goals introduced in each experimental stage was specified. In the first stage, goals required coordinated activity conducive to division of labor and hence to status and role differentiation. In the second stage, goals were conducive to friction between groups. In the third stage, goals were conducive to interdependent and cooperative activity between groups.

No special techniques by adults to manipulate interaction were used. There were no lectures, exhortations, emotional appeals, or discussions led by adults. Rather, carefully designed problem situations were introduced. When the group members reached a decision and took a course of action, they were given an effective hand by staff members in carrying it out.

STAGE I: FORMATION OF IN-GROUPS

The predictions concerning group formation and the conditions of interaction conducive to it were formulated in the following hypotheses:

1. A definite group structure consisting of differentiated status positions and reciprocal roles will be produced when a number of individuals (without previously established interpersonal relations) interact with one another under conditions (a) which situationally embody goals that have common appeal value to the individuals and (b) which require interdependent activities for their attainment.

2. When individuals interact under conditions stated in hypothesis 1, concomitant with the formation of group structure, norms regulating their behavior in relations with one another and activities commonly engaged in will be standardized.

In line with the findings of the 1949 and 1953 experiments, these two hypotheses were once more verified in the Robbers Cave experiment. The change from togetherness situations to more and more stabilized groups took place during interaction in a series of problem situations over a week's period. Each of the problem situations had common goals which could not be ignored by the individuals and which required coordinated efforts for their attainment.

The emergence of differentiated statuses was ascertained in daily observations and independent status ratings made twice a day by staff members. The criterion for formation of group structures was stabilization of statuses occupied by members for two consecutive days, as revealed in high agreement between independent ratings of different observers. At the end of a week this criterion was satisfied. Each group had adopted a name, "Rattlers" and "Eagles" respectively. Each had appropriated a bunkhouse, hide-out, and swimming place as its own. The boys put the names of their groups on flags and T-shirts. The Eagles had named their swimming place ("Moccasin Creek"). The

Rattlers appropriated the baseball field, which was closer to their area and which they had cleared for the coming competitive events when informed that another group was in the vicinity.

The sort of conditions which were introduced during this stage can be illustrated by representative problem situations. One was introduced by putting canoes near the bunkhouse of each group. When the group members discovered them, they wanted to take them to their special swimming place over rough terrain some distance away. The problem was discussed immediately and a plan carried out with the enthusiastic collaboration of group members.

Another typical problem situation was making available to the subjects the ingredients of a meal in unprepared form (e.g., meat, watermelon, Kool-Aid) at a time when they were hungry. Turning these ingredients into a meal required preparation, division into portions, and serving, in which participation of all was necessary.

STAGE II: PRODUCTION OF INTERGROUP FRICTION

The formation of negative intergroup attitudes and stereotypes was planned in order to create the problem of reducing them. The main hypotheses for this stage were:

1. In the course of competition and frustrating relations between two groups, unfavorable stereotypes will come into use in relation to the out-group and its members and will be standardized in time, placing the out-group at a certain social distance.
2. The course of relations between two groups which are in a state of competition will tend to produce an increase in in-group solidarity.
3. Functional relations between groups which are of consequence to the groups in question will tend to bring about changes in the pattern of relations within in-groups involved.

To test these predictions, a series of competitive events and reciprocally frustrating situations was planned. As in the previous experiment, prizes were to be awarded to the group that accumulated the higher score in a tournament. There was great enthusiasm over this tournament in both groups. When the boys learned of the presence of another group during the last days of Stage I, each group to a man expressed intense desires to compete with that other group with a great confidence in themselves, and issued a challenge to the other group. Thus it appeared to the subjects that the tournament was the consequence of their own challenges. This strong tendency to want to compete with another group stemmed from their experiences and activities in the general culture.

In this experiment it proved unnecessary to introduce planned situations which were mutually frustrating. A series of mutually frustrating situations arose when the Eagles were defeated in a tug-of-war contest toward the end of the first day of the tournament. The Eagles burned the Rattlers' flag, which had been left on the backstop of the athletic field. The following morning the Rattlers arrived first at the athletic field and discovered their burned emblem. This seemed an outrage which must have been the vengeful deed of the Eagles. They drew up a strategy to destroy the Eagle flag if the Eagles admitted the misdeed.

So when the Eagles arrived at the field and admitted they had burned the flag, the Rattlers immediately went into action according to plan. The Eagles' flag was seized; the Eagles responded with some violence and in turn seized the remaining Rattler flag. Through all, the groups were scuffling and shouting derogatory names.

During the rest of this experimental stage, name-calling, physical encounters, and "raids" followed one another. After the skirmishes over the flags, the Rattlers staged a "raid" on the Eagle cabin, causing quite a bit of inconvenience and frustration to the Eagles. . . . The Rattlers displayed blue jeans seized as booty on which they painted "The Last of the Eagles." This raid was later reciprocated by the Eagles, who left the Rattlers' cabin in confusion. However, this was a mild affair compared to the Rattlers' retaliation some days later, which took place after the Rattlers lost the tournament.

In the competitive events, the success of one group meant the failure of the other. In the reciprocally frustrating engagements that flared up, unfavorable invectives were hurled across group lines. Physical encounters intensified intergroup hostility. Within six days the intergroup conflict produced such an unfavorable image of the out-group, with accompanying derogatory stereotypes, that each group was dead set against having any more to do with the other. Thus there arose extreme social distance between the two groups.

Estimation of time by groups on the verge of victory and defeat. Each engagement in the competitive series implied considerable effort and zeal, which were reflected in characteristic psychological reactions and contributed to the building up of unfavorable attitudes toward the out-group. One of the noteworthy incidents is exemplified in the second tug-of-war. The Rattlers had won the first tug-of-war. The Eagles had retaliated by burning the Rattler flag, which initiated the series of conflict situations .

Before the Eagles came to the second tug-of-war on the next day, they devised a strategy to win. After the pulling started, on a prearranged signal the Eagles all sat down on the ground and dug in their feet. The confident Rattlers were on their feet pulling strenuously, but they were becoming exhausted and rapidly lost ground. After seven minutes, the Rattlers adopted the enemy strategy and dug in too.

Greatly exhausted during their initial pull in a standing position, the Rattlers were being pulled gradually across the line. At the fortieth minute of the contest, a time limit of an additional 15 minutes was announced. At the end of this time, the Rattlers had not yet been pulled completely over the line. The contest was declared a tie, to the indignation of the Eagles and the relief and satisfaction of the weary Rattlers.

The Rattlers, thus relieved of certain defeat had the contest lasted longer, were accusing the Eagles of employing "dirty" strategy and telling each other that the contest had appeared to them as if it would never end. The Eagles, on the other hand, were remarking to each other that the precious time flew too fast on the verge of their victory.

On the following day the participant observers of each group asked the members of their respective groups individually, "How long did the tug-of-war last after both groups sat down and dug in?" The actual duration was 48 minutes. The Eagle estimates ranged from 20 to 45 minutes. The Rattler estimates ranged from 1 hour to $3\frac{1}{2}$ hours. Thus there was no overlapping at all between the estimates of time made by the two groups. Deliberately, the question was worded without specifying a time unit. The Eagles all gave their judgments in minute units. The Rattlers gave theirs in hour units.

Impact of intergroup events on in-group relations. The nature of in-group relations is essential in understanding intergroup relations. The reverse is equally true; for an adequate understanding of in-group relations, the understanding of relations between groups is also essential. A striking illustration was the downfall of Craig from the leadership status in the Eagle group as intergroup competition and conflict developed during Stage II. Craig rose to leadership during Stage I, when more peaceful activities were engaged in. But with the advent of Stage II, which required leadership that could stand in the front line in contests and engagements against an adversary, Craig did not live up to expectations. For example, he deserted the rope during the first tug-of-war when it became evident that the Eagles were losing. Several days later, he kept himself at a safe distance when the Eagles attempted a retaliatory raid on the Rattlers. Therefore, Mason, a high-status Eagle, rose steadily and took over leadership in the group with his exemplary daring and front-line action in various contests and conflicts with the Rattlers.

In various events, defeats caused temporary confusion, bickering, and blaming each other within both groups. On the whole, however, the cumulative effect of intergroup friction was to intensify in-group solidarity. Temporary dissension within the group was followed typically by renewed efforts at in-group coordination, planning new tactics or engaging in acts directed against the out-group, and the like.

The change of leadership in the Eagles, reciprocal bickering, and maneuvering for positions within groups were family affairs. The Eagles were like members of a family or good friends who join hands immediately against an outside intrusion.

One of the telling indications of increased in-group solidarity was exhibited in both groups at Carlton Lake, a public beach a few miles from the camp. At the end of Stage II, each group was taken there separately. This was a test situation. The public beach was crowded with people and full of other distractions. However, each group behaved there as if the boys were by themselves; they were altogether preoccupied with their own business and their own fun.

These are examples of the general finding that intergroup relations, both in conflict and in the period of friendship between groups which followed, had significant consequences for the properties of interaction and the relations of members within the group structures involved.

Summary of observational findings in Stage II. The recurrent observations during Stage II indicate that intergroup friction which is consequential in the scheme of group activities (1) brings about unfavorable attitudes and stereotypes in relation to the out-group, (2) increases in-group solidarity, and (3) changes the pattern of relations within groups when such changes become necessary for effective dealings in intergroup relations. These results substantiate further the findings concerning intergroup friction in the 1949 experiment.[1]

[1] In the 1953 study, this stage was not completed. In a frustration episode, the subjects attributed the plan to the camp administration. Since testing the hypothesis required that the source of frustration be attributed to the experimental out-group, the 1953 study was terminated at this point.

Checking observational findings with other methods. At the end of Stage II, sociometric choices, ratings of stereotypes of the in-group and the out-group, and judgments of performance by in-group and out-group were obtained in order to check the validity of observational findings.

Sociometric choices. Sociometric questions were asked informally of every member of each group individually. Two of the criterion questions concerned friendship preferences. They were worded to specify choices from the *entire camp* and not just from one's in-group. The other two criterion questions concerned effective initiative in the group, i.e., choosing who gets things started and who gets things done.

The friendship choices were overwhelmingly toward in-group members. Sociograms constructed on the basis of weighted scores (4 for the first choices, 3 for second, 2 for third, and 1 for the rest) for the four criteria reveal clearly the unique hierarchical group structures formed among the Rattlers and Eagles.

Stereotyped images of in-group and out-group. Ratings of fellow group members and members of the out-group were obtained on a number of adjectives, of which six were critical. These critical terms were chosen from those actually used by subjects in referring to their own group or to the out-group during the height of intergroup friction. Three were favorable terms *(brave, tough, friendly)* and three were unfavorable *(sneaky, smart alecks, stinkers)*. The rating technique was essentially like Avigdor's, ranging from "all of them are . . ." to "none of them are. . . ."

As predicted from observational data, ratings of fellow group members were almost exclusively favorable (100 percent by Rattlers and 94.3 percent by Eagles). In contrast, ratings of the out-group after the intense intergroup friction were predominantly unfavorable. The ratings made by Rattlers of Eagle members were 53 percent unfavorable and 34.9 percent favorable. The ratings made by the Eagles of the Rattlers were 76.9 percent unfavorable and only 15.4 percent favorable. (Other ratings fell in the category "some of them are. . . .") These significant differences between favorable and unfavorable designations of the in-group and out-group confirmed observational findings. They will be discussed further in giving results of Stage III, where shifts in these ratings brought about by changed intergroup relations constitute important substantiating evidence.

Judgments of performance by in-group and out-group. It was predicted that an individual group member would have formed attitudes toward his own group and the out-group which would influence significantly his appraisal of the activities of other individuals in the respective groups. This hypothesis was made on the basis of observations that the individual members tend to depreciate the achievements of the adversary and magnify the achievements of their fellows. This unit illustrates how precise methods derived from the laboratory can be utilized as an integral aspect of field study in lifelike conditions.

The task was introduced as a contest between the two groups, with a $5 reward to the winning group. Since social distance between the groups was so great that neither wanted to be in a situation with the other, this prize and the news that the staff had made wagers on the outcome of the event were inducements to take part. Once in the situation, members of each group participated with considerable zeal.

The contest was to be as follows: Each group was to collect beans which were scattered in two marked-off areas, one for each group, and then the number supposedly collected by each individual was to be judged. As far as subjects were concerned, both excellence in performance and accuracy in judgment were required to win the reward. The time for collecting beans was one minute. The beans were put in sacks with necks bound by a rubber hose so that they could not be counted.

After the collection the two groups went to a large hall where, according to announcement, the performance of each person (viz., beans collected) was projected by an opaque projector and judged by every other person. As each individual's supposed performance was projected, he stood up to insure proper identification.

Actually the same number of beans was projected each time for 5 seconds. Pretests with different subjects had shown that this number (35) could not be counted in 5 seconds but that subjects felt they could just about count if they tried a little harder. Thus, the number and timing reduced possible objections that exposure was too brief, but prevented accurate counting. Subjects did not suspect that the same number was projected each time. When the performance attributed to the Rattler leader was projected, admiring whistles were heard from his group.

The results of this unit were in numerical form, indicating the average amount of overestimation or underestimation of the number presented (35 in every case) as the performance by fellow group members or by members of the out-group. Thus the Rattlers tended to overestimate performance by fellow group members, the mean discrepancy between judgment and number projected being 3.40. In contrast, Rattlers tended to underestimate performance by Eagles with a mean discrepancy of –.29. Members of the Eagle group overestimated their own performance considerably more, the mean discrepancy being 11.80. In contrast, the Eagles' estimates of Rattler performance diverged from the actual number presented by only 4.56.

These differences between judgments of performance attributed to in-group members and of performance attributed to members of the out-group were highly significant and in the expected direction. It was concluded that the differing attitudes formed by individuals toward their own group and toward an antagonistic group affected their judgments. These results confirm the overall behavioral trends through reactions made in quantitative form by single individuals.

STAGE III: REDUCTION OF INTERGROUP CONFLICT AND STEREOTYPES

By the end of Stage II, each group saw the out-group as the "villain" and placed itself on the side of the angels, justifying its deeds and unfavorable stereotypes toward the out-group. Solidarity and cooperativeness within the in-groups did not lead to cooperativeness and solidarity between groups.

Choice of measure for reducing intergroup friction. Various measures have been proposed for reducing the intergroup frictions that prevail today. A few of these are listed here with brief notes explaining why they were not included among the experimental conditions in Stage III:

1. Disseminating favorable *information* in regard to the out-group was not chosen as the experimental measure. As we shall see in discussing the general problem of attitude change in Chapter 16, information not related to the goals currently in focus in the activities of the groups in question is relatively ineffective.

2. In small groups like those in this study, it is possible to devise sufficiently attractive rewards to make individual achievement supreme. This may reduce tension between small groups by splitting the memberships on the basis of *"every man for himself."* Such a solution, however, has little relevance for actual intergroup tensions. In real life, social distance and intergroup conflict are in terms of membership in groups and of group alignments.

3. The resolution of conflict through leaders alone was not utilized. Group leaders, even when meeting apart from their groups around a conference table, cannot be taken independently of the dominant trends and prevailing intergroup attitudes of the membership in their respective groups. If the leader is too much out of step with these, he will cease to be followed. It is more realistic, therefore, to study the influence of leadership within the framework of prevailing trends and attitudes of the groups involved. This will give us leads concerning the conditions under which leadership can be effective in reducing intergroup tensions.

4. The "common enemy" approach is effective in pulling two or more groups together against another group. This was utilized in the 1949 experiment and yielded effective results. But bringing some groups together against others means larger conflicts, even though it may patch up frictions among a few groups temporarily.

5. Another measure advanced, both in theoretical and practical works, centers around social contacts among members of groups who stand at given social distances on occasions which are pleasant in themselves. This measure was tried out in the first phase of Stage III of this study.

6. In the second phase of Stage III, the measure that was effectively used was the introduction of superordinate goals which necessitated cooperative interaction between the groups.

Phase 1: Social contacts in reducing intergroup conflict. Before getting to the introduction of superordinate goals, contact in social situations was arranged. In this series of contact situations during the first two days of Stage III, both groups were left free in close physical proximity to interact with one another in situations which were pleasant in themselves. The staff members appeared to be out of supervision range on these occasions, as much as possible.

There were seven different contact situations, including eating together in the same dining hall, watching a movie together, and shooting fire crackers in the same area. These contact situations had no effect in reducing intergroup friction. If anything, they were utilized by members of both groups as opportunities for further name-calling and conflict. For example, they used mealtimes in the same place for "garbage fights," throwing mashed potatoes, leftovers, bottle caps, and the like accompanied by the exchange of derogatory names.

Thus, in line with our hypothesis to this effect, *contact between groups does not in itself produce a decrease in an existing state of intergroup tension.* Because of its implications for learning theories and for practitioners in the intergroup relations area, special note should be made of the fact that these activities, carried out by the two groups in close physical proximity, were satisfying in themselves.

Phase 2: Interaction between groups toward superordinate goals. Following the social contact situations, a series of superordinate goals was introduced which afforded challenging problem situations for both groups. These superordinate goals necessitated intergroup interaction toward common ends in problem situations which were real to the members of both groups. The goals were selected so that they would become focal to members in both groups; therefore, they could not be ignored or postponed easily. The attainment of superordinate goals could not be achieved through the energy and resources of one group alone but required the combined efforts and resources of both groups. This is why they are called *superordinate goals.*

The first of the two hypotheses tested during this period was:

1. When groups in a state of friction are brought into contact under conditions embodying superordinate goals, which are compelling but which cannot be achieved by the efforts of one group alone, they will tend to cooperate toward the common goal.

However, it is too much to expect that a state of friction, unfavorable stereotypes, and mutual social distance developed in a series of encounters over a period will be eliminated in a single episode of cooperation toward a common end. Therefore, the second hypothesis was:

2. Cooperation between groups necessitated by a series of situations embodying superordinate goals will have a cumulative effect in the direction of reduction of existing tension between groups.

Accordingly, during the following six days, a series of problem situations embodying such goals was introduced. The situations were varied in nature and required varied kinds of consideration, planning, and execution on the part of the subjects. But no matter how varied they were, all had an essential feature in common: they all involved goals that became focal for both groups under the given circumstances. These goals were urgent to the subjects; they had to be attended to. Psychological selectivity favored them. Yet their attainment clearly depended on communication, planning, and joint action by both groups. Thus the problem situations created a state of interdependence. The goal was highly desired by both groups, yet it could not be attained by the efforts and energies of one group alone.

All of the superordinate goals and problem situations introduced cannot be described here. Three of them are summarized below.

1. Both groups were warned several hours in advance that there was trouble in the water-supply system. Water came from a tank on top of a hill about a mile away. The tank was supplied with water pumped from a reservoir approximately two miles' walking distance from the camp. The terrain between camp and tank and reservoir was mountainous, rough, thickly wooded, and bushy. Both groups had had first-hand acquaintance with these places

during Stage I, when each went on separate overnight camp-outs in the area. They had filled their canteens from a large faucet on the tank. So the water-supply system was real in the subjects' experience.

The problem situation was created by turning off a valve at the water tank and stuffing the open faucet on the tank with pieces of sacking. Several hours after a first warning, the water in the pipes leading to the camp was all drained through use. Therefore both groups were summoned to a central place at which the main pipe line in the camp divided into smaller lines supplying various points throughout the camp area. After demonstrating that the main pipe line and accessories were bone dry, the camp administration declared its inability to cope with the water situation within a reasonable time. It was explained that the defect might be leakage somewhere along the length of pipe line, at the pump by the reservoir, or in the supply tank. In order to make the outcome credible, it was stated that in the past vandals had been known to tamper with the supply system. Therefore, to solve the problem several parts of the system had to be attended to and about 20-25 men were required to discover the difficulty that day. By this time the Eagles were getting thirsty; the Rattlers still had a little water in their canteens.

Both groups promptly volunteered to tackle the situation. The details that volunteered for various segments of the water system were made up of either all Rattlers or all Eagles.

The announced plan was for all details to meet at the water tank after inspecting the pipe line and pump. In a little over an hour, all details congregated by the large tank. Since they were thirsty and hot, the first object of attention was the faucet on the tank. No water came out of the faucet. The members of the two groups took over the procedure. They tried to ascertain whether there was water in the tank.

When the faucet had been stopped up by the staff earlier in the day, the ladder, which leaned against the tank for climbing atop it, had been laid aside in the weeds about 30 feet away. Now the ladder was discovered by the boys. Almost to a man, Eagles and Rattlers were on top of the tank to look through the opening there and see if there was water in the tank. In short order, they came to the conclusion that the tank was practically full. Then the majority of both Eagles and Rattlers rushed again to the faucet. They discovered now that the faucet was stopped up with pieces of sack. Immediately they tackled the task of removing it. They pooled their available implements (mostly knives) and took turns at the work. Members of each group were mindful of and receptive to suggestions from members of the other group. There was common rejoicing at even the appearance of a few drops of water as efforts proceeded. This work lasted over half an hour. Then a Rattler suggested getting help from staff members. When the task was completed with staff help and the valve leading to the camp was turned on, there were expressions of satisfaction from all with the accomplishment, in which members of both groups had had an active and effective part.

This first cooperative action toward a common goal did not eliminate the stabilized intergroup friction. An hour later at supper, there was once again an exchange of invectives across group lines.

2. Another in the series of superordinate goals was the problem of acquiring the use of a much-desired feature-length movie. Both groups were called to-

gether and the possibility of procuring either *Treasure Island* or *Kidnapped* from the neighboring town was put to both groups. It was announced that the camp administration could put up half of the money to secure one film. (Since this was toward the end of the camp period, one group could not have provided the remaining sum alone without being destitute for the rest of the period.)

Following this announcement, suggestions poured in from both groups on a division of the needed sum. They made computations and agreed on a figure for each group to contribute. Then they computed the amount each member would have to pay to secure the desired film. Both groups decided together on the film to be selected.

After supper that evening the film chosen *(Treasure Island)* was shown. Both groups felt that they had chosen it and had a part in getting it. As a test situation, five rows of benches were placed in the hall with an aisle between them. Both groups were called to the hall at the same time. Despite the cooperative efforts they had carried out in getting the film, the seats chosen by individual members to watch it followed group lines on the whole.

3. The most striking episodes of intergroup activities toward superordinate goals took place during a camp-out at Cedar Lake, an out-of-the-way spot in the hills about 60 miles from the camp. Previously, both groups were asked separately to name the activities they would like to enjoy during the last days of camp. Overnight camping was high on the list of both groups.

Cedar Lake had an attractive camping and picnic area overlooking a clear-water lake surrounded by hills. Since it was far off the main roads, there were no people, shops, or refreshment stands within miles. It afforded an ideal place for controlling experimental conditions for the introduction of super-ordinate goals.

Each group was taken in a separate truck to Cedar Lake early on the morning of the fifth day of this stage. Both groups were enthusiastic over the prospect of the overnight camp; but they stated a preference to enjoy the overnight camping by themselves, and not with the other group. Both groups, on their own initiative, loaded their respective trucks for an early start. When the trucks arrived in midmorning, each group went first to the swimming area, which is separated from the picnic area by a wooded valley. In the meantime, plans for the problem situations to be introduced were prepared in the picnic area.

Near lunch time, both groups returned to the picnic area. After the early breakfast, the trip, and the swim they were getting quite hungry by this time. At the picnic area there were separate tables and facilities and also a centrally located table on which eating and cooking utensils, mustard, and pickles had been placed. The groups rushed to this central table. The only means of transportation visible at the time was an old truck parked nearby.

A staff member announced in a voice audible to everyone that he was leaving to get food from a store some miles away. The groups were now standing about 15 yards apart. They watched the truck that was going to bring food. The truck made all kinds of noises, but simply would not start, as planned.

Several Rattlers suggested giving it a push so that it would start. This suggestion was not followed since the truck was parked facing uphill (as planned). The tug-of-war rope was lying piled up in plain sight. One Rattler suggested, "Let's get 'our' tug-of-war rope and have a tug-of-war against the truck." There was a little discussion of this idea and its practicality. Someone said: "Twenty of us can pull it for sure." Members in both groups voiced approval of this plan. Therefore they got into action. There was a little discussion concerning how to operate. This problem was settled by feeding the rope through the front bumper so that there were 2 lines for the pull. On the whole, the Rattlers pulled one line and the Eagles pulled the other.

It took considerable effort to pull the truck. Several tries were necessary. During these efforts, a rhythmic chant of "Heave, heave" arose to accent the times of greatest effort. This rhythmic chant of "Heave, heave" had been used earlier by the Eagles during the tug-of-war contests in the period of intergroup competition and friction. Now it was being used in a cooperative activity involving both groups. When, after some strenuous efforts, the truck moved and started there was jubilation over the common success.

While the truck went for food, the question arose of taking turns in the preparation of meals or of joint preparation by both groups. The Eagles, with some dissensions, decided to prepare their own meals separately. Preparing food in their own areas implied two sets of activities: dividing food for each group; preparing it in their respective areas. A few days earlier, both groups would have insisted upon separate facilities and independent activities even though this implied more work for each.

Now, however, when the truck returned with the food, the groups did not bother to divide the food into two parts for meals in their respective areas. They simply started preparing it together. In this instance actual cooperation in preparing a meal proceeded without discussion and even in a direction contrary to the prior decision of one group. That evening at Cedar Lake the meal was also prepared jointly.

The truck pull was repeated in the afternoon when the truck "stalled" again before going to get supper provisions. This time both groups knew what to do, and carried out the plan with the same success. But on this second occasion the two lines of rope were not pulled separately by the two groups. Members from both groups intermingled on both lines of the rope. Henceforth group lines were blurred on such cooperative occasions.

The same tool in the service of friction and harmony. It will be remembered that the tug-of-war rope was used in the service of intense competition during Stage II. At the end of that stage the Rattlers used the same rope in activities within their own group. They had spent several days chopping at a dead tree at their hide-out. When the trunk was chopped through, the tree did not fall down. The fall was prevented by surrounding trees. As it stood, the tree was a hazard. It might have fallen down at an inopportune moment. Therefore the Rattlers used the tug-of-war rope to pull the trunk to a safe position. They rejoiced in loud tones over their victory in tug-of-war "against the tree."

As we have seen at the Cedar Lake campout, the Rattlers introduced "their" tug-of-war rope against the truck in a cooperative intergroup effort to get food for all. Here we see how the same weapon used in intergroup friction can be put into use for intergroup harmony.

Summary of observations in Stage III. Only a few high points of the observations during this stage have been summarized. On the basis of the observational data, it was concluded: (a) When the groups in a state of friction interacted under conditions created by introducing superordinate goals, they did cooperate toward the common goal. (b) A series of such joint activities toward common, superordinate goals had the cumulative effect of reducing the prevailing friction between groups and unfavorable stereotypes toward the out-group.

In the closing hours of the experiment, the two groups decided together on their own initiative to put on a joint program at a campfire, entertaining each other with skits and songs. Also on their own initiative both groups requested that they leave the experimental site together in one bus. Thus, these two groups, which formed separately, met for the first time as rivals, engaged in sharp conflict which culminated in mutual antagonism and social distance, now appeared as friendly copartners.

Part XIII

Applied psychology

Chapter 36

Use of the Premack principle in controlling the behavior of nursery school children*

L. E. Homme, P. C. deBaca, J. V. Devine, R. Steinhorst, and E. J. Rickert

One of the basic principles that make human behavior so interesting (and so variable!) is that any stimulus to which an organism is sensitive can, through learning, come to function as a reinforcer for any response that the organism is capable of making. Whether we are attempting to find ways to modify ongoing behavior or merely attempting to understand behavior that at first glance may seem puzzling, it is helpful not to have too many preconceptions about just what is, or is not, functioning as a reinforcer. . . .

Premack's principle (Premack, 1959) can be stated: if behavior B is of higher probability than behavior A, then behavior A can be made more probable by making behavior B contingent upon it.

In a preliminary exploration of nursery school procedures, three 3-year-old subjects (Ss) were available three hours a day, five days a week, for about one month. On the first day, in the absence of any aversive control, verbal instructions usually had little effect on the Ss' behavior. When they were instructed to sit in their chairs, Ss would often continue what they were doing—running around the room, screaming, pushing chairs, or quietly working jigsaw puzzles. Taking Premack seriously, such behaviors were labeled as high probability behaviors and used in combination with the signals for them as reinforcers. These high probability behaviors were then made contingent on desired behaviors. For example, sitting quietly in a chair and looking at the blackboard would be intermittently followed by the sound of the bell, with the instruction: "Run and scream." The Ss would then leap to their feet and run around the

*From *Journal of the Experimental Analysis of Behavior* 6:544, 1963. Copyright 1963 by Society for the Experimental Analysis of Behavior, Inc.

room screaming. At another signal they would stop. At this time they would get another signal and an instruction to engage in some other behavior which, on a quasi-random schedule, might be one of high or low probability. At a later stage, *S*s earned tokens for low probability behaviors which could later be used to "buy" the opportunity for high probability activities.

With this kind of procedure, control was virtually perfect after a few days. For example when *S*s were requested to "sit and look at the blackboard" (an activity which in the past had intermittently been interrupted by the signal for some higher probability behavior), they were under such good control that an observer, new on the scene, almost certainly would have assumed extensive aversive control was being used.

An examination of high probability behaviors quickly showed that many, if not most of them, were behaviors which ordinarily would be suppressed through punishment. Extrapolating from this we were able to predict the reinforcing properties of some behaviors which had never been emitted. For example, throwing a plastic cup across the room and kicking a wastebasket had never been observed but proved to be highly reinforcing activities after they had once been evoked by instructions. (Some unpredicted behaviors proved to be highly reinforcing, e.g., pushing the experimenter around the room in his caster-equipped chair.)

In summary, even in this preliminary, unsystematic application, the Premack hypothesis proved to be an exceptionally practical principle for controlling the behavior of nursery school *S*s.

Chapter 37

Marketing eight hidden needs*

Vance Packard

As psychologists learn more about your motivations—your reasons for behaving—chances become greater that your behavior can be effectively controlled by other people—especially by the advertisers. As you read the following excerpt from Packard's book, think about this possibility of controlling human behavior . . . do you really know why you chose Brand X over Brand Y? Who influenced your choice? Do you want to be manipulated in your buying habits?

> *"The home freezer becomes a frozen island of security."*
> *—From a report, Weiss and Geller advertising agency.*

In searching for extra psychological values that they could add to products to give them a more potent appeal, the depth merchandisers came upon many gratifying clues by studying our subconscious needs, yearnings, and cravings. Once the need was identified, and certified to be compelling, they began building the promise of its fulfillment into their sales presentations of such unlikely products as air conditioners, cake mixes, and motorboats. Here we will explore some of the more picturesque applications in merchandising eight of our hidden needs.

Selling emotional security. The Weiss and Geller advertising agency became suspicious of the conventional reasons people gave for buying home freezers. In many cases it found that economically, the freezers didn't make sense when you added up the initial cost, the monthly cost added on the electric bill, and the amount of frozen leftovers in the box that eventually would be thrown out. When all factors were added, the food that was consumed from the freezer often became very costly indeed.

Its curiosity aroused, the agency made a psychiatric pilot study. The probers found significance in the fact that the home freezer first came into widespread popularity after World War II when many families were filled with inner anxieties because of uncertainties involving not only food but just about every-

---

*From *The Hidden Persuaders,* by Vance Packard, 1958. By permission of the author, David McKay Co., Inc., New York, and Longmans Green & Co., London.

thing else in their lives. These people began thinking fondly of former periods of safety and security, which subconsciously took them back to childhood where there was the mother who never disappointed and love was closely related with the giving of food. The probers concluded: "The freezer represents to many the assurance that there is always food in the house, and food in the home represents security, warmth, and safety." People who feel insecure, they found, need more food around than they can eat. The agency decided that the merchandising of freezers should take this squirrel factor into account in shaping campaigns.

The same agency found that the air conditioner has a hidden security value of another sort that can be exploited. Some people, its psychiatric probers found, need to feel protected and enclosed and to keep the windows closed at night while they sleep so that nothing "threatening" can enter. These people, it seems, are subconsciously yearning for a return to the security of the womb.

While the womb-seekers are a highly vulnerable market for air conditioners (already a half-billion-dollar-a-year business), another type of person offers a real challenge to the conditioner salesman. The agency's probers found that there is a latent claustrophobia in many of us. For those of us in this class the conditioner, far from being a symbol of security, becomes a threat. Its sealed world gives us a feeling of being closed in. The agency concluded that a way would have to be found to give such people open windows and still persuade them to buy air conditioners, but they didn't say how to do it. (Another agency man advised us that many people still feel guilty about installing an air conditioner because "God made bad weather so you should put up with it." He said, "There is a lot of that attitude, amazingly, left in America.")

Dr. Dichter advised marketers of do-it-yourself tools and gadgets that they were missing a bet if they were not selling men security as well as gadgets. He advised: "A man concentrating on his tools or his machinery is in a closed world. He is free from the strains of interpersonal relationships. He is engaged in a peaceful dialogue with himself."

At a showing of children's furniture in mid-1956 (National Baby and Children's Show) a combination of high chair, bathinette, and toilet trainer was displayed. The president of the firm said it was calculated to give the child a "home" and a "feeling of security." Then he added: "Things are getting to the point where manufacturers are getting more and more to be psychologists."

Selling reassurance of worth. In the mid-fifties *The Chicago Tribune* made a depth study of the detergent and soap market to try to find out why these products had failed to build brand loyalty, as many other products have done. Housewives tend to switch from one brand to another. This, the *Tribune* felt, was lamentable and concluded that the soap and detergent makers were themselves clearly to blame. They had been old-fashioned in their approach. "Most advertising," it found, "now shows practically no awareness that women have any other motive for using their products than to be clean, to protect the hands, and to keep objects clean." The depth-wise soap maker, the report advised, will realize that many housewives feel they are engaged in unrewarded and unappreciated drudgery when they clean. The advertiser should thus foster the wife's feeling of "worth and esteem." His "advertising should exalt the role of housekeeping—not in self-conscious, stodgy ways or with embarrassingly direct praise—but by various implications making it known what an important and proud thing it is or should be to be a housewife performing a role often regarded . . . as drudgery."

Dr. Smith, in his book on motivation research, makes the point that luggage makers can increase sales if they remind the public that they are selling a form of reassurance. Nice new luggage, he advises, gives a man a feeling of being important and gives him more bearing when he goes out into the world.

Even the all-wise doctor is sometimes badly in need of reassurance, and according to Dr. Dichter, the shrewd pharmaceutical house will sell it to him, and thus win the doctor's gratitude and recommendation of at least its general type of medication when a prescription is to be ordered. Dr. Dichter made a depth study of 204 doctors for pharmaceutical advertisers in order that they could be more effective "in influencing the prescription motivation of physicians." The drug houses should understand, he counseled, that the doctor feels a little threatened by the growth of factory-compounded, ready-mixed medicines. The doctors probed revealed deep resentment of drug ads that relegated the doctor to the position of a pill dispenser (rather than chief diagnostician and healer). The shrewd drug house, Dr. Dichter counseled, will not claim too much credit for the good results or go over the doctor's head to the public. Instead, it will seek to re-enforce the doctor's self-image as the "all-powerful healer," and put the spotlight in ads on the doctor rather than overstress the "medical qualities of the drug."

Selling ego-gratification. This in a sense is akin to selling reassurance of worth. A maker of steam shovels found that sales were lagging. It had been showing in its ads magnificent photos of its mammoth machines lifting great loads of rock and dirt. A motivation study of prospective customers was made to find what was wrong. The first fact uncovered was that purchasing agents, in buying such machines, were strongly influenced by the comments and recommendations of their steam-shovel operators, and the operators showed considerable hostility to this company's brand. Probing the operators, the investigators quickly found the reason. The operators resented pictures of the ad that put all the glory on the huge machine and showed the operator as a barely visible figure inside the distant cab. The shovel maker, armed with this insight, changed its ad approach and began taking its photographs from over the operator's shoulder. He was shown as the complete master of the mammoth machine. This new approach, *Time* magazine reported, is "easing the operators' hostility."

One of the most forthright instances of selling ego-gratification is that done by the vanity press that brings out books completely subsidized by the author. During the early fifties 10 percent of all books published in America were of this variety. One of the most active of the vanity publishers, Exposition Press, brings out as many as two hundred books a year. Its publisher, Mr. Edward Uhlan, states: "Our authors must be prepared psychologically and financially to lose money. Other houses may promise riches . . . we just offer immortality!" He not only prints the author's words and name in deathless type but sets up author luncheons, autographing parties in local bookstores, newspaper reviews and radio interviews. Mr. Uhlan says he has had authors so anxious to get themselves in print that they have expressed willingness to sell their automobiles and mortgage their homes to pay Uhlan for publishing their books. One offered to sell his 150-acre ranch in New Mexico. Mr. Uhlan, a candid man, comments: "I have often felt that the desk in my office might be exchanged profitably for an analyst's couch."

Selling creative outlets. The director of psychological research at a Chicago ad agency mentioned casually in a conversation that gardening is a "pregnancy activity." When questioned about this she responded, as if explaining the most obvious thing in the world, that gardening gives older women a chance to keep on growing things after they have passed the child-bearing stage. This explains, she said, why gardening has particular appeal to older women and to men, who of course can't have babies. She cited the case of a woman with eleven children who, when she passed through menopause, nearly had a nervous collapse until she discovered gardening, which she took to for the first time in her life and with obvious and intense delight.

Housewives consistently report that one of the most pleasurable tasks of the home is making a cake. Psychologists were put to work exploring this phenomenon for merchandising clues. James Vicary made a study of cake symbolism and came up with the conclusion that "baking a cake traditionally is acting out the birth of a child" so that when a woman bakes a cake for her family she is symbolically presenting the family with a new baby, an idea she likes very much. Mr. Vicary cited the many jokes and old wives' tales about cake making as evidence: the quip that brides whose cakes fall obviously can't produce a baby yet; the married jest about "leaving a cake in the oven"; the myth that a cake is likely to fall if the woman baking it is menstruating. A psychological consulting firm in Chicago also made a study of cake symbolism and found that "women experience making a cake as making a gift of themselves to their family," which suggests much the same thing.

The food mixes—particularly the cake mixes—soon found themselves deeply involved in this problem of feminine creativity and encountered much more resistance than the makers, being logical people, ever dreamed possible. The makers found themselves trying to cope with negative and guilt feelings on the part of women who felt that use of ready mixes was a sign of poor housekeeping and threatened to deprive them of a traditional source of praise.

In the early days the cake-mix packages instructed, "Do not add milk, just add water." Still many wives insisted on adding milk as their creative touch, overloaded the cakes or muffins with calcium, and often the cakes or muffins fell, and the wives would blame the cake mix. Or the package would say, "Do not add eggs." Typically the milk and eggs had already been added by the manufacturer in dried form. But wives who were interviewed in depth studies would exclaim: "What kind of cake is it if you just need to add tap water!" Several different psychological firms wrestled with this problem and came up with essentially the same answer. The mix makers should always leave the housewife something to do. Thus Dr. Dichter counseled General Mills that it should start telling the housewife that she and Bisquick *together* could do the job and not Bisquick alone. Swansdown White Cake Mix began telling wives in large type: "You Add Fresh Eggs . . ." Some mixes have the wife add both fresh eggs and fresh milk.

Marketers are finding many areas where they can improve sales by urging the prospective customer to add his creative touch. A West Coast firm selling to home builders found that although its architects and designers could map houses to the last detail it was wise to leave some places where builders could add their own personal touch. And Dr. Dichter in his counseling to pharmaceutical houses advised them that in merchandising ready-mixed medical compounds they would be wise to leave the doctors ways they could add personal touches so that each doctor could feel the compound was "his own."

Selling love objects. This might seem a weird kind of merchandising but the promoters of Liberace, the TV pianist, have manipulated—with apparent premeditation—the trappings of Oedipus symbolism in selling him to women past the child-bearing age (where much of his following is concentrated). The TV columnist John Crosby alluded to this when he described the reception Liberace was receiving in England, where, according to Mr. Crosby, he was "visible in all his redundant dimples" on British commercial TV. Mr. Crosby quoted the *New Statesman and Nation* as follows: "Every American mom is longing to stroke the greasy, roguish curls. The wide, trustful childlike smile persists, even when the voice is in full song." TV viewers who have had an opportunity to sit in Mr. Liberace's TV presence may recall that in his TV presentations a picture of his real-life mom is frequently flashed on screen, beaming in her rocking chair or divan while her son performs.

Selling sense of power. The fascination Americans show for any product that seems to offer them a personal extension of power has offered a rich field for exploitation by merchandisers. Automobile makers have strained to produce cars with ever-higher horsepower. After psychiatric probing a Midwestern ad agency concluded that a major appeal of buying a shiny new and more powerful car every couple of years is that "it gives him [the buyer] a renewed sense of power and reassures him of his own masculinity, an emotional need which his old car fails to deliver."

One complication of the power appeal of a powerful new car, the Institute for Motivational Research found, was that the man buying it often feels guilty about indulging himself with power that might be regarded as needless. The buyer needs some rational reassurance for indulging his deep-seated desires. A good solution, the institute decided, was to give the power appeals but stress that all that wonderful surging power would provide "the extra margin of safety in an emergency." This, an institute official explains, provides "the illusion of rationality" that the buyer needs.

The McCann-Erickson advertising agency made a study for Esso gasoline to discover what motivates consumers, in order more effectively to win new friends for Esso. The agency found there is considerable magic in the word power. After many depth interviews with gasoline buyers the agency perfected an ad strategy that hammered at two words, with all letters capitalized: TOTAL POWER.

This need for a sense of power, particularly in men, has been observed and very thoroughly exploited by marketers interested in the boat-buying habits of Americans. Although the owner of a pleasure boat is not going anywhere in particular or at least not in a hurry, Americans prefer power boats to sailboats by a margin of eight to one. The Institute for Motivational Research studied American attitudes toward boat buying and concluded that the average buyer sees his boat as a very satisfying way of fulfilling his need for power. One man, an executive, who was invited to chat at length on the subject said that with a good power boat "you can show you are all man and let her rip—without having the fear you are bound to have on the road." The institute found that many men seem to use their boats to express their sense of power in "almost a sexual way," and it outlined what it found to be a "power profile" in the average enthusiast's boat-buying habits. If the man has owned five boats the "power profile" structure is apt to shape up like this: first boat, $3\frac{1}{2}$ horsepower; second boat, 5 horsepower; third boat, two tens; fourth boat, 20 to 25 horsepower; fifth boat, the sky is the limit in horsepower. The institute counsels: "Manufacturers, eying profits, should explore to the fullest the psychological ways and means of tapping these motives."

Selling a sense of roots. When the Mogen David wine people were seeking some way to add magic to their wine's sales appeal (while it was still an obscure brand), they turned to motivation research via their ad agency. Psychiatrists and other probers listening to people talk at random about wine found that many related it to old family-centered or festive occasions. Some talked in an almost homesick way about wine and the good old days that went with it. A hard-hitting copy platform was erected based on these homey associations. The campaign tied home and mother into the selling themes. One line was: "The good old days—the home sweet home wine—the wine that grandma used to make." As a result of these carefully "motivated" slogans, the sales of Mogen David doubled within a year and soon the company was budgeting $2,000,000 just for advertising—the biggest ad campaign in the history of the wine industry.

Selling immortality. Perhaps the most astounding of all the efforts to merchandise hidden needs was that proposed to a conference of Midwestern life-insurance men. The conference invited Edward Weiss, head of Weiss and Geller, to tell members of the assembled North Central Life Advertisers Association (meeting in Omaha in April, 1955) how to put more impact into their messages advertising insurance. In his speech, called "Hidden Attitudes Toward Life Insurance" he reported on a study in depth made by several psychologists. (In an aside he pointed out that one of the serious problems in selling insurance to women is how to do it without reminding them that they are getting older. If they start brooding about their advancing age the whole sales message may be lost on them. He further agreed this called for real "creative" thinking.)

The heart of his presentation, however, was the findings on selling life insurance to the male, who is the breadwinner in most families and the one whose life is to be insured. Weiss criticized many of the current selling messages as being blind to the realities of this man who usually makes the buying decision. Typically, he demonstrated, current ads either glorified the persistence and helpfulness of the insurance agent or else portrayed the comfortable pattern of life the family had managed to achieve after the breadwinner's death, thanks to the insurance. Both approaches, said Mr. Weiss, are dead wrong. In a few cases, he conceded, the breadwinner may be praised for his foresight, but still he is always depicted as someone now dead and gone.

One of the real appeals of life insurance to a man, his probers found, is that it assures the buyer of "the prospect of immortality through the perpetuation of his influence for it is not the fact of his own *physical* death that is inconceivable; it is the prospect of his *obliteration*." The man can't stand the thought of obliteration. Weiss reported that when men talked at the conscious and more formal level about insurance they talked of their great desire to protect their loved ones in case of any "eventuality." In this their desire for immortality was plain enough. But Weiss said there was strong evidence that this socially commendable acceptance of responsibility was not always the real and main desire of the prospective customer. Weiss said it appeared to be true for many men but not all. "In many instances," he went on, "our projective tests revealed the respondent's fierce desire to achieve immortality in order to *control* his family after death. These men obtain insurance against obliteration through the knowledge that they will continue to *dominate* their families; to *control* the family standard of living, and to guide the education of their children long after they are gone."

Then Mr. Weiss asked how advertising could be more effective in reassuring both these types on the prospect for the kind of immortality they yearned for. In short, how could the appeals promise both protection and control without alienating one or the other of the potential buyers? He said: "I suggest that such advertising may become more effective as it is concentrated on the emotional problems of the buyer himself rather than picturing the comfort of his surviving family." He proposed that in picturing the security and unity of the surviving family the "living personality" of the breadwinner always be present by the picture or implication. Not only should he be there in the family picture, "but he, and he alone, is the hero—eternally shielding, providing, comforting and governing."

Chapter 38

The theoretical assumptions of management*

Douglas McGregor

Each one of us has a number of assumptions about human nature that strongly influence the conduct of our everyday affairs. The following article demonstrates the usefulness and the desirability of systematically examining these assumptions not only in industry, but in every setting in which we must deal with people.

Behind every managerial decision or action are assumptions about human nature and human behavior. A few of these are remarkably pervasive. They are implicit in most of the literature of organization and in much current managerial policy and practice:

1. *The average human being has an inherent dislike of work and will avoid it if he can.*

This assumption has deep roots. The punishment of Adam and Eve for eating the fruit of the Tree of Knowledge was to be banished from Eden into a world where they had to work for a living. The stress that management places on productivity, on the concept of "a fair day's work," on the evils of featherbedding and restriction of output, on rewards for performance—while it has a logic in terms of the objectives of enterprise—reflects an underlying belief that management must counteract an inherent human tendency to avoid work. The evidence for the correctness of this assumption would seem to most managers to be incontrovertible.

2. *Because of this human characteristic of dislike of work, most people must be coerced, controlled, directed, threatened with punishment to get them to put forth adequate effort toward the achievement of organizational objectives.*

The dislike of work is so strong that even the promise of rewards is not generally enough to overcome it. People will accept the rewards and demand continually higher ones, but these alone will not produce the necessary effort. Only the threat of punishment will do the trick.

266

The current wave of criticism of "human relations," the derogatory comments about "permissiveness" and "democracy" in industry, the trends in some companies toward recentralization after the postwar wave of decentralization— all these are assertions of the underlying assumption that people will only work under external coercion and control. The recession of 1957-58 ended a decade of experimentation with the "soft" managerial approach, and this assumption (which never really was abandoned) is being openly espoused once more.

3. *The average human being prefers to be directed, wishes to avoid responsibility, has relatively little ambition, wants security above all.*

This assumption of the "mediocrity of the masses" is rarely expressed so bluntly. In fact, a good deal of lip service is given to the ideal of the worth of the average human being. Our political and social values demand such public expressions. Nevertheless, a great many managers will give private support to this assumption, and it is easy to see it reflected in policy and practice. Paternalism has become a nasty word, but it is by no means a defunct managerial philosophy.

I have suggested elsewhere the name Theory X for this set of assumptions. In later chapters of this book I will attempt to show that Theory X is not a straw man for purposes of demolition, but is in fact a theory which materially influences managerial strategy in a wide sector of American industry today. Moreover, the principles of organization which comprise the bulk of the literature of management *could only have been derived from assumptions such as those of Theory X*. Other beliefs about human nature would have led inevitably to quite different organizational principles.

Theory X provides an explanation of some human behavior in industry. These assumptions would not have persisted if there were not a considerable body of evidence to support them. Nevertheless, there are many readily observable phenomena in industry and elsewhere which are not consistent with this view of human nature.

Such a state of affairs is not uncommon. The history of science provides many examples of theoretical explanations which persist over long periods despite the fact that they are only partially adequate. Newton's laws of motion are a case in point. It was not until the development of the theory of relativity during the present century that important inconsistencies and inadequacies in Newtonian theory could be understood and corrected.

The growth of knowledge in the social sciences during the past quarter century has made it possible to reformulate some assumptions about human nature and human behavior in the organizational setting which resolve certain of the inconsistencies inherent in Theory X. While this reformulation is, of course, tentative, it provides an improved basis for prediction and control of human behavior in industry.

SOME ASSUMPTIONS ABOUT MOTIVATION

At the core of any theory of the management of human resources are assumptions about human motivation. This has been a confusing subject because there have been so many conflicting points of view even among social scientists. In recent years, however, there has been a convergence of research findings and a growing acceptance of a few rather basic ideas about motivation. These ideas appear to have considerable power. They help to explain the inadequacies of Theory X as well as the limited sense in which it is correct. In addition, they provide the basis for an entirely different theory of management.

The following generalizations about motivation are somewhat oversimplified. If all of the qualifications which would be required by a truly adequate treatment were introduced, the gross essentials which are particularly significant for management would be obscured. These generalizations do not misrepresent the facts, but they do ignore some complexities of human behavior which are relatively unimportant for our purposes.

Man is a wanting animal—as soon as one of his needs is satisfied, another appears in its place. This process is unending. It continues from birth to death. Man continuously puts forth effort—works, if you please—to satisfy his needs.

Human needs are organized in a series of levels—a hierarchy of importance. At the lowest level, but preeminent in importance when they are thwarted, are the physiological needs. Man lives by bread alone, when there is no bread. Unless the circumstances are unusual, his needs for love, for status, for recognition are inoperative when his stomach has been empty for a while. But when he eats regularly and adequately, hunger ceases to be an important need. The sated man has hunger only in the sense that a full bottle has emptiness. The same is true of the other physiological needs of man—for rest, exercise, shelter, protection from the elements.

A satisfied need is not a motivator of behavior! This is a fact of profound significance. It is a fact which is unrecognized in Theory X and is, therefore, ignored in the conventional approach to the management of people. I shall return to it later. For the moment, an example will make the point. Consider your own need for air. Except as you are deprived of it, it has no appreciable motivating effect upon your behavior.

When the physiological needs are reasonably satisfied, needs at the next higher level begin to dominate man's behavior—to motivate him. These are the safety needs, for protection against danger, threat, deprivation. Some people mistakenly refer to these needs as needs for security. However, unless man is in a dependent relationship where he fears arbitrary deprivation, he does not demand security. The need is for the "fairest possible break." When he is confident of this, he is more than willing to take risks. But when he feels threatened or dependent, his greatest need is for protection, for security.

The fact needs little emphasis that since every industrial employee is in at least a partially dependent relationship, safety needs may assume considerable importance. Arbitrary management actions, behavior which arouses uncertainty with respect to continued employment or which reflects favoritism or discrimination, unpredictable administration of policy—these can be powerful motivators of the safety needs in the employment relationship at every level from worker to vice president. In addition, the safety needs of managers are often aroused by their dependence downward or laterally. This is a major reason for emphasis on management prerogatives and clear assignments of authority.

When man's physiological needs are satisfied and he is no longer fearful about his physical welfare, his social needs become important motivators of his behavior. These are such needs as those for belonging, for association, for acceptance by one's fellows, for giving and receiving friendship and love.

Management knows today of the existence of these needs, but it is often assumed quite wrongly that they represent a threat to the organization. Many studies have demonstrated that the tightly knit, cohesive work group may, under proper conditions, be far more effective than an equal number of separate individuals in achieving organizational goals. Yet management, fearing group hostility to its own objectives, often goes to considerable lengths to control and direct human efforts in ways that are inimical to the natural "groupiness" of human beings. When man's social needs—and perhaps his safety needs, too— are thus thwarted, he behaves in ways which tend to defeat organizational objectives. He becomes resistant, antagonistic, uncooperative. But this behavior is a consequence, not a cause.

Above the social needs—in the sense that they do not usually become motivators until lower needs are reasonably satisfied—are the needs of greatest significance to management and to man himself. They are the egoistic needs, and they are of two kinds:

1. Those that relate to one's self-esteem: needs for self-respect and self-confidence, for autonomy, for achievement, for competence, for knowledge;

2. Those that relate to one's reputation: needs for status, for recognition, for appreciation, for the deserved respect of one's fellows.

Unlike the lower needs, these are rarely satisfied; man seeks indefinitely for more satisfaction of these needs once they have become important to him. However, they do not usually appear in any significant way until physiological, safety, and social needs are reasonably satisfied. Exceptions to this generalization are to be observed, particularly under circumstances where, in addition to severe deprivation of physiological needs, human dignity is trampled upon. Political revolutions often grow out of thwarted social and ego, as well as physiological, needs.

The typical industrial organization offers only limited opportunities for the satisfaction of egoistic needs to people at lower levels in the hierarchy. The conventional methods of organizing work, particularly in mass production industries, give little heed to these aspects of human motivation. If the practices of "scientific management" were deliberately calculated to thwart these needs—which, of course, they are not—they could hardly accomplish this purpose better than they do.

Finally—a capstone, as it were, on the hierarchy—there are the needs for self-fulfillment. These are the needs for realizing one's own potentialities, for continued self-development, for being creative in the broadest sense of that term.

The conditions of modern industrial life give only limited opportunity for these relatively dormant human needs to find expression. The deprivation most people experience with respect to other lower-level needs diverts their energies into the struggle to satisfy *those* needs, and the needs for self-fulfillment remain below the level of consciousness.

Now, briefly, a few general comments about motivation:

We recognize readily enough that a man suffering from a severe dietary deficiency is sick. The deprivation of physiological needs has behavioral consequences. The same is true, although less well recognized, of the deprivation of higher-level needs. The man whose needs for safety, association, independence, or status are thwarted is sick, just as surely as is he who has rickets. And his sickness will have behavioral consequences. We will be mistaken if we attribute his resultant passivity, or his hostility, or his refusal to accept responsibility to his inherent "human nature." These forms of behavior are *symptoms* of illness—of deprivation of his social and egoistic needs.

The man whose lower-level needs are satisfied is not motivated to satisfy *those* needs. For practical purposes they exist no longer. (Remember my point about your need for air.) Management often asks, "Why aren't people more productive? We pay good wages, provide good working conditions, have excellent fringe benefits and steady employment. Yet people do not seem to be willing to put forth more than the minimum effort." It is unnecessary to look far for the reasons.

Consideration of the rewards typically provided the worker for satisfying his needs through his employment leads to the interesting conclusion that most of these rewards can be used for satisfying his needs *only when he leaves the job.* Wages, for example, cannot be spent at work. The only contribution they can make to his satisfaction on the job is in terms of status differences resulting from wage differentials. (This, incidentally, is one of the reasons why small and apparently unimportant differences in wage rates can be the subject of so much heated dispute. The issue is not the pennies involved, but the fact that the status differences which they reflect are one of the few ways in which wages can result in need satisfaction in the job situation itself.)

Most fringe benefits—overtime pay, shift differentials, vacations, health and medical benefits, annuities, and the proceeds from stock purchase plans or profit-sharing plans—yield needed satisfaction only when the individual leaves the job. Yet these, along with wages, are among the major rewards provided by management for effort. It is not surprising, therefore, that for many wage earners *work is perceived as a form of punishment* which is the price to be paid for various kinds of satisfaction away from the job. To the extent that this is their perception, we would hardly expect them to undergo more punishment than is necessary.

Under today's conditions management has provided relatively well for the satisfaction of physiological and safety needs. The standard of living in our country is high; people do not suffer major deprivation of their physiological needs except during periods of severe unemployment. Even then, the social legislation developed since the thirties cushions the shock.

But the fact that management has provided for these physiological and safety needs has shifted the motivational emphasis to the social and the egoistic needs. Unless there are opportunities *at work* to satisfy these higher-level needs, people will be deprived; and their behavior will reflect this deprivation. Under such conditions, if management continues to focus its attention on physiological needs, the mere provision of rewards is bound to be ineffective, and reliance on the threat of punishment will be inevitable. Thus one of the assumptions of Theory X will appear to be validated, but only because we have mistaken effects for causes.

People *will* make insistent demands for more money under these conditions. It becomes more important than ever to buy the material goods and services which can provide limited satisfaction of the thwarted needs. Although money has only limited value in satisfying many higher-level needs, it can become the focus of interest if it is the only means available.

The "carrot and stick" theory of motivation which goes along with Theory X works reasonably well under certain circumstances. The *means* for satisfying man's physiological and (within limits) safety needs can be provided or withheld by management. Employment itself is such a means, and so are wages, working conditions, and benefits. By these means the individual can be controlled so long as he is struggling for subsistence. Man tends to live for bread alone when there is little bread.

But the "carrot and stick" theory does not work at all once man has reached an adequate subsistence level and is motivated primarily by higher needs. Management cannot provide a man with self-respect, or with the respect of his fellows, or with the satisfaction of needs for self-fulfillment. We can create conditions such that he is encouraged and enabled to seek such satisfactions for himself, or we can thwart him by failing to create those conditions.

But this creation of conditions is not "control" in the usual sense; it does not seem to be a particularly good device for directing behavior. And so management finds itself in an odd position. The high standard of living created by our modern technological know-how provides quite adequately for the satisfaction of physiological and safety needs. The only significant exception is where management practices have not created confidence in a "fair break"—and thus where safety needs are thwarted. But by making possible the satisfaction of lower-level needs, management has deprived itself of the ability to use control devices on which the conventional assumptions of Theory X has taught it to rely: rewards, promises, incentives, or threats and other coercive devices.

The philosophy of management by direction and control—*regardless of whether it is hard or soft*—is inadequate to motivate because the human needs on which this approach relies are relatively unimportant motivators of behavior in our society today. Direction and control are of limited value in motivating people whose important needs are social and egoistic.

People, deprived of opportunities to satisfy at work the needs which are now important to them, behave exactly as we might predict—with indolence, passivity, unwillingness to accept responsibility, resistance to change, willingness to follow the demagogue, unreasonable demands for economic benefits. It would seem that we may be caught in a web of our own weaving.

Theory X explains the *consequences* of a particular managerial strategy; it neither explains nor describes human nature although it purports to. Because its assumptions are so unnecessarily limiting, it prevents our seeing the possibilities inherent in other managerial strategies. What sometimes appear to be new strategies—decentralization, management by objectives, consultative supervision, "democratic" leadership—are usually but old wine in new bottles because the procedures developed to implement them are derived from the same inadequate assumptions about human nature. Management is constantly becoming disillusioned with widely touted and expertly merchandised "new approaches" to the human side of enterprise. The real difficulty is that these new approaches are no more than different tactics—programs, procedures, gadgets—within an unchanged strategy based on Theory X.

In child rearing, it is recognized that parental strategies of control must be progressively modified to adapt to the changed capabilities and characteristics of the human individual as he develops from infancy to adulthood. To some extent industrial management recognizes that the human *adult* possesses capabilities for continued learning and growth. Witness the many current activities in the fields of training and management development. In its *basic* conceptions of managing human resources, however, management appears to have concluded that the average human being is permanently arrested in his development in early adolescence. Theory X is built on the least common human denominator: the factory "hand" of the past. As Chris Argyris has shown dramatically in his *Personality and Organization,* conventional managerial strategies for the organization, direction, and control of the human resources of enterprise are admirably suited to the capacities and characteristics of the child rather than the adult.

There have been few dramatic break-throughs in social science theory like those which have occurred in the physical sciences during the past half century. Nevertheless, the accumulation of knowledge about human behavior in many specialized fields has made possible the formulation of a number of generalizations which provide a modest beginning for a new theory with respect to the management of human resources. . . .

1. *The expenditure of physical and mental effort in work is as natural as play or rest.* The average human being does not inherently dislike work. Depending upon controllable conditions, work may be a source of satisfaction (and will be voluntarily performed) or a source of punishment (and will be avoided if possible).

2. *External control and the threat of punishment are not the only means for bringing about effort toward organizational objectives. Man will exercise self-direction and self-control in the service of objectives to which he is committed.*

3. *Commitment to objectives is a function of the rewards associated with their achievement.* The most significant of such rewards, e.g., the satisfaction of ego and self-actualization needs, can be direct products of effort directed toward organizational objectives.

4. *The average human being learns, under proper conditions, not only to accept but to seek responsibility.* Avoidance of responsibility, lack of ambition, and emphasis on security are generally consequences of experience, not inherent human characteristics.

5. *The capacity to exercise a relatively high degree of imagination, ingenuity, and creativity in the solution of organizational problems is widely, not narrowly, distributed in the population.*

6. *Under the conditions of modern industrial life, the intellectual potentialities of the average human being are only partially utilized.*

These assumptions involve sharply different implications for managerial strategy than do those of Theory X. They are dynamic rather than static: They indicate the possibility of human growth and development; they stress the necessity for selective adaptation rather than for a single absolute form of control. They are not framed in terms of the least common denominator of the factory hand, but in terms of a resource which has substantial potentialities.

Above all, the assumptions of Theory Y point up the fact that the limits on human collaboration in the organizational setting are not limits of human nature but of management's ingenuity in discovering how to realize the potential represented by its human resources. Theory X offers management an easy rationalization for ineffective organizational performance: It is due to the nature of the human resources with which we must work. Theory Y, on the other hand, places the problems squarely in the lap of management. If employees are lazy, indifferent, unwilling to take responsibility, intransigent, uncreative, uncooperative, Theory Y implies that the causes lie in management's methods of organization and control.